Chapter and Unit Tests
with Answer Key

HOLT

World History
The Human Journey

HOLT, RINEHART AND WINSTON
A Harcourt Education Company
Austin • Orlando • Chicago • New York • Toronto • London • San Diego

Cover description: Depiction of French costumes
Cover credit: Nawrocki Stock Photo

Printed in the United States of America

ISBN 0-03-065734-2

8 9 054 05

Contents

Chapter/Unit Tests

Chapter/Unit Tests

Contents

Chapter/Unit Tests

Unit 8 (Modern Unit 6) The World Since 1945

Name ______________________ Class ______________ Date ____________

Chapter Test Form A

The Emergence of Civilization

FILL IN THE BLANK *(3 points each)* For each of the following statements, fill in the blank with the appropriate word, name, or phrase.

1. A ____________________ of a people includes the set of beliefs, knowledge, and patterns of living the people have developed.

2. The ____________________ was a slow process that shifted people from food gathering to food producing and revolutionized early human life.

3. Anthropologists call humans and other humanlike creatures ____________________.

4. Some advanced peoples who lived near rivers built ____________________ systems to bring water to their fields and crops.

5. The ____________________ of some wild animals, such as goats and pigs, provided early peoples with another source of food.

6. Characteristics of a ____________________ include the ability to produce extra food, towns with some form of government, and people doing specialized jobs.

7. An ____________________ is an object that reveals information about the lives of early peoples.

8. A ____________________ as societies advanced caused some people to specialize in farming and some people to make tools and other goods.

9. Like some peoples today, many early humans were ____________________ who wandered from place to place, often over great distances.

10. Before the development of agriculture, prehistoric peoples practiced a hunting and ____________________ way of life.

UNDERSTANDING IDEAS *(3 points each)* For each of the following, write the letter of the best choice in the space provided.

______ **1.** The world's first civilizations developed in
- **a.** Europe.
- **b.** caves.
- **c.** river valleys.
- **d.** the Old Stone Age.

______ **2.** The spread of ideas and other aspects of a culture is called
- **a.** cultural diffusion.
- **b.** culture shock.
- **c.** a division of labor.
- **d.** civilization.

Name ______________________ Class ______________ Date ____________

______ **3.** Advanced civilizations developed along all of the following rivers EXCEPT
a. the Amazon.
b. the Indus.
c. the Nile.
d. the Huang.

______ **4.** Humans developed the first calendars to help them in
a. practicing their religion.
b. choosing new leaders.
c. farming their lands.
d. keeping track of deaths.

______ **5.** One advance made by Cro-Magnons is that they
a. painted pictures on cave walls.
b. followed animals over a land bridge to America.
c. were the first to use stone tools.
d. were the first to make use of fire.

______ **6.** The order of human development, from earliest to latest, is the
a. Iron Age, Bronze Age, and Stone Age.
b. Stone Age, Iron Age, and Bronze Age.
c. Iron Age, Stone Age, and Bronze Age.
d. Stone Age, Bronze Age, and Iron Age.

______ **7.** Early *Homo sapiens* differed from the first humans because they
a. used stone tools.
b. walked upright.
c. buried their dead.
d. may have developed in Africa.

______ **8.** The first metal that people used was probably
a. bronze.
b. copper.
c. iron.
d. steel.

______ **9.** The balance of power shifted from women to men because
a. women were required to raise the children.
b. religious practices called for it.
c. women could not make pottery and clothing.
d. men took over the job of farming.

______ **10.** Scientists think Neanderthals probably had religious beliefs because they
a. wore animal skins as clothing.
b. buried meat and tools with their dead.
c. built temples in caves.
d. were mentally alert.

TRUE/FALSE *(2 points each)* Mark each statement *T* if it is true or *F* if it is false.

______ **1.** Donald Johanson and Mary Leakey are famous for their studies of the Cro-Magnons and Neanderthals.

______ **2.** Two characteristics that often mark civilizations are a system of writing and a system of government.

_______ **3.** Bronze was used to make tools because it was more plentiful than copper and deposits of it were easy to find.

_______ **4.** Neolithic people were less advanced in their food gathering and tool making techniques than were Paleolithic people.

_______ **5.** The development of agriculture changed human life by allowing people to settle in towns.

PRACTICING SKILLS *(5 points each)* The chart below diagrams the development of the major ethnic and racial groups in the world today. Study the chart and answer the questions that follow.

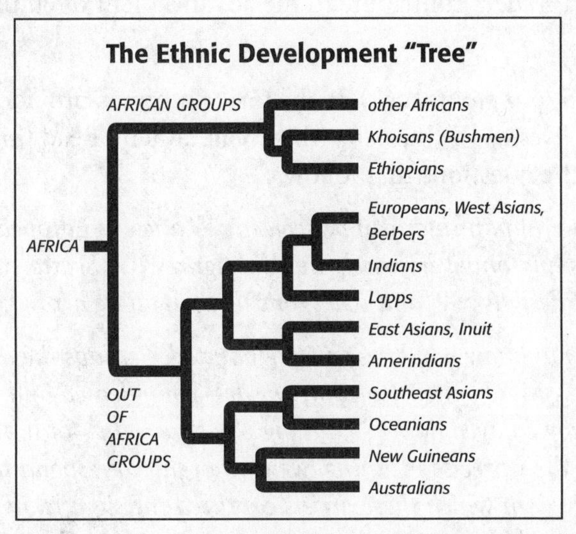

From "The Origins of Humankind" from *The History Atlas of Africa* by Samuel Kasule. Published by Macmillan Inc., New York, 1998.

1. According to the chart, what is the geographic origin of all races and ethnic groups in the world today?

____

2. Are the original people of East Asia (China, Japan, etc.) more closely related to the people of Southeast Asia (Vietnam, Thailand, etc.) or to the people of Europe? Explain how you know.

____

COMPOSING AN ESSAY *(20 points)* On a separate sheet of paper, write a brief essay in response to one of the following.

1. How did the development of language and writing help early human societies?

2. Why would people who created towns and cities also be likely to have developed some form of government?

Name ______________________ Class ______________ Date ______________

Chapter Test Form B

The Emergence of Civilization

SHORT ANSWER *(10 points each)* Provide brief answers for each of the following.

1. How do a culture and a civilization differ?

2. What evidence shows that Cro-Magnons were more advanced than other early humans?

3. How did the geography of river valleys aid in establishing early civilizations?

4. How and why did advances in farming affect the power of women in early societies?

5. In what ways did traders contribute to the advancement of cultures?

PRIMARY SOURCES *(10 points each)* Prehistoric paintings provide anthropologists with clues about the lives of the humans who created them. Read this modern-day passage and answer the questions that follow.

> *The first flowering [of painting] can be seen in . . . ancient European caves. . . . There are no landscapes and only very rarely human figures. . . . Scattered among the animals, there are abstract designs . . . [and] chevrons that might be arrows. . . .*
>
> *Even now, we do not know why these people painted. Perhaps the designs were part of a religious ritual. . . . Maybe their function was less complicated and the people painted simply because they enjoyed doing so, taking pleasure in art for art's sake. . . . Even if we are baffled by their precise meaning, we cannot fail to respond to the perceptiveness and . . . sensitivity with which these artists captured the significant outlines of a mammoth, the cocked heads of a herd of antlered deer or the looming bulk of a bison.*

1. What evidence do these paintings provide to indicate that the artists were hunters and gatherers?

2. What theories does the passage offer that suggest this culture was highly advanced compared to the earliest humans?

COMPOSING AN ESSAY *(30 points)* Write an essay on one of the following subjects. Remember to use examples to support your essay.

1. Explain how the growth of agriculture led to the development of civilization.

2. Contrast life in the Paleolithic Age with life in the Neolithic Age.

Name ______________________ Class ______________ Date ______________

Chapter Test Form A

The First Civilizations

MATCHING *(3 points each)* In the space provided, write the letter of the name or term that matches each description. Some answers will not be used.

______ **1.** formed city-states and developed the first civilization in the Fertile Crescent

______ **2.** united Egypt into one kingdom about 3200 B.C.

______ **3.** traders who lived in what is now Turkey and were first to use coins in their business dealings

______ **4.** biblical figure who led his people out of slavery in Egypt and presented them with the Ten Commandments that Yahweh had revealed to him

______ **5.** conquered much of the Fertile Crescent and Egypt and became the first to effectively govern a large empire

______ **6.** founded a religion in Persia that probably influenced Judaism and Christianity

______ **7.** turned to trade because they lacked fertile lands and became the greatest traders of ancient times

______ **8.** one of the first known female rulers who reigned as pharaoh of the New Kingdom of Egypt

______ **9.** compiled a collection of laws that governed business, work, and property rights and set harsh punishments for violators

______ **10.** established an empire in Mesopotamia that reached from the Persian Gulf to the Mediterranean Sea

a. Assyrians
b. Chaldeans
c. Hammurabi
d. Hatshepsut
e. Hebrews
f. Lydians
g. Menes
h. Moses
i. Phoenicians
j. Sargon
k. Sumerians
l. Zoroaster

UNDERSTANDING IDEAS *(3 points each)* For each of the following, write the letter of the best choice in the space provided.

______ **1.** The Egyptians built the pyramids to be
a. centers for celebrations.
b. temples for worship.
c. tombs for their rulers.
d. symbols of their power.

______ **2.** The writing the ancient Egyptians used is called
a. cuneiform.
b. papyrus.
c. ziggurats.
d. hieroglyphics.

_____ **3.** Which factor was most important in holding ancient empires together?
a. trade
b. strong rulers
c. religious beliefs
d. farming

_____ **4.** Which characteristic did Babylonian and Hebrew society have in common?
a. sets of written laws
b. election of their leaders
c. belief in the same gods
d. creation of city-states

_____ **5.** What brought about the collapse of Egypt's Old Kingdom?
a. invasions by outsiders
b. disputes over religion
c. weak rulers and civil wars
d. revolts against high taxes

_____ **6.** The main reason a civilization developed in Egypt was
a. the Nile River.
b. help from friendly peoples.
c. the building of pyramids.
d. conquest by outsiders.

_____ **7.** Which people conquered the greatest amount of territory?
a. the Akkadians
b. the Assyrians
c. the Babylonians
d. the Persians

_____ **8.** The Hebrews differed from most other ancient peoples because they
a. traded with their neighbors.
b. practiced monotheism.
c. did not believe in war.
d. were never ruled by others.

_____ **9.** Why was the Fertile Crescent frequently invaded?
a. It had water and good land.
b. No one lived there.
c. Its people were traders.
d. The Egyptians were weak.

_____ **10.** The alphabet we use today is modeled on an alphabet that was first developed by the
a. Sumerians.
b. Egyptians.
c. Phoenicians.
d. Hebrews.

TRUE/FALSE *(2 points each)* Mark each statement *T* if it is true or *F* if it is false.

_____ **1.** A dynasty is a form of government that unites different territories and people under one ruler.

_____ **2.** The use of money to purchase goods and services is known as the barter system.

_____ **3.** The most important contribution of the ancient Hebrews to Western civilization was ethical monotheism.

_____ **4.** The Hittites and the Chaldeans were among the peoples who invaded the Fertile Crescent.

______ **5.** The ancient Hebrews believed that the god Osiris judged people after death, determining the destination of their souls in the afterlife.

PRACTICING SKILLS *(5 points each)* Study the map and answer the questions that follow.

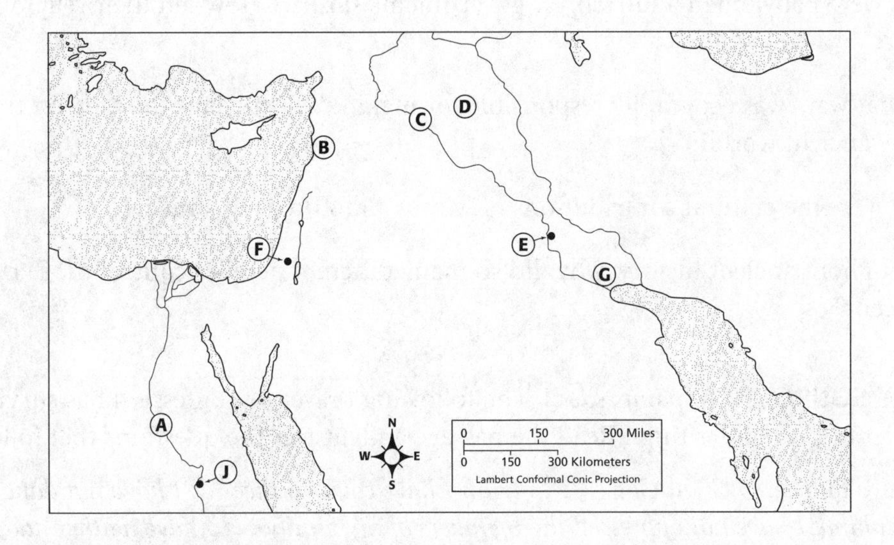

1. Which letter on the map shows where the Phoenicians lived?

____

2. What location does the letter *E* represent?

____

COMPOSING AN ESSAY *(20 points)* On a separate sheet of paper, write a brief essay in response to one of the following.

1. Compare and contrast the religious beliefs of the Sumerians and ancient Egyptians.

2. Explain how Egypt's geography allowed a great civilization to develop there.

Name ______________________ Class ______________ Date ____________

Chapter Test Form B

The First Civilizations

SHORT ANSWER *(10 points each)* Provide brief answers for each of the following.

1. What is the difference between a money economy and a barter system?
2. How were Babylonian and Hebrew governments similar? How did their religions differ?
3. In what ways was geography responsible for making Phoenicians the greatest traders of the ancient world?
4. How were the cultural contributions of Moses and Zoroaster similar?
5. Throughout ancient history, why did so many different peoples control the Fertile Crescent?

PRIMARY SOURCES *(10 points each)* The following prayer or confession has survived from ancient Egyptian writings. Read the passage and answer the questions that follow.

Homage to thee, O Great God. . . . In truth I have come to thee . . . I have not done evil to mankind. I have not oppressed the members of my family . . . I have neither added to nor filched away land. I have not encroached upon the fields of others. . . . I have not carried away the milk from the mouths of children. I have not driven away the cattle which were upon their pastures. . . .

Deliver me from Baba who feeds upon the entrails [insides] of the mighty on the day of the great judgment. Behold that I have come before you without sin, without guilt, without a witness against me, without anyone against whom I have borne false witness; therefore let nothing evil be done unto me. . . . I am pure of mouth and pure of hands; therefore let it be said unto me by those who shall behold me, "Come in peace; come in peace."

1. From the content of the passage and what you know about ancient Egyptians' religious beliefs, to whom is this prayer directed and for what purpose?
2. What clues does this prayer provide about the significance of agriculture in ancient Egypt?

COMPOSING AN ESSAY *(30 points)* Write an essay on one of the following subjects. Remember to use examples to support your essay.

1. Summarize the ways in which Sumerian and Egyptian civilization were similar. Consider geographic, economic, technological, and cultural factors in forming your comments.
2. Explain the role of trade in advancing culture and civilization in the ancient Mediterranean world.

Name ______________________ Class ______________ Date ____________

Chapter Test Form A

Ancient Indian Civilizations

MATCHING *(3 points each)* In the space provided, write the letter of the name that matches each description. Some answers will not be used.

______ **1.** ruler who reigned during the golden age of the Gupta empire

______ **2.** the most famous of the Hindu scriptures

______ **3.** the Indo-Aryans' great works of religious literature

______ **4.** priests who conducted Indo-Aryan religious rituals; the name given to priests and scholars in the Indian caste system

______ **5.** the language of the Indo-Aryans

______ **6.** founder of Buddhism who became known as the Buddha, or "the Enlightened One"

______ **7.** ruler who expanded the Mauryan Empire to include nearly all of India

______ **8.** mathematician who was one of first people to use algebra

______ **9.** a collection of explanations and teachings that became the basis for the Hindu religion

______ **10.** famous Buddhist university that became a center of Indian knowledge and learning

a. Aryabhata
b. Aśoka
c. Bhagavad Gita
d. Brahmins
e. Chandra Gupta II
f. Chandragupta Maurya
g. Nalanda
h. Pariahs
i. Sanskrit
j. Siddhartha Gautama
k. Upanishads
l. Vedas

UNDERSTANDING IDEAS *(3 points each)* For each of the following, write the letter of the best choice in the space provided.

______ **1.** The rise of ancient Harappan civilization was encouraged by
a. mild climates and monsoons on the Deccan.
b. land that was enriched and watered by the Indus River.
c. the heavy rains of the lower Ganges River.
d. the fertile plains that bordered the Bay of Bengal.

______ **2.** All of the following were important in Harappan culture EXCEPT
a. cities.
b. farming.
c. rebellions.
d. trade.

_____ **3.** What similarity did the Harappans have with the Indo-Aryans?
a. the color of their skin
b. a nomadic way of life
c. the structure of their society
d. the raising of livestock

_____ **4.** The people who entered India about 1750 B.C. and gradually shaped its social structure and religious development were the
a. Harappans.
b. Indo-Aryans.
c. Hindus.
d. Hindu Kush.

_____ **5.** Ancient Indian civilization produced all the following scientific and technological advances EXCEPT
a. inoculation.
b. plastic surgery.
c. mummification.
d. Arabic numerals.

_____ **6.** The young man who became the Buddha made a discovery that shaped his religious philosophy and teachings. What was it?
a. that challenges and tragedies were an everyday part of life
b. that some Indians led lives of luxury and advantage
c. that Indians were not united under one ruler
d. that the authority of the Brahmins should not be questioned

_____ **7.** The sequence of India's history, from early to late, is the
a. Vedic Age, Gupta Empire, and Maurya Empire.
b. Maurya Empire, Gupta Empire, and Vedic Age.
c. Vedic Age, Maurya Empire, and Gupta Empire.
d. Gupta Empire, Maurya Empire, and Vedic Age.

_____ **8.** The word that best describes the position of women in early Indian society is
a. enslaved.
b. independent.
c. equal.
d. obedient.

_____ **9.** Why has the period of Gupta rule been called a golden age in India's history?
a. The arts, sciences, and learning flourished.
b. The Buddhist and Hindu religions were founded.
c. India's greatest religious books were written.
d. Indian artisans produced beautiful objects from gold.

_____ **10.** All of the following were direct or indirect results of the Vedic Age EXCEPT
a. the caste system.
b. great works of literature.
c. the unification of India.
d. the Hindu religion.

TRUE/FALSE *(2 points each)* Mark each statement *T* if it is true or *F* if it is false.

______ **1.** Typhoons bring much of the year's rainfall to most of India.

______ **2.** Much of what we know of Harappan civilization comes from the ruins of Harappa and Mohenjo Daro.

______ **3.** Early civilization in southern India followed patterns of development that were different from those in the north.

______ **4.** Freedom of religion existed in both the Maurya and Gupta empires.

______ **5.** The Maurya Empire was larger and lasted longer than the Gupta Empire.

PRACTICING SKILLS *(5 points each)* Study the map and answer the questions that follow.

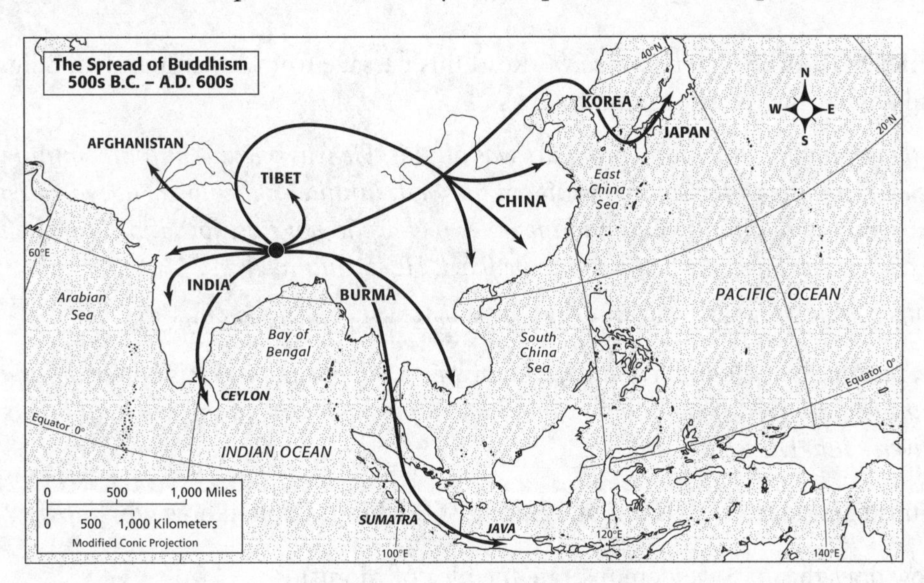

1. Which people had the most direct influence on Buddhism in Japan? Explain why.

____

2. Did Buddhism affect life in Japan before it did so in Ceylon? Explain why or why not.

____

COMPOSING AN ESSAY *(20 points)* On a separate sheet of paper, write a brief essay in response to one of the following.

1. Identify beliefs that early Hindus and Buddhists shared, as well as Hindu beliefs that were rejected by the Buddha.

2. Compare and contrast the reasons that the Maurya and Gupta empires collapsed.

Name ______________________ Class ______________ Date ____________

Chapter Test Form B

Ancient Indian Civilizations

SHORT ANSWER *(10 points each)* Provide brief answers for each of the following.

1. How did geography shape the development of an advanced Harappan civilization?

2. Who were the Indo-Aryans, and how did they differ from the Harappans?

3. What are the Vedas and the Upanishads, and how are they important in Indian history?

4. What was Indo-Aryan government like before the Maurya and Gupta empires came to power?

5. How can the position of women in early Indian society best be described?

PRIMARY SOURCES *(10 points each)* Read this passage from an early Indian religious text and answer the questions that follow.

> *In the beginning Brahman [Brahma] was all this. He was one and infinite: infinite in the east, infinite in the south, infinite in the west, infinite in the north, above and below and everywhere infinite. East and the other regions do not exist for Him . . . no beneath, no above. The Supreme Self is not to be fixed. He is unlimited. . . .*
>
> [T]*he Self of all things, which exists everywhere, being all-pervading. . . .*
>
> *He, the One and Undifferentiated, who by the . . . application of His powers produces, in the beginning, different objects for a hidden purpose, and, in the end, withdraws the universe into Himself. . . .*

1. Is this passage from a Hindu or a Buddhist teaching? Explain how you know.

2. How does this passage demonstrate the idea of monism?

COMPOSING AN ESSAY *(30 points)* Write an essay on one of the following subjects. Remember to use examples to support your essay.

1. Compare and contrast the way early civilization developed in northern India with the way it developed in southern India.

2. Summarize the achievements of the Maurya and Gupta empires in the arts, architecture, and sciences.

Name ______________________ Class ______________ Date ____________

Chapter Test Form A

Ancient Chinese Civilization

FILL IN THE BLANK *(3 points each)* For each of the following statements, fill in the blank with the appropriate name, term, or phrase.

1. Cheng, who assigned himself the title Shih Huang Ti, meaning "first emperor," founded the ______________________ dynasty in 221 B.C.

2. Followers of the great philosopher ______________________ collected his ideas and teachings on a work called the *Analects.*

3. ______________________ washes into the Huang River and gives it a yellow tint.

4. A therapy called ______________________ is perhaps the best known early Chinese contribution to medicine.

5. The belief that an emperor was supported by the gods in his rule of China was called the ______________________.

6. One reason Han rulers were more effective than earlier Chinese rulers was because the Han established a centralized ______________________ to govern China.

7. To protect their crops, early Chinese farmers built earthen walls called ______________________ along the Huang River.

8. Ancient Chinese believed everything resulted from the balance between two forces they called ______________________ and ______________________.

UNDERSTANDING IDEAS *(3 points each)* For each of the following, write the letter of the best choice in the space provided.

______ **1.** The Chinese dynasty that lasted longest was the
a. Shang.
b. Zhou.
c. Qin.
d. Han.

______ **2.** All the early dynasties in China created strong central governments EXCEPT the
a. Shang.
b. Han.
c. Qin.
d. Zhou.

_____ **3.** One Chinese contribution to the world was the invention of
a. paper.
b. writing.
c. photography.
d. the steam engine.

_____ **4.** One way in which Chinese writing differs from Western writing is that Chinese writing
a. is easier to learn.
b. uses a smaller alphabet.
c. consists of symbols.
d. is written left to right.

_____ **5.** The biggest problems the Huang River caused in China resulted from the river's
a. lack of water.
b. shallow depth.
c. yellow water.
d. devastating floods.

_____ **6.** The belief that people required harsh laws to control them was part of the Chinese philosophy of
a. Daoism.
b. Legalism.
c. Confucianism.
d. Mahayana Buddhism.

_____ **7.** Which emperor started a university to train government workers and set up a program to store grain for use in lean years?
a. Di-xin
b. Liu Bang
c. Chang Jung
d. Liu Ch'e

_____ **8.** Shang religious practices and beliefs included all of the following EXCEPT
a. ancestor worship.
b. the use of oracle bones.
c. a belief in reincarnation.
d. festivals when planting and harvesting crops.

_____ **9.** The importance of family, respect for elders, and reverence for ancestors form the basis of
a. Confucianism.
b. Daoism.
c. Legalism.
d. Mahayana Buddhism.

_____ **10.** Humbleness, thoughtfulness, and withdrawal from the world to contemplate nature are all teachings of
a. Legalism.
b. Confucianism.
c. Daoism.
d. Mahayana Buddhism.

TRUE/FALSE *(2 points each)* Mark each statement *T* if it is true or *F* if it is false.

_____ **1.** The teachings and principles of Daoism were compiled in a book called the *Dao De Jing.*

_____ **2.** The art of writing that was developed by the early Chinese is called animism.

_____ **3.** Mothers and mothers-in-law held positions of great respect in early Chinese society.

_______ **4.** Texts known as the Five Classics were used to train civil servants and scholars in ancient China.

_______ **5.** Among the contributions the early Chinese made to technology were the invention of the sundial and the water clock.

_______ **6.** China's economy during the Shang dynasty was based mainly on trade.

_______ **7.** Women enjoyed the same rights and power as men in early Chinese society.

_______ **8.** The first dynasty to rule in China was the Qin.

PRACTICING SKILLS *(5 points each)* In the 400s B.C. the Warring States competed to control China. Study the map of the Warring States and answer the questions that follow.

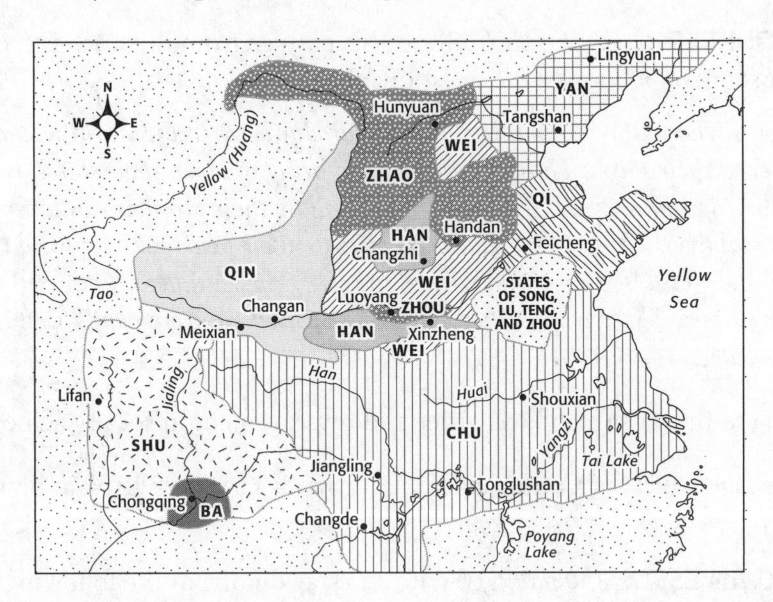

1. What state lay to the west of Zhao?

____

2. Which state controlled the most territory?

____

COMPOSING AN ESSAY *(20 points)* On a separate sheet of paper, write a brief essay in response to one of the following.

1. Explain how geography influenced the development of early Chinese culture and shaped Chinese attitudes toward foreigners.

2. Summarize and contrast the reasons for the rise and fall of the Zhou, Qin, and Shang dynasties.

Name ______________________ Class ______________ Date ____________

Chapter Test Form B

Ancient Chinese Civilization

SHORT ANSWER *(10 points each)* Provide brief answers for each of the following.

1. Why did the flooding of the Huang River become a more serious problem with the passage of time?

2. What factors explain why the early Chinese referred to foreigners as "barbarians"?

3. What conditions and beliefs explain the religious practices of Shang-era Chinese?

4. What was family life for women like in early Chinese society?

5. What scientific, medical, and technological advances did the early Chinese make?

PRIMARY SOURCES *(10 points each)* Read this passage from the teachings of one early Chinese philosopher and answer the questions that follow.

> *The ancients who wished to manifest their clear character to the world would first bring order to their states. Those who wished to bring order to their states, would first regulate their families. Those who wished to regulate their families would first cultivate their personal lives. Those who wished to cultivate their personal lives would first rectify [improve] their minds. Those who wished to rectify their minds would first make their wills sincere. Those who wished to make their wills sincere would first extend their knowledge.*

1. According to the passage, how is order and improvement in society achieved?

2. Is this passage typical of Confucianism, Daoism, or Legalism? Explain how you know.

COMPOSING AN ESSAY *(30 points)* Write an essay on one of the following subjects. Remember to give examples to support your essay.

1. Explain how the Han dynasty illustrates the ideas of Confucianism and how the Qin showed the influence of Legalism.

2. Which dynasty—the Shang, Qin, or Han—did the most to advance Chinese civilization? Explain and support your opinion.

Name ______________ Class ________ Date ________

Unit Test Form A

The Beginnings of Civilization

UNDERSTANDING IDEAS *(3 points each)* For each of the following, write the letter of the best choice in the space provided.

_____ **1.** One of the characteristics that makes a culture also a civilization is
a. a highly developed agriculture.
b. having religious beliefs.
c. the domestication of animals.
d. a division of labor.

_____ **2.** The rulers responsible for a "golden age" in early India were the
a. Indo-Aryans.
b. Han.
c. Gupta.
d. Maurya.

_____ **3.** The first civilizations in India, China, Egypt, and Mesopotamia all
a. developed along rivers.
b. were organized into city-states.
c. were ruled by pharaohs.
d. disappeared for some unknown reason.

_____ **4.** Which of the following is NOT evidence that Neanderthals and Cro-Magnons were more advanced than earlier prehistoric humans?
a. They both lived in colder regions of the world.
b. They both hunted and lived in caves.
c. Neanderthals buried tools with their dead.
d. Cro-Magnons painted on cave walls.

_____ **5.** Ancient civilization in the Fertile Crescent probably reached its highest point under the rule of the
a. Hittites.
b. Chaldeans.
c. Hebrews.
d. Sumerians.

_____ **6.** The Chinese philosophy that emphasizes family and ancestors, proper behavior, and duty to society is
a. Buddhism.
b. Confucianism.
c. Daoism.
d. yin and yang.

_____ **7.** Early leaders who are known for the written laws they provided to their people include all of the following EXCEPT
a. Asóka in India.
b. the Babylonian leader Hammurabi.
c. the Hebrew leader Moses.
d. Liu Ch'e in China.

_____ **8.** The order of prehistoric human development, from early to late, is the
a. Stone Age, Iron Age, and Bronze Age.
b. Iron Age, Bronze Age, and Stone Age.
c. Stone Age, Bronze Age, and Iron Age.
d. Iron Age, Stone Age, and Bronze Age.

______ **9.** All of the following regions grew as the result of invasions by outsiders. Which region did invasion affect the MOST?
a. China
b. Egypt
c. India
d. Mesopotamia

______ **10.** Early Chinese civilization reached its height under
a. Zhou and Han rulers.
b. Han and Gupta rulers.
c. Gupta and Qin rulers.
d. Qin and Maurya rulers.

MATCHING *(3 points each)* In the space provided, write the letter of the name or term that matches each description. Some answers will not be used.

______ **1.** family of rulers

______ **2.** belief in only one god

______ **3.** human or early humanlike creature

______ **4.** system of government in which one ruler holds total power

______ **5.** government organized into different levels and tasks

______ **6.** the set of beliefs, knowledge, and patterns of living that a group of people develop

______ **7.** object that reveals information about the lives of early peoples

______ **8.** belief that spirits inhabit all objects

______ **9.** belief that all things are of the same essence as God

______ **10.** government officials who run the day-to-day business of government

a. animism
b. artifact
c. autocracy
d. bureaucracy
e. civil servants
f. culture
g. domestication
h. dynasty
i. hieroglyphics
j. hominid
k. monism
l. monotheism

TRUE/FALSE *(2 points each)* Mark each statement *T* if it is true or *F* if it is false.

______ **1.** The early Chinese, Egyptian, and Sumerian writing systems were similar because they all used symbols or drawings of objects to represent words.

______ **2.** Early civilizations in Egypt, China, and India made great advances in science and technology, while those in Mesopotamia did not.

______ **3.** An event that happened in 1500 B.C. took place about 1,500 years ago.

_______ **4.** The Indo-Aryans, a people who came to India from north of the Black and Caspian Seas, brought religious beliefs that became the basis of Hinduism.

_______ **5.** Buddhism and Daoism, a religion and a philosophy that each began in early China, had a great influence on other civilizations as they spread across Asia.

PRACTICING SKILLS *(5 points each)* Study the map below about the beginnings of civilization and answer the questions that follow.

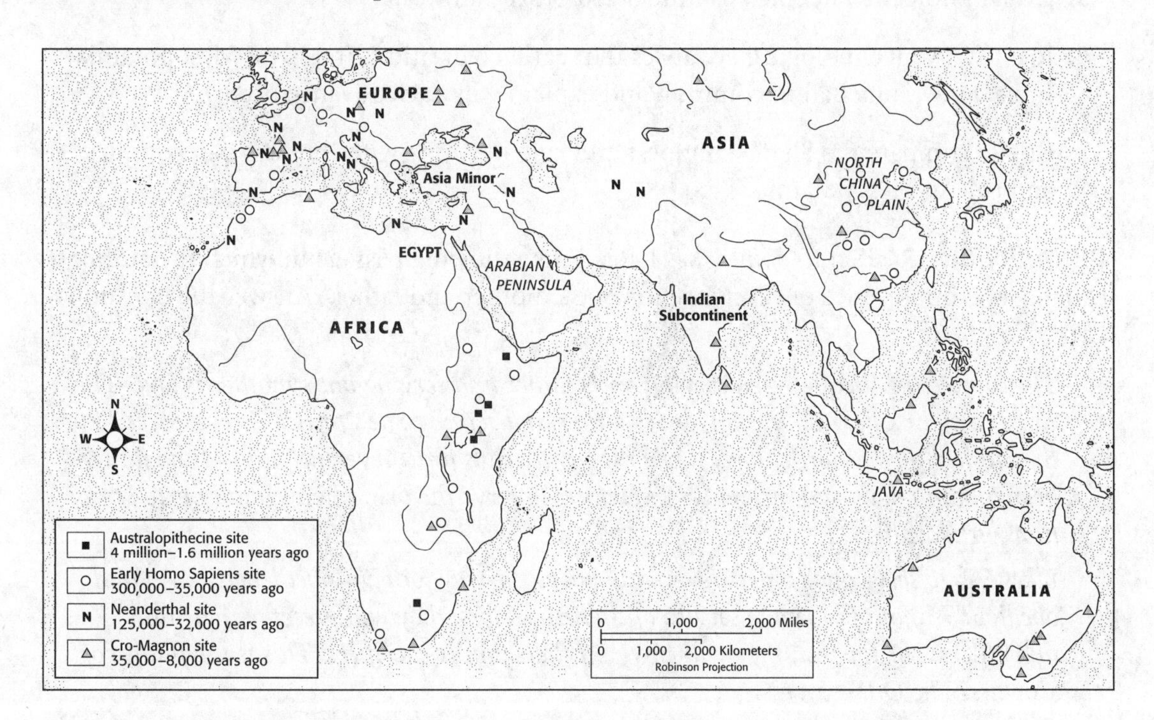

1. Most of the Neanderthal sites are located on which continent?

____

2. What was the general pattern of migration that human beings followed over time?

____

COMPOSING AN ESSAY *(20 points)* On a separate sheet of paper, write a brief essay in response to one of the following.

1. Describe the impact of the Neolithic agricultural revolution on the development of civilization. In forming your answer, consider the characteristics of civilization and think about how each civilization depended on the Neolithic agricultural revolution or developed as a result of it.

2. Summarize the important achievements of the early Egyptians, Indians, and Chinese in mathematics, medicine, science, and technology.

Name ______________________ Class ______________ Date ____________

Unit Test Form B

The Beginnings of Civilization

SHORT ANSWER *(10 points each)* Provide brief answers for each of the following

1. Explain how experts learn about early peoples who left no written record.
2. Explain the difference between a culture and a civilization. Is it possible for either to exist without the other?
3. Explain how the Phoenicians influenced other cultures.
4. Identify two technological advances that early civilizations in Egypt, Mesopotamia, India, and China had in common and explain why each advance occurred.
5. Briefly compare the Shang conquest and rule in China with the Assyrian conquest and rule in Mesopotamia.

PRIMARY SOURCES *(10 points each)* Read the following passage in which the author explains the importance of reverence for one's mother and father. Answer the questions that follow.

> *The connecting link between serving one's father and serving one's mother is love. The connecting link between serving one's father and serving one's prince is reverence. Thus the mother [brings forth] love, while the prince calls forth reverence. But to the father belong both—love and reverence. Therefore, to serve the prince with filialty is to serve him with loyalty.*
>
> *Likewise, to serve one's elders reverently paves the way for civic obedience. Loyal and obedient without fail in the service of their superiors, they will preserve their rank and offices. For the rest, they will carry on their family sacrifices. This is the filialty of scholars. The Odes say:*
>
> *Rise early and retire late,*
> *Not to discredit those [from whom you are born].*

1. What are the author's views on the relationship of people's attitudes toward families and their roles in society?
2. Which religion or philosophy that you have studied in Unit 1 is this passage discussing? What clues in the passage support your conclusion?

COMPOSING AN ESSAY *(30 points)* Write an essay on one of the following subjects.

1. Choose two of the major world religions you have studied in Unit 1: Judaism, Hinduism, and Buddhism. Describe three basic beliefs held by followers of each of the two religions.
2. Identify the geographic factors that allowed ancient Egypt and ancient China to develop in relative isolation and explain how this isolation affected the culture that developed in each region. Remember to use examples to support your essay.

Name ______________________ Class ______________ Date ____________

Chapter Test Form A

The Greek City-States

FILL IN THE BLANK *(3 points each)* For each of the following statements, fill in the blank with the appropriate name, term, or phrase.

1. The Delian League was an alliance of city-states formed to protect themselves against an attack by ______________________.

2. The archon ______________________ eased tensions in Athens by outlawing the practice of enslaving people who could not pay their debts.

3. City-states that were governed by nobles were known as ______________________, which meant "rule by the best."

4. At the Battle of Thermopylae, a Spartan army fought to the death against an army from ______________________.

5. When the Spartans invaded the Peloponnesus and founded their city-state, they called the native people ______________________ and turned them into slaves.

6. Early Greeks were entertained and informed about their history by traveling poets who recited ______________________ about great heroes, deeds, and events.

7. The most important economic activity in Athens was ______________________.

8. With its ally Sparta, ______________________ was victorious in the Persian Wars.

9. Athens reached its peak of democracy, power, and wealth under the leadership of ______________________.

10. The Greek poet ______________________ is credited with writing the *Iliad* and the *Odyssey*, two of the greatest works in world literature.

UNDERSTANDING IDEAS *(3 points each)* For each of the following, write the letter of the best choice in the space provided.

______ **1.** Which requirement did a resident of Sparta have to meet to be a citizen?
- **a.** be born in Sparta
- **b.** be a Greek who had served in the military
- **c.** be descended from one of the Spartan invaders
- **d.** be male and not enslaved

______ **2.** Which group had full political rights in Athens?
- **a.** all citizens
- **b.** all adult males who were born in Athens
- **c.** all male and female adults
- **d.** all adult males who paid taxes

______ **3.** All these factors kept the Greeks divided EXCEPT
a. a lack of democracy.
b. the Peloponnesian War.
c. mountains and rivers.
d. the growth of city-states.

______ **4.** The geographic feature that was most important to the growth of Greek trade was
a. a good river system.
b. dry climate and poor soil.
c. the long uneven coastline.
d. mountains to the north.

______ **5.** The central idea of the polis was based on
a. strict religious beliefs and practices.
b. dependence on overseas colonies and trade.
c. the unity, common ancestry, and national identity of all Greeks.
d. territory, community, and political and economic independence.

______ **6.** Which activity was LEAST important to life in Athens?
a. education
b. military training
c. politics and government
d. athletics and fitness

______ **7.** Which activity was most important to the Spartans?
a. military service
b. religious festivals
c. trade and business
d. taking part in government

______ **8.** The metics of Athens were most like which residents of Sparta?
a. helots
b. equals
c. half-citizens
d. nobles

______ **9.** From first to last, the correct sequence of leaders who brought democratic change to Athens is
a. Draco, Peisistratus, Solon, Cleisthenes, and Pericles.
b. Draco, Solon, Cleisthenes, Peisistratus, and Pericles.
c. Draco, Cleisthenes, Solon, Peisistratus, and Pericles.
d. Draco, Solon, Peisistratus, Cleisthenes, and Pericles.

______ **10.** The earliest Greek civilization developed
a. in the Peloponnesus.
b. on the island of Crete.
c. in a river valley.
d. at Athens and Sparta.

TRUE/FALSE *(2 points each)* Mark each statement *T* if it is true or *F* if it is false.

______ **1.** In both Athens and Sparta, all free men paid taxes, but only male citizens could own land or hold government office.

______ **2.** The pedagogues set up schools in Athens where older boys studied government, mathematics, and other subjects.

______ **3.** One condition that promoted the rise of democracy in Athens was fostering anger and discontent among the poor.

_______ **4.** Slavery existed in both Athens and Sparta, but the number of slaves in each society was not very great.

_______ **5.** An erupting volcano and tidal waves caused the decline and eventual fall of the first Greek civilization on the island of Crete.

PRACTICING SKILLS *(5 points each)* Study the chart below and answer the questions that follow.

THE ATHENIAN GOVERNMENT (5th century, B.C.)

LEGISLATIVE

The Assembly
Consisted of all male citizens over 20 years old.
Made the laws and voted policy and taxes.

The Council of 500
Chosen by lot to serve one year. Proposed laws to the Assembly.

EXECUTIVE	JUDICIAL
Nine Archons and the Commander in Chief Elected annually by the Assembly. Directed policy and the armed forces. **Other Officials** Chosen by lot to serve one year.	**Juries** Consisted of members of the Assembly, who were chosen by lot. Tried all law cases.

1. Which Athenian government body is an example of direct democracy?

____

2. What type of democracy is illustrated by the nine archons? Explain why.

____

COMPOSING AN ESSAY *(20 points)* On a separate sheet of paper, write a brief essay in response to one of the following.

1. Describe how hoplites and tyrants aided the growth of democracy in Greek city-states.

2. Explain the causes and consequences of the Peloponnesian War.

Name ______________________ Class ______________ Date ______________

Chapter Test Form B

The Greek City-States

SHORT ANSWER *(10 points each)* Provide brief answers for each of the following.

1. Explain how Greece's geography both encouraged and discouraged trade.

2. Identify the geographic and political conditions that kept Greece divided.

3. Explain why the Delian League was formed and how it helped to divide the Greeks, as well as unite them.

4. Describe the difference between a representative democracy and a direct democracy.

5. Compare the class structure of Athens and Sparta.

PRIMARY SOURCES *(10 points each)* The excerpt below describes children's education in one of the Greek city-states. Read the passage and answer the questions that follow.

> *Lycurgus [a great Spartan leader] did not permit children to be taught by slaves, but he had them enrolled at the age of seven in companies or classes, where they received uniform discipline and instruction. The major emphasis in their education was on perfect obedience. The old men witnessed the children's lessons and exercises and drills, and often started quarrels among the students to test which ones would be brave and which would be cowards when they later faced real dangers. The young studied only enough of reading and writing to be able to perform their civic duties. They were taught mainly to endure pain and to persevere in battle.*

1. What were the goals of the instruction at this school?

2. Did this school likely exist in Athens or in Sparta? Explain how you know.

COMPOSING AN ESSAY *(30 points)* Write an essay on one of the following subjects.

1. Summarize the process by which many Greek city-states evolved from kingdoms to more democratic forms of government.

2. During the Age of Pericles, when Athenian democracy reached its height, Athens chose some of its officials by holding a drawing for the job. Is this a democratic way of selecting leaders? Explain why or why not.

Name ______________________ Class ______________ Date ____________

Chapter Test Form A

Greece's Golden and Hellenistic Ages

MATCHING *(3 points each)* In the space provided, write the letter of the name or term that matches each description. Some answers will not be used.

_____ **1.** philosopher who taught that the aim of life is to seek pleasure and avoid pain

_____ **2.** great teacher who was sentenced to death for criticizing Greek leaders and democracy

_____ **3.** Father of History and the first great historian of the Western world

_____ **4.** Athenian sculptor who created statues of the gods that decorated the Parthenon and the Temple of Olympia

_____ **5.** scientist who used math and physics to invent important labor-saving machines

_____ **6.** medical pioneer who taught that disease comes from natural causes and not from the gods

_____ **7.** philosopher who wrote about government, justice, and the nature of physical and spiritual things

_____ **8.** thinker who developed approaches to organizing information that are now part of modern science

_____ **9.** philosopher who believed that everything could be explained in terms of mathematics

_____ **10.** public speaker who warned the Greeks about the threat to their freedom posed by the kingdom of Macedon

a. Archimedes
b. Aristotle
c. Demosthenes
d. Epicurus
e. Euripides
f. Herodotus
g. Hippocrates
h. Phidias
i. Plato
j. Pythagoras
k. Socrates
l. Sophocles

UNDERSTANDING IDEAS *(3 points each)* For each of the following, write the letter of the best choice in the space provided.

_____ **1.** The leader who ended the independence of the city-states and united Greece under his rule was
a. Alexander the Great.
b. Philip II of Macedon.
c. King Darius of Persia.
d. Demosthenes.

_____ **2.** One change in art during the golden age was that
a. painting was introduced.
b. sculpture was introduced.
c. figures became more life-like and realistic.
d. animals became subjects of art.

_____ **3.** In the Hellenistic Age, people who lived outside Greece were considered "Greek" if they
a. were married to a Greek.
b. adopted Greek culture.
c. had Greek ancestors.
d. spoke the Greek language.

_____ **4.** Aristotle wanted to reduce government corruption by
a. establishing a democracy.
b. letting women vote.
c. uniting the city-states.
d. combining democracy with monarchy and aristocracy.

_____ **5.** Alexander the Great controlled his empire by all of the following methods EXCEPT
a. dividing it into several large and small kingdoms.
b. letting some conquered peoples help in their rule.
c. marrying two Persian noblewomen.
d. spreading Greek culture into conquered regions.

_____ **6.** Art in the golden age expressed all of the following values EXCEPT
a. the glorification of humans and human actions.
b. the desire for all Greeks to be united.
c. a belief in order, harmony, and simplicity.
d. a belief that beautiful things should also be useful.

_____ **7.** The Greeks' conquests under Alexander mixed Asian and Mediterranean cultures to create a way of life that became known as
a. Hellenic culture.
b. the golden age.
c. Hellenistic culture.
d. the Age of Pericles.

_____ **8.** The golden age was the period of time when the Greeks reached new heights of
a. culture.
b. military power.
c. trade.
d. empire.

_____ **9.** Which was NOT a change that occurred in Greek society during the Hellenistic Age?
a. Old values faded, and women won new rights.
b. People's loyalty to their city-states increased.
c. Education became more widespread.
d. The expansion of trade spread prosperity.

_____ **10.** One theme missing from plays in the golden age was
a. traditional Greek values.
b. the relationship between people and the gods.
c. making fun of people and ideas.
d. the glorification of war, conquest, and empire.

TRUE/FALSE *(2 points each)* Mark each statement *T* if it is true or *F* if it is false.

_______ **1.** To honor Athena, the people of Athens built a temple called the Acropolis.

_______ **2.** The Greeks were the first people to write dramas.

_______ **3.** Philip II of Macedon was the son of Alexander the Great.

_______ **4.** The Stoic philosophers believed that people should accept their fate.

_______ **5.** The Skeptic philosophers believed that all knowledge is uncertain.

PRACTICING SKILLS *(5 points each)* Study the map and use its information to answer the questions that follow.

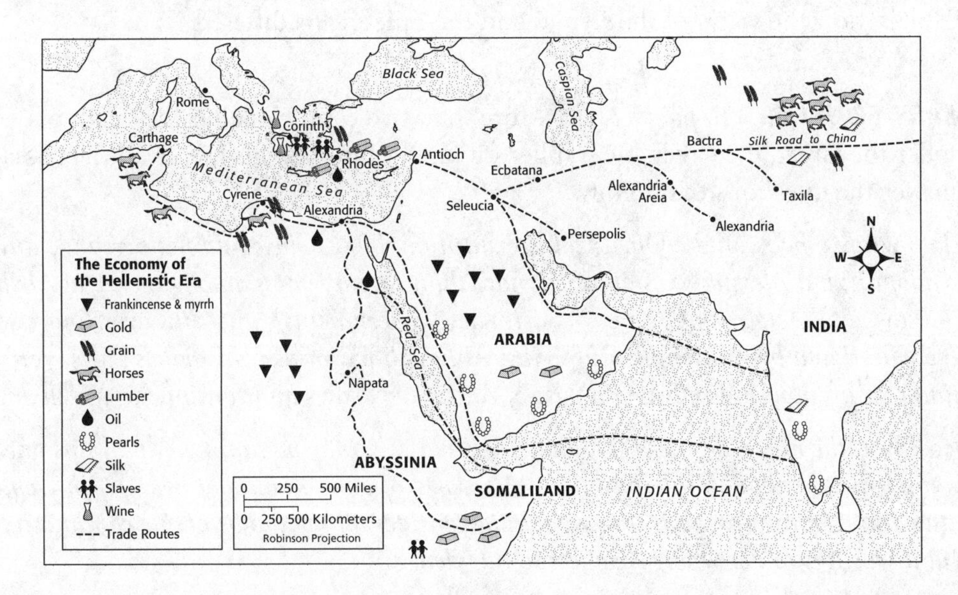

1. What items from mainland Greece could have been traded in the rest of the empire?

____

2. What evidence suggests that Alexandria, Egypt, was a leading center of trade?

____

COMPOSING AN ESSAY *(20 points)* On a separate sheet of paper, write a brief essay in response to one of the following.

1. Describe how Alexander the Great tried to unite Persian and Greek culture and explain why he made the effort to do this.

2. Identify and explain three Greek accomplishments in mathematics along with the applications that remain useful today.

Name ______________________ Class ______________ Date ______________

Chapter Test Form B

Greece's Golden and Hellenistic Ages

SHORT ANSWER *(10 points each)* Provide brief answers for each of the following.

1. Identify two goals of Greek art in the golden age and explain how each was achieved.

2. Explain how Socrates differed from most Greek teachers and why that difference made powerful Greeks his enemies.

3. Identify and explain two nonmilitary methods that Alexander the Great used to help unify his empire.

4. Name three contributions, other than their value as entertainment, that Greek comedy and tragedy made to society.

5. Explain how the views of the Cynics and the Epicureans differed.

PRIMARY SOURCES *(10 points each)* More than two centuries after the death of Alexander the Great, the Greek biographer Plutarch examined his life. Read the passage and answer the questions that follow.

> *Plato wrote a book on the One Ideal Constitution, but . . . he could not persuade anyone to adopt it; but Alexander established more than seventy cities among the savage tribes, and sowed all Asia with Grecian magistracies [governments], and thus overcame its uncivilized and brutish manner of living. Although few of us read Plato's* Laws, *yet hundreds of thousands have made use of Alexander's laws and continue to use them. . . .*
>
> *Moreover, the much-admired Republic [of Zeno] . . . may be summed up in this one main principle: that all inhabitants of this world of ours should not live . . . [in] separate cities and communities, but that we should consider all men to be of one community. . . . But it was Alexander who gave effect to the idea.*

1. Whom does Plutarch admire more, Alexander or Plato? Explain why.

2. Does Plutarch's attitude toward non-Greeks express Hellenistic values? Explain why or why not.

COMPOSING AN ESSAY *(30 points)* Write an essay on one of the following subjects. Remember to use examples to support your essay.

1. What caused the middle ranks of society to expand during the Hellenistic Age, and how did this process affect society and traditional Greek culture?

2. For what reasons might Greek city-states have decided to ignore Demosthenes' warnings about the threat posed by Philip II of Macedon?

Name ______________________________ Class ______________ Date ____________

Chapter Test Form A

The Roman World

FILL IN THE BLANK *(3 points each)* For each of the following statements, fill in the blank with the appropriate name, term, or phrase.

1. Because of the ________________________, many Romans demanded that the city of Carthage be destroyed.

2. The Romans depended on the ________________________ to bring water from the mountains.

3. The ________________________ culture had the strongest outside influence on Roman culture.

4. The murder of ________________________ resulted in a power struggle that eventually brought the republic to an end.

5. Struggles known as the ________________________ won the common people more rights during the Roman Republic.

6. In the A.D. 400s, as the power of Rome declined, two peoples called the Visigoths and the ________________________ attacked the city and looted it.

7. During emergencies in the republic, a ________________________ could be appointed to rule with total authority for up to six months.

8. During the ________________________, the Roman Empire grew and prospered for about 200 years.

9. The spread of Christianity in the Roman Empire was furthered when the emperor ________________________ converted to the faith.

10. Conflict between ________________________, trained fighters who were usually slaves, was a popular form of entertainment in the Roman Empire.

UNDERSTANDING IDEAS *(3 points each)* For each of the following, write the letter of the best choice in the space provided.

______ **1.** Julius Caesar came to power in Rome
- **a.** as a member of Senate.
- **b.** because he had an army.
- **c.** by defeating Hannibal.
- **d.** when Cleopatra gave him her support.

______ **2.** All these elements of Roman culture are a major influence in the world today EXCEPT their
- **a.** alphabet.
- **b.** language.
- **c.** early religion.
- **d.** republican system of government.

______ **3.** The Roman Republic became the Roman Empire when
a. the Senate gave Octavian the title Augustus.
b. the Romans first expanded outside Italy.
c. the First Triumvirate was established.
d. the patricians took control of government.

______ **4.** Which was NOT a cause of the Roman Empire's decline?
a. government weaknesses
b. invasions by Germans
c. economic problems
d. the rise of Christianity

______ **5.** Diocletian tried to slow the Roman Empire's decline by
a. turning half of the empire over to a co-emperor.
b. giving land to invading barbarian tribes.
c. expanding the size of the Senate.
d. increasing the personal freedoms of Romans.

______ **6.** Christianity gained popularity in the Roman Empire because
a. followers were allowed to continue worshipping their traditional gods.
b. Jesus had pledged his loyalty to the emperor.
c. it offered hope to people who were poor or suffering.
d. its leaders sought the protection and support of wealthy Romans.

______ **7.** Which statement does NOT describe the economy of the Roman Empire?
a. A widespread trade network developed.
b. Most Romans lived well, and few were truly poor.
c. Farming was an important occupation.
d. Slavery existed throughout the empire.

______ **8.** The conflict between Rome and Carthage was known as the
a. Pax Romana.
b. Social War.
c. Punic Wars.
d. Conflict of the Orders.

______ **9.** One reason Roman leaders finally accepted Christianity is because the
a. Christians agreed to pay taxes.
b. northern barbarian tribes adopted the faith.
c. leaders feared Christianity less than Judaism.
d. number of Christians grew too large to punish.

______ **10.** Struggles with the patricians during the early days of the republic gained the plebeians all of the following EXCEPT
a. the right to hold an important public office.
b. the creation of written laws.
c. control of the government.
d. the right to join the army.

TRUE/FALSE *(2 points each)* Mark each statement *T* if it is true or *F* if it is false.

______ **1.** Before they established their republic, the Romans were ruled by the Greeks.

______ **2.** Most of the settlements in the Roman Empire were on coasts because travel inland was difficult.

______ **3.** The common people of early Rome were known as plebeians.

______ **4.** Christians who were put to death for their beliefs became known as Zealots.

______ **5.** Before Christianity arrived, most Romans were Jews.

PRACTICING SKILLS *(5 points each)* Study the bar graph and answer the questions that follow.

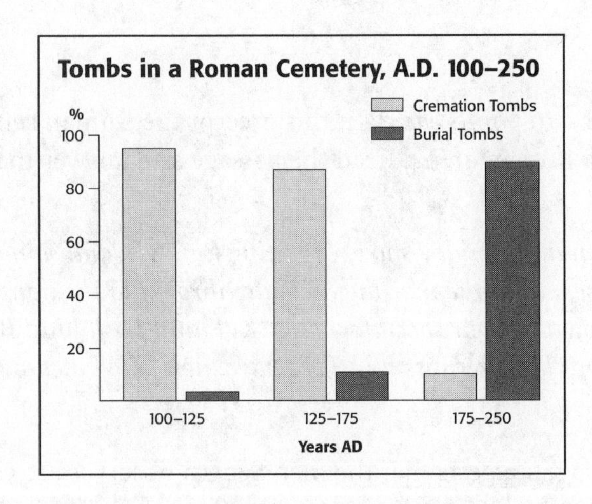

1. What happened to the remains of most dead Romans in A.D. 125?

____

2. After A.D. 140, most Roman expansion occurred to the east, where people buried their dead. What does the graph suggest about how Roman culture was influenced by this expansion?

____

COMPOSING AN ESSAY *(20 points)* On a separate sheet of paper, write a brief essay in response to one of the following.

1. Describe the basic structure of government during the Roman Republic, including the main functions of each governing body and elected official.

2. Summarize Rome's early policies on governing conquered peoples. Then describe the changes in those policies and explain how they weakened the empire.

Name ______________________ Class ______________ Date ____________

Chapter Test Form B

The Roman World

SHORT ANSWER *(10 points each)* Provide brief answers for each of the following.

1. What are the Twelve Tables, and how did they affect the power distribution between plebeians and patricians in the early Roman Republic?

2. What were Rome's policies toward the peoples they conquered, and how did those policies change over time?

3. Why did Diocletian believe that dividing the Roman Empire would strengthen it?

4. How did political and economic conditions in the Roman Empire aid the spread of Christianity as the Roman Empire declined?

5. What was the Romans' transportation network like, and in what ways did it benefit the empire?

PRIMARY SOURCES *(10 points each)* In this excerpt the Roman senator Seneca describes his visit to a Roman arena. Read the passage and answer the questions that follow.

> *I chanced to stop in at a midday show, expecting fun, wit, and some relaxation. . . . It was just the reverse. . . . in the morning men are thrown to the lions and the bears, at noon they are thrown to their spectators. . . . "Kill him! Lash him! Burn him! . . ." And when the show stops for intermission, "Let's have men killed meanwhile! Let's not have nothing going on!"*

1. What in this passage suggests that the men Seneca observes are criminals and not trained fighters?

2. What opinion does Seneca seem to have about this form of entertainment?

COMPOSING AN ESSAY *(30 points)* Write an essay on one of the following subjects. Remember to use examples to support your essay.

1. Describe the various ways that the principle of checks and balances operated in the government of the Roman Republic. Remember to cite examples to support your answer.

2. The 200-year-period during which Roman armies expanded the Empire by conquering new lands and peoples is known as the Pax Romana. Translate this term and explain why it is, or is not, an appropriate label for this time span in Roman history.

Name ______________________ Class ______________ Date ____________

Chapter Test Form A

Africa

MATCHING *(3 points each)* In the space provided, write the letter of the name or term that matches each description. Some answers will not be used.

_____ **1.** poems, songs, and stories that are passed by word of mouth from one generation to another

_____ **2.** vast area of dry grasslands

_____ **3.** the first kingdom to be established in West Africa

_____ **4.** a people who settled in what is now Zimbabwe

_____ **5.** an East African language that has Persian and Arabic influences

_____ **6.** the Muslim ruler of Mali whose travels made others aware of West African power and wealth

_____ **7.** a family of related languages that is one of Africa's largest language groups

_____ **8.** a king of Aksum whose religious conversion helped Christianity become a powerful influence in Eastern Africa

_____ **9.** a Songhai ruler who helped turn his kingdom into a center of trade and learning

_____ **10.** a prosperous African kingdom that declined after A.D. 150, possibly because its land was no longer fertile

a. Mohammed I Askia
b. Bantu
c. ʿĒzānā
d. Ghana
e. Great Zimbabwe
f. Kush
g. oral traditions
h. Mansa Mūsā
i. Mombasa
j. savannas
k. Shona
l. Swahili

UNDERSTANDING IDEAS *(3 points each)* For each of the following, write the letter of the best choice in the space provided.

_____ **1.** Which of the following does NOT describe most early African societies?
a. They were nomadic.
b. They were matrilineal.
c. They were religious.
d. They herded, farmed, or fished.

_____ **2.** Which ancient African kingdom conquered part of Egypt and copied its culture by building pyramids?
a. Aksum
b. Great Zimbabwe
c. Kush
d. Songhai

______ **3.** The two major natural regions of Sub-Saharan Africa are the
a. deserts and grasslands.
b. grasslands and rain forest.
c. deserts and rain forest.
d. mountains and deserts.

______ **4.** In most early African societies the farming was done by
a. women.
b. men.
c. children.
d. slaves.

______ **5.** All of the following peoples set up trading centers along the East African coast EXCEPT
a. Arabs.
b. Ghanaians.
c. Indonesians.
d. Persians.

______ **6.** Which is NOT a reason that gold mining was important in the early African economies?
a. West African kingdoms traded gold to obtain salt.
b. The kingdoms of East Africa traded gold for needed salt, tools, and cloth.
c. Rulers adorned themselves with gold to oversee ceremonies.
d. Farmers used gold to buy more land so they could grow more crops.

______ **7.** Linguists are experts who
a. trace people's ancestors.
b. study languages.
c. record oral traditions.
d. study ancient civilizations.

______ **8.** The center of learning in Sub-Saharan Africa in the 1300s and 1400s was
a. Alexandria.
b. Great Zimbabwe.
c. Mogadishu.
d. Timbuktu.

______ **9.** The strength and wealth of Ghana, Mali, and Songhai depended on
a. the support of the powerful rulers in Egypt and Arabia.
b. large scale agriculture.
c. control of the trade routes across the Sahara.
d. adapting Egyptian culture to life in the rain forest.

______ **10.** Aksum became a prosperous kingdom MAINLY because
a. trade routes from the Red Sea into Egypt and Africa passed through it.
b. it had a powerful king.
c. it traded gemstones and ivory to Mediterranean kingdoms.
d. Christianity became its official religion.

TRUE/FALSE *(2 points each)* Mark each statement *T* if it is true or *F* if it is false.

______ **1.** The African region where farming is difficult because of uncertain rainfall is called the Sahel.

______ **2.** The main source of information about early African society is the writings of African kings.

______ **3.** One major source of the salt that was traded in Africa was the Sahara.

______ **4.** Trade spread the Islamic religion into both East Africa and West Africa.

______ **5.** Mali and Songhai both became important centers of Christian learning.

PRACTICING SKILLS *(5 points each)* Study the map and answer the questions that follow.

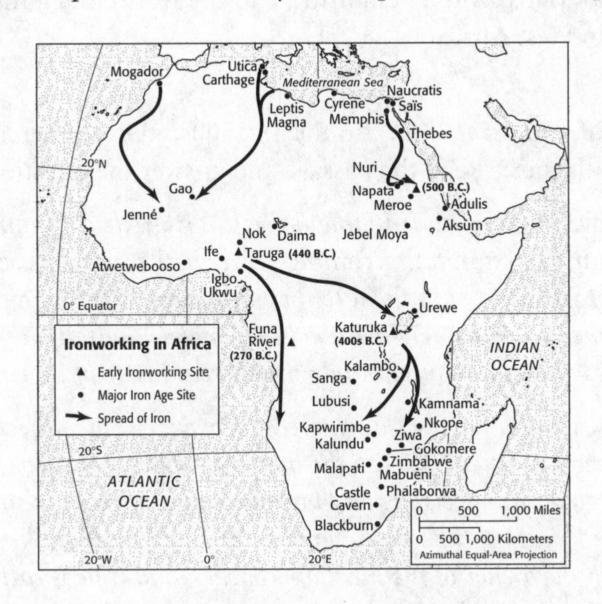

1. Where was the first African ironworking center?

____

2. What was the general pattern of ironworking technology's spread into Africa?

____

COMPOSING AN ESSAY *(20 points)* On a separate sheet of paper, write a brief essay in response to one of the following.

1. Explain how the location of the East African kingdoms shaped their development.

2. Explain how the location of the West African kingdoms shaped their development.

Name ______________________ Class ______________ Date ______________

Chapter Test Form B

Africa

SHORT ANSWER *(10 points each)* Provide brief answers for each of the following.

1. How would family organization and ownership and inheritance of property work in a matrilineal society?

2. What challenges did Africa's geography present to communicating and trading with the peoples of the continent's interior?

3. How did Christianity and Islam become established in Sub-Saharan Africa?

4. Where are Great Zimbabwe and Timbuktu located and what importance do they have in African history?

5. In what ways did Mansa Mūsā demonstrate to the world that a highly advanced society existed in West Africa?

PRIMARY SOURCES *(10 points each)* In the A.D. 500s, a Greek merchant visiting Aksum wrote about his travels there. Read the passage and answer the questions that follow.

> *The country known as . . . Sasu [in Ethiopia] is . . . [the site of] many gold mines. The king of the Axumites [Aksumites] accordingly, every other year . . . sends . . . special agents. . . . They take along with them to the mining district oxen, lumps of salt, and iron, and when they reach its neighborhood they make a halt at a certain spot and form an encampment, which they fence round with a great hedge of thorns.*
>
> *Within this they live, and having slaughtered the oxen, cut them in pieces, and lay the pieces on top of the thorns, along with the lumps of salt and the iron. Then come the natives bringing gold in nuggets . . . and lay one or two or more of these upon what pleases them—the pieces of flesh or the salt or the iron, and then they retire to some distance off. Then the owner of the meat approaches, and if he is satisfied he takes the gold away, and upon seeing this its owner comes and takes the flesh or the salt or the iron. . . .*

1. What kind of activity is being described in this passage?

2. What does this description suggest about the languages the agents and natives spoke?

COMPOSING AN ESSAY *(30 points)* Write an essay on one of the following subjects. Remember to use examples to support your answer.

1. Explain the importance of gold in the kingdoms of East and West Africa.

2. Identify common factors present in the decline of the early African kingdoms and the later trading states of East and West Africa. Explain which factor seems to have been the most important in causing the collapse of early African kingdoms.

Name ______________________ Class ______________ Date ____________

Chapter Test Form A

The Americas

MATCHING *(3 points each)* In the space provided, write the letter of the name or term that matches each description. Some answers will not be used.

_____ **1.** people of the Yucatán peninsula who developed the only complete writing system in early America

_____ **2.** people of the Ohio Valley region who built mounds, often in the shape of animals

_____ **3.** earliest civilization in Mexico that flourished from about 1200 B.C. to 400 B.C.

_____ **4.** official language of the Inca Empire that remains widely spoken in South America today

_____ **5.** North American city where some 30,000 Native Americans lived about A.D. 1200

_____ **6.** pyramid-building people of central Mexico in the A.D 800s to 1100s who introduced metalworking to the region

_____ **7.** early southwestern people who built irrigation networks to grow cotton and other crops

_____ **8.** early culture in Andean South America that mysteriously disappeared between 400 B.C. and 200 B.C.

_____ **9.** warriors who ruled an empire in central Mexico in the A.D 1400s

_____ **10.** people in what is now the southwestern United States who built structures of sun-dried bricks

a. Aztec
b. Beringia
c. Cahokia
d. Chavín
e. Hohokam
f. Hopewell
g. Inca
h. Maya
i. Olmec
j. Pueblo
k. Quechua
l. Toltec

UNDERSTANDING IDEAS *(3 points each)* For each of the following, write the letter of the best choice in the space provided.

_____ **1.** The major crops grown by native North American people included
a. coffee and cocoa.
b. potatoes and tomatoes.
c. corn and beans.
d. wheat and rice.

_____ **2.** Which two civilizations were NOT in existence at the same time?
a. Inca and Aztec
b. Hopewell and Mississippian
c. Maya and Toltec
d. Mississippian and Inca

______ **3.** The mounds built by the Mississippians seem to have been for what purpose?
a. religious
b. defense
c. trade
d. burial

______ **4.** The two most advanced Native American civilizations were the
a. Hohokam and Aztec.
b. Aztec and Maya.
c. Maya and Inca.
d. Aztec and Inca.

______ **5.** Why did some peoples in the Pacific Northwest hold potlaches?
a. to bury the dead
b. to sacrifice captives
c. to thank the gods for a good harvest
d. to give away their possessions

______ **6.** Which is NOT true of Plains peoples in A.D. 1400s?
a. They hunted buffalo on foot and used the hides for clothing.
b. European settlers pushed some peoples off their lands.
c. Drought ended farming in some areas.
d. Their main work animals were dogs.

______ **7.** All the following peoples built pyramid-shaped buildings EXCEPT the
a. Inca.
b. Aztec.
c. Maya.
d. Toltec.

______ **8.** The reason farming developed more slowly in the Americas than elsewhere was that early Americans
a. never settled in towns.
b. relied only on hunting to provide food.
c. had no horses or plows.
d. lived in areas where it was too cold to grow crops.

______ **9.** Mayan religion was closely connected to
a. agriculture.
b. medicine.
c. science.
d. warfare.

______ **10.** Scientists believe that the first people in the Americas
a. developed from hominids in the Mississippi valley.
b. arrived from North and West Africa.
c. sailed to South America from islands in Southeast Asia.
d. migrated from Asia by crossing what is now the Bering Strait.

Name ________________ Class ________________ Date ________________

TRUE/FALSE *(2 points each)* Mark each statement *T* if it is true or *F* if it is false.

______ **1.** The first farming in the Americas took place on the Great Plains.

______ **2.** The Inca built a system of paved roads to improve transportation, communication, and unity within their empire.

______ **3.** The Aztec made human sacrifices so that the sun would rise each day.

______ **4.** Aztec farmers used mud to make chinampas, or raised fields for farming.

______ **5.** The Inca recorded information on quipu, a series of knots on parallel strings.

PRACTICING SKILLS *(5 points each)* Study the map and answer the questions that follow.

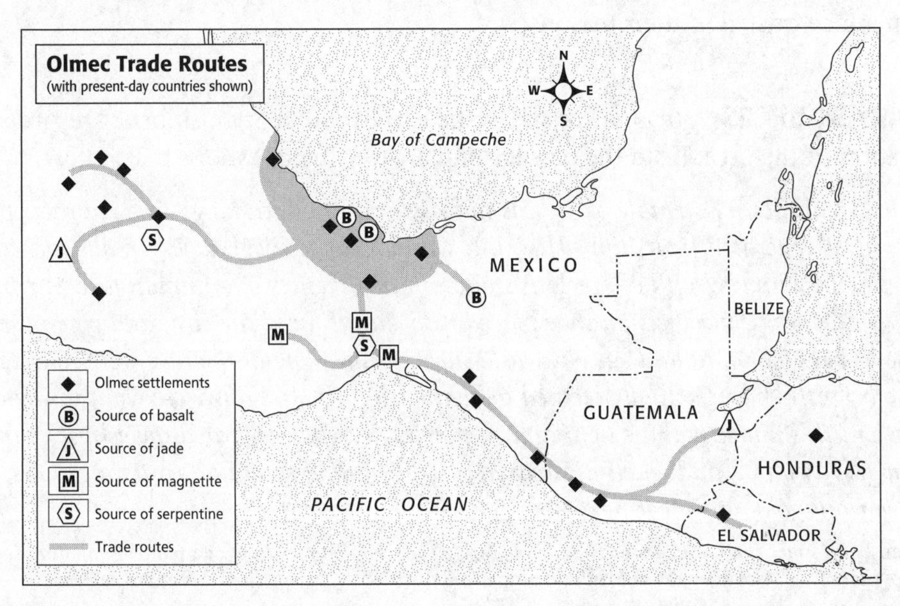

1. The Olmec used jade, basalt, and other stone for their crafts and rock carvings. Which did craftworkers in the villages near the Gulf of Campeche likely use most?

____

2. From where did villages along the Pacific Ocean most likely obtain jade?

____

COMPOSING AN ESSAY *(20 points)* On a separate sheet of paper, write a brief essay in response to one of the following.

1. Briefly describe the types of societies that developed in the Southwest, Pacific Coast, Great Plains, and Eastern Woodlands culture areas of North America.

2. Explain how changes in climate affected early and later cultures in North America.

Name ______________________ Class ______________ Date ____________

Chapter Test Form B

The Americas

SHORT ANSWER *(10 points each)* Provide brief answers for each of the following.

1. What changes in climate allowed early hunter-gathers to migrate to North America?

2. How did later climate changes shape the lives of peoples who lived in North America?

3. In what ways was the religion and technology of the Maya people tied to their economy?

4. How did the development of farming affect the way Native American people lived?

5. For what reason did the Maya and the Aztec practice human sacrifice? What difference existed in their reasons?

PRIMARY SOURCES *(10 points each)* In the early 1600s a Spanish priest recorded this observation of the Inca. Read the passage and answer the questions that follow.

> *[T]he wealthiest . . . temple of all was that [where] the Inca kings . . . kept their principal and most venerated [worshipped] idol. It was an impressive image, . . . all worked in finest gold with a wealth of precious stones, in the likeness of a human face, surrounded by rays, as we depict the sun; they placed it so that it faced the east, and when the sun rose its rays fell on it; and since it was a sheet of finest metal the rays were reflected from it so brightly that it actually seemed to be the sun. The Indians were wont to say that the sun lent this image both its light and its power. . . . They regarded the eclipse of the sun as a grave matter, and when it occurred . . . they made great and costly sacrifices, offering up various gold and silver figures. . . .*

1. Why did the Inca worship the idol in the temple? Whom or what did it represent?

2. What explanation does the writer suggest regarding why the Inca were so concerned about eclipses?

COMPOSING AN ESSAY *(30 points)* Write an essay on one of the following subjects. Remember to use examples to support your essay.

1. Compare and contrast the practices and policies of the Incas and Aztecs in controlling their empires. Then explain which group seemed the better rulers and why.

2. Describe ways in which the peoples of the Southwest, Pacific Coast, Great Plains, and Eastern Woodlands culture areas were generally alike and identify ways in which geography and resources made each cultural area unique.

Name ______________________ Class ______________ Date ______________

Unit Test Form A

The Growth of Civilizations

UNDERSTANDING IDEAS *(3 points each)* For each of the following, write the letter of the best choice in the space provided.

______ **1.** In its early years, Christianity spread through the Roman Empire because its teachings especially appealed to
a. the poor and oppressed.
b. wealthy merchants.
c. the Roman army.
d. Roman philosophers.

______ **2.** Cities that became important centers of culture and learning include all of the following EXCEPT
a. Alexandria in Egypt.
b. Athens in Greece.
c. Timbuktu in Songhai.
d. Sparta in Greece.

______ **3.** The central idea of the Greek polis relied upon
a. strict religious beliefs and practices.
b. the migrations of families following their herds.
c. territory, community, and political and economic independence.
d. scientific advances and a highly developed culture.

______ **4.** Which is NOT true of Greece's golden age?
a. Thebes became the cultural center of Greece.
b. Democracy in Athens reached its height.
c. The arts and sciences flourished.
d. The Peloponnesian War took place.

______ **5.** The LEAST important factor in the development of powerful kingdoms in East and West Africa was
a. gold.
b. location.
c. agriculture.
d. trade.

______ **6.** Which is NOT true of Greek and Maya civilizations?
a. Both were organized into city-states.
b. They developed at about the same time.
c. The religions of each had many gods.
d. Each civilization made advances in astronomy.

______ **7.** One way the Inca controlled their empire was by
a. making human sacrifices of rebels.
b. forcing heavy taxes on conquered peoples.
c. moving peoples within the empire to minimize regional differences.
d. publicly punishing troublemakers by making them fight wild beasts.

______ **8.** Which two societies have the LEAST in common?
a. Hopewell and Mali
b. Greek and Roman
c. Spartan and Aztec
d. Aksum and Kush

______ **9.** Which two empires depended on a highly developed road network to help hold them together?
a. Inca and Roman
b. Roman and Hellenistic
c. Hellenistic and Aztec
d. Aztec and Inca

______ **10.** During the Ice Age, people migrated from Asia across what is now the Bering Strait to settle in
a. East Africa.
b. West Africa.
c. Eastern Europe.
d. North America.

MATCHING *(3 points each)* In the space provided, write the letter of the name or term that matches each description. Some answers will not be used.

______ **1.** blind poet credited with writing the Greek epics the *Iliad* and the *Odyssey*

______ **2.** statesman under whose rule Athens experienced its greatest power and prosperity

______ **3.** united Greece under his rule

______ **4.** leader whose assassination led to a power struggle that brought the Roman Republic to an end

______ **5.** first emperor of the Roman Empire

______ **6.** ruler whose travels made the world aware of West Africa's advanced civilization and wealth

______ **7.** philosopher who developed approaches to organizing information that are now part of modern science

______ **8.** emperor whose conversion to Christianity helped it spread throughout the Roman Empire

______ **9.** created a huge empire under Greek rule

______ **10.** ended Athenian practice of enslaving people who did not pay their debts

a. Alexander the Great
b. Aristotle
c. Augustus
d. Constantine
e. Homer
f. Julius Caesar
g. King ʻĒzānā
h. Mansa Mūsā
i. Pericles
j. Philip II of Macedon
k. Socrates
l. Solon

TRUE/FALSE *(2 points each)* Mark each statement *T* if it is true or *F* if it is false.

______ **1.** One way that Alexander the Great tried to unify his empire was by encouraging his soldiers to marry local women in conquered lands.

______ **2.** Some early Native American peoples of the Southwest practiced farming by irrigating their crops.

______ **3.** Mountainous geography was an obstacle to unity in early Greece.

______ **4.** Farming and buffalo were important to the Plains peoples in North America.

______ **5.** In the Roman Republic, all citizens participated in government regardless of their wealth, race, or gender.

PRACTICING SKILLS *(5 points each)* The map below shows trade at the height of the Roman Empire in A.D. 117. Study the map and answer the questions that follow.

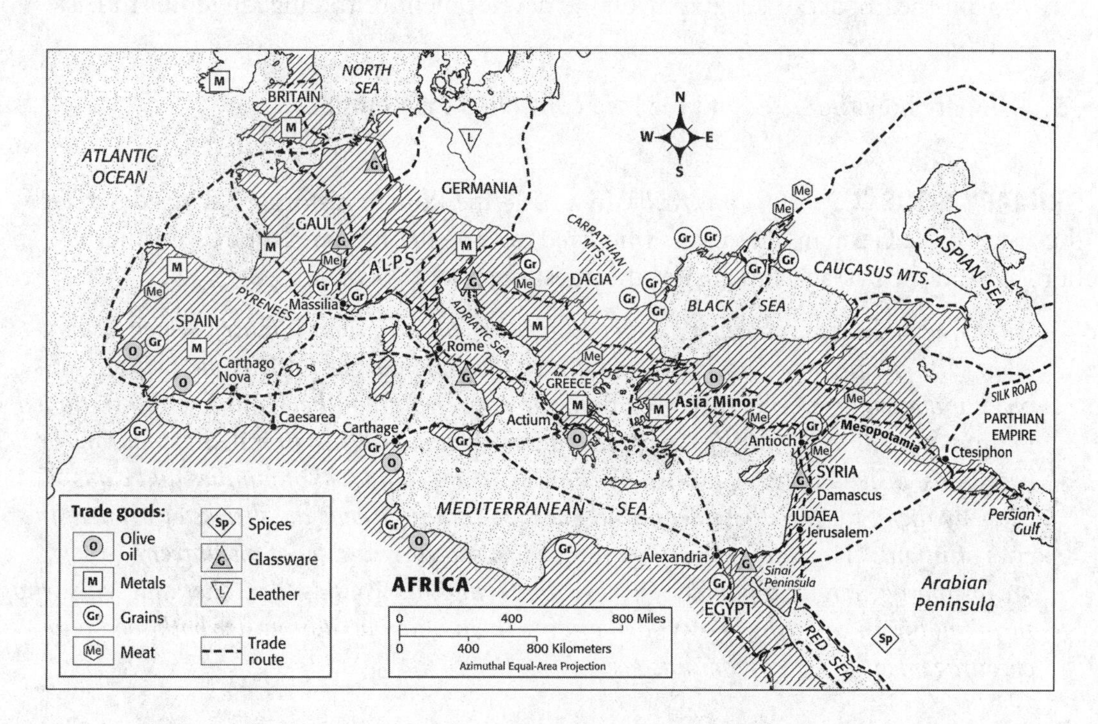

1. From what regions in and outside of the Empire did the Romans obtain leather?

____

2. Would Romans have likely used more olive oil or spices in their cooking? Why?

____

COMPOSING AN ESSAY *(20 points)* On a separate sheet of paper, write a brief essay in response to one of the following. Be sure to support your essay with examples.

1. What characteristics of government and democracy that developed in Athens and Rome can be found in American government today?

2. Why do you think civilizations in North America developed differently from those in East and West Africa?

Name ______________________ Class ______________ Date ______________

Unit Test Form B

The Growth of Civilizations

SHORT ANSWER *(10 points each)* Provide brief answers for each of the following

1. Name two geographic features of Greece and explain how they influenced Greece's civilization and culture.

2. Describe three characteristics of Greek art in Greece's golden age.

3. Identify three specific ways in which the world contains legacies from Roman culture.

4. Explain the impact of geography on the development of trading kingdoms in East and West Africa.

5. Compare how the Aztec and the Inca controlled their empires.

PRIMARY SOURCES *(10 points each)* In A.D. 98 the Roman historian Tacitus described the army of the German barbarians who lived outside the Roman Empire's northern border. Read the passage and answer the questions that follow.

> *On the whole, one would say that their chief strength is in their infantry, which fights along with the cavalry; admirably adapted to the action of the latter is the swiftness of certain foot-soldiers, who are picked from the entire youth of their country, and stationed in front of the line. . . . [W]hat most stimulates their courage is, that their squadrons or battalions, instead of being formed by chance . . . are composed of families and clans. Close by them, too, are those dearest to them, so that they hear the shrieks of women, the cries of infants.* They *are to every man the most sacred witnesses of his bravery—*they *are his most generous applauders. The soldier brings his wounds to mother and wife, who shrink not from counting or even demanding them and who administer both food and encouragement to the combatants. . . .*

1. What factors does Tacitus identify in the organization of the German army that he believes account for its success?

2. In what ways does Tacitus believe German women contribute to the bravery of German soldiers in battle?

COMPOSING AN ESSAY *(30 points)* Write an essay on one of the following subjects. Remember to use examples to support your essay.

1. Compare government in the Greek polis and the Roman Empire, and explain why the government that evolved in each society was not appropriate for the other.

2. Trace the evolution of religion in the Mediterranean world, beginning with the early Greeks and continuing through the Roman Empire. Consider similarities and differences in religious beliefs in each culture and period, as well as how religion affected Greek and Roman society.

Name ______________________ Class ______________ Date ____________

Chapter Test Form A

Modern Chapter **1** **The Byzantine Empire and Russia**

FILL IN THE BLANK *(3 points each)* For each of the following statements, fill in the blank with the appropriate name, term, or phrase.

1. Nobles called ______________________ formed councils that advised the rulers of Kievan Russia.

2. Ivan IV considered himself heir to the Roman and Byzantine empires and took the title of ______________________, the Russian word for caesar.

3. Under the emperor ______________________, Byzantine scholars organized Roman law.

4. A Turkish people called the ______________________ controlled territory south of Kiev and weakened Kievan Russia by interfering with its trade.

5. Rurik was a leader of a people called the ______________________, who gradually gained control of the region around Kiev.

6. The actions of Ivan IV earned him the nickname ______________________.

7. Town meetings called *veche* gave the people of ______________________ a voice in their government.

8. The religious conversion of ruler ______________________ helped to establish Christianity in Kievan Russia.

9. In the late 1500s, the city of ______________________ became the center of the Russian Orthodox Church.

10. Russia's first code of laws was known as the ______________________.

UNDERSTANDING IDEAS *(3 points each)* For each of the following, write the letter of the best choice in the space provided.

______ **1.** The Eastern Orthodox Church and the Roman Catholic Church emerged from the split of the
- **a.** Byzantine Empire.
- **b.** Russian Orthodox Church.
- **c.** Roman Empire.
- **d.** Christian Church.

______ **2.** Which of the following did NOT contribute to the growth of Kievan Russia?
- **a.** help from allies in western Europe
- **b.** a network of rivers that crossed the region
- **c.** trade with the Byzantines
- **d.** the arrival of the Vikings

_____ **3.** Government in Kievan Russia was controlled by the
a. emperors.
b. princes.
c. people.
d. clergy.

_____ **4.** The Byzantine Empire was saved around A.D. 1100 by
a. the rule of a wise and powerful emperor.
b. an alliance with the Ottoman Turks.
c. a strong navy that used a chemical weapon known as "Greek fire."
d. an army of western Europeans that reclaimed Western Asia Minor from the Turks.

_____ **5.** Which was NOT a reason for the Byzantine Empire's growth and power?
a. a strong emperor and central government
b. the Justinian Code
c. alliances with Germanic tribes to the north
d. the fall of Rome

_____ **6.** An important reason for the decline of the Byzantine Empire was
a. wars and invasions by outsiders.
b. high taxes and the loss of Mediterranean trade.
c. the spread of the Mongol Empire.
d. friction resulting from the Iconoclastic Controversy.

_____ **7.** Rulers who helped Moscow expand its power and territory in Russia included all EXCEPT
a. Great Prince Ivan I.
b. Ivan the Great.
c. Ivan the Terrible.
d. Yaroslav the Wise.

_____ **8.** The Mongols who controlled Russia until the late 1400s
a. allowed self-government, but levied heavy taxes.
b. were converted to Christianity by Cyril and Methodius.
c. tried to prevent Russia's economic development.
d. were finally driven out by Ivan I.

_____ **9.** The practice of removing people from church membership whose opinions conflict with its leaders or beliefs is called
a. heresy.
b. holy wisdom.
c. excommunication.
d. martyrdom.

_____ **10.** The Byzantine culture is best known for its
a. expression of Islamic values and beliefs.
b. religious art and architecture.
c. beautiful metalwork and pottery.
d. hand-woven wool carpets with intricate designs.

TRUE/FALSE *(2 points each)* Mark each statement *T* if it is true or *F* if it is false.

_______ **1.** The Seljuq Turks weakened the Byzantine Empire by capturing much of Asia Minor.

_______ **2.** A dispute over the Pravda Russkia split the Russian Orthodox Church.

_______ **3.** The great culture that developed in the Byzantine Empire caused Constantinople to be known as the "third Rome."

_______ **4.** The Iconoclastic Controversy was a controversy about the use of religious icons in Christian worship.

_______ **5.** Two major agricultural regions in Russia are the steppe and the taiga.

PRACTICING SKILLS *(5 points each)* Study the map of Constantinople and answer the questions that follow.

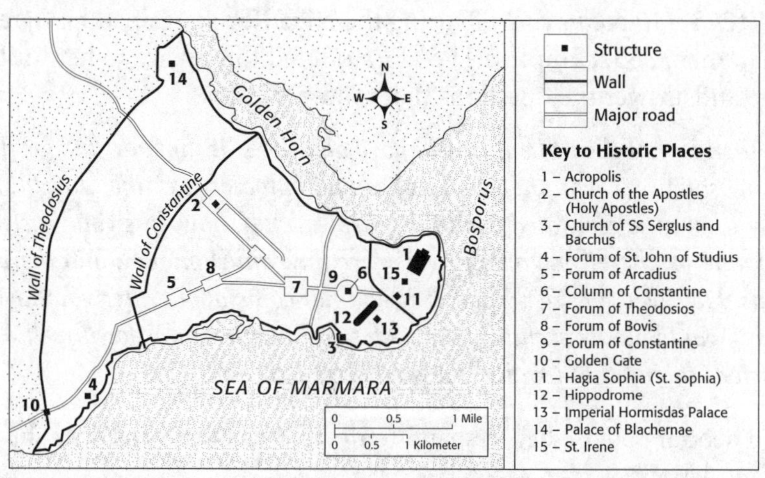

1. In what direction from the Church of the Apostles is the Column of Constantine?

____

2. About how far is the Forum of Arcadius from the Hagia Sophia?

____

COMPOSING AN ESSAY *(20 points)* On a separate sheet of paper, write a brief essay in response to one of the following.

1. How was geography important in the Byzantine Empire's wealth and decline?

2. Why did Kievan Russia gradually decline and finally collapse in the 1200s?

Name ______________________ Class ______________ Date ______________

Chapter Test Form B

The Byzantine Empire and Russia

SHORT ANSWER *(10 points each)* Provide brief answers for each of the following.

1. What controversy helped to split the Christian Church into the Eastern Orthodox Church and the Roman Catholic Church?

2. What geographic features assisted the growth of Kievan Russia?

3. What three factors led to the collapse of Kievan Russia?

4. What did Ivan the Great and Ivan the Terrible do that earned them each their nicknames?

5. Why was Constantinople known as the "second Rome" and Moscow as the "third Rome?"

PRIMARY SOURCES *(10 points each)* During the Nika Revolt against the Byzantine emperor Justinian in A.D. 532, Empress Theodora offered this advice to her husband. Read the passage and answer the questions that follow.

My opinion then is that the present time, above all others, is inopportune for flight, even though it bring safety. . . . For one who has been an emperor it is unendurable to be a fugitive. May I never be separated from this purple. . . . If, now, it is your wish to save yourself, O Emperor, there is no difficulty. For we have much money, and there is the sea, here the boats. However consider whether it will not come about after you have been saved that you would gladly exchange that safety for death. For as for myself, I approve a certain ancient saying that royalty is a good burial-shroud.

1. What does Theodora advise her husband to do, and what reasons does she give for her recommendation?

2. What decision does Theodora seem to have made for herself in this situation, and for what reason has she made this decision?

COMPOSING AN ESSAY *(30 points)* Write an essay on one of the following subjects.

1. Which of the Byzantine Empire's strengths do you think was most responsible for the fact that it endured about 1,000 years? Explain and support your opinion.

2. In what ways were the Mongols both a help and an obstacle in the creation of a Russian state?

Name ______________________ Class ______________ Date ____________

Chapter Test Form A

Modern Chapter **2**

The Islamic World

MATCHING *(3 points each)* In the space provided, write the letter of the name or term that matches each description. Some answers will not be used.

_____ **1.** Islamic leader whose murder started a split in the Muslim community

_____ **2.** Muslims who believed that religious matters should be settled by agreement among the Muslim people

_____ **3.** holy book containing rules and instructions that guide the lives of Muslims

_____ **4.** became the leader of Islam after Muhammad's death and expanded its influence

_____ **5.** Berber leader in North Africa whose Muslim army invaded and conquered Spain

_____ **6.** means "submission to [the will of] God" in Arabic

_____ **7.** strong leader whose conquests expanded Islam into the Persian Empire

_____ **8.** group of Muslims who believed that imams should decide religious and worldly matters

_____ **9.** early Islamic doctor who compiled a medical encyclopedia that was used in Europe for centuries

_____ **10.** character in literature who is the basis for *The Thousand and One Nights,* Muslim folktales that are among the most widely read stories in history

a. Abū Bakr
b. al-Idrīsī
c. al-Rāzī
d. Islam
e. Qur'an
f. Scheherazade
g. Shi'ah
h. Sufi
i. Sunni
j. Tāriq
k. 'Umar
l. 'Uthmān

UNDERSTANDING IDEAS *(3 points each)* For each of the following, write the letter of the best choice in the space provided.

_____ **1.** The Islamic leader who was considered the "successor to the Prophet," had the title of
a. ayatollah.
b. caliph.
c. imam.
d. sultan.

_____ **2.** Early Muslims' advances in geography and astronomy were MOST related to their interest in
a. Islam.
b. conquest.
c. culture.
d. trade.

______ **3.** The bedouins of the Arabian Peninsula followed a lifestyle that was shaped by
a. trade.
b. religion.
c. their environment.
d. hunting and gathering.

______ **4.** Before Muhammad founded Islam he had been a
a. prophet.
b. trader.
c. sheikh.
d. teacher.

______ **5.** The people who became the ruling force in the Islamic world in the 1100s were the
a. Arabs.
b. caliphs.
c. Moors.
d. Turks.

______ **6.** By 750 the Muslim Empire had spread into all of the following places EXCEPT
a. Constantinople.
b. India.
c. North Africa.
d. Spain.

______ **7.** Which group had MORE rights and freedoms in the Qur'an than under traditional Arab law?
a. slaves
b. single men
c. married men
d. women

______ **8.** Muslim contributions to science included
a. advances in geography, medicine, and astronomy.
b. the invention of paper and the astrolabe.
c. creation of the Arabic numerals that we use today.
d. discovery that Earth was not flat.

______ **9.** The reason that Islam divided into two main branches was
a. a dispute over who should be caliph, or leader of the faith.
b. controversy over the place of sin in Islamic teaching.
c. a conflict over the meaning of the Qur'an.
d. differences over the role of religious leaders in the Muslim community.

______ **10.** Which was NOT a way that Islam spread?
a. through religious wars by Muslims against non-Muslims
b. by forcing conquered peoples who followed other religions to convert to Islam
c. when political leaders who were Muslims expanded their empires
d. through trade between Muslim and non-Muslim peoples

TRUE/FALSE *(2 points each)* Mark each statement *T* if it is true or *F* if it is false.

______ **1.** The term *Muslim* means "People of the Book."

______ **2.** Muslims consider Muhammad to be the prophet of Islam.

______ **3.** Muslims who settled in Spain became known as Berbers.

______ **4.** The Turks spread Islam into Asia Minor and across northern India.

______ **5.** Muhammad accepted the Bible as part of God's teachings.

PRACTICING SKILLS *(5 points each)* Study this map on the spread of Islam in Southeast Asia and answer the questions that follow.

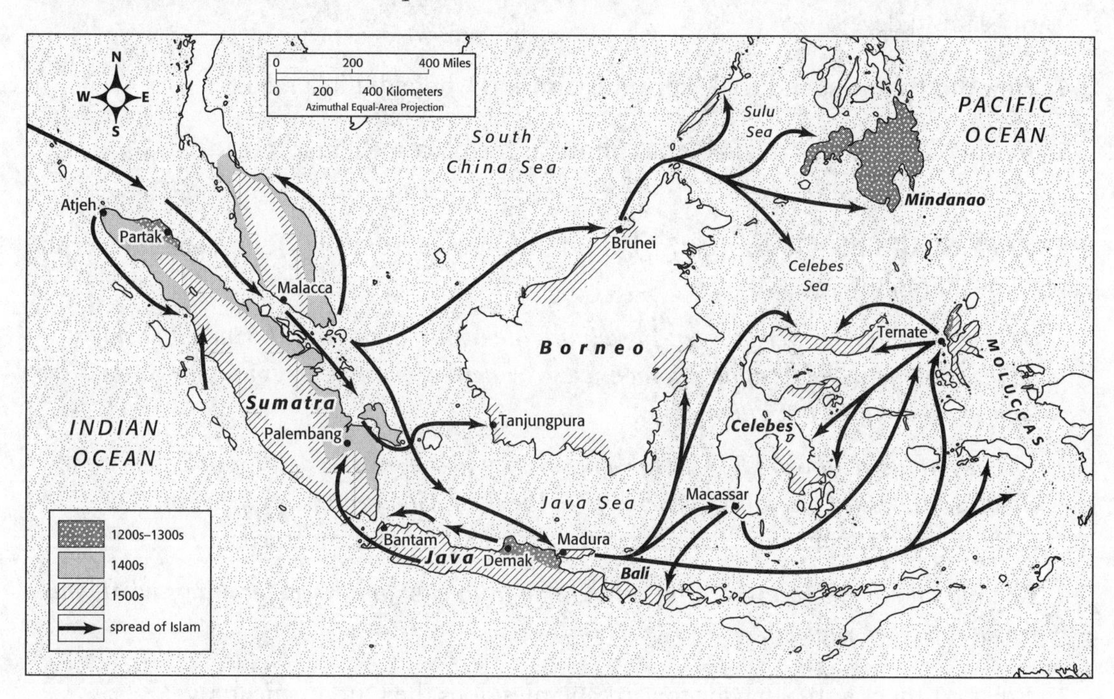

1. Was Borneo or Mindanao influenced by Islam first?

____

2. From where did Islam reach Celebes?

____

COMPOSING AN ESSAY *(20 points)* On a separate sheet of paper, write a brief essay in response to one of the following.

1. What influences caused the bedouins to become Muslims? How did their conversion to Islam help the faith to spread?

2. How did Muslims' religious beliefs affect the Islamic world's art and architecture?

Name ______________________ Class ______________ Date ____________

Chapter Test Form B

Modern Chapter **2**

The Islamic World

SHORT ANSWER *(10 points each)* Provide brief answers for each of the following.

1. What part did Muhammad play in the founding and spread of Islam?

2. Why did the bedouins' acceptance of Islam help to spread the faith?

3. What disagreement over religious leaders and their roles caused two main branches of Islam to develop?

4. How did conquest and trade spread Islam, and where did it spread?

5. In what ways did Islam affect the culture of the places where it spread?

PRIMARY SOURCES *(10 points each)* Read the passage from the Qur'an and answer the questions that follow.

> *Be just: the unjust never prosper. Be valiant: die rather than yield. Be merciful: slay neither old men, children, nor women. Destroy neither fruit trees, grain, nor cattle. Keep your word even to your enemies.*
>
> *The law of life requires: sincerity to God, severity to self, justice to all people, service to elders. Kindness to the young, generosity to the poor. Good counsel to friends. Forbearance with enemies. Indifference to fools. Respect to the learned. . . .*
>
> *Do unto all men as you would they should do unto you, and reject for others what you would reject for yourself.*

1. What attitudes and behavior toward enemies does the Qur'an encourage?

2. What general instruction does the Qur'an provide about how people should treat one another?

COMPOSING AN ESSAY *(30 points)* Write an essay on one of the following subjects.

1. How did the rise of Turkish power in the Middle East change the role of caliphs in Muslim society and affect how Islam was spread?

2. Which do you think was more significant: the influence of Islamic culture on the regions to which it spread, or the influence of those regions on the development of Islamic culture? Explain your opinion and support it with examples.

Name ______________________ Class ______________ Date ____________

Chapter Test Form A

Modern Chapter 3

The Civilizations of East Asia

FILL IN THE BLANK *(3 points each)* For each of the following statements, fill in the blank with the appropriate name, term, or phrase.

1. A form of Buddhism known as ______________________ became very popular among warriors and artists in Japan.

2. Construction of China's Grand Canal began under the emperors of the ______________________ dynasty.

3. The Mongol leader Temujin took the name ______________________, meaning "Universal Ruler," and created a huge empire across Asia.

4. In Southeast Asia, the culture of ______________________ was the one that was most influenced by China.

5. A ______________________ was a warrior in feudal Japan who was similar to a knight in Europe during the same time period.

6. Because of poets such as Li Bo and Du Fu, Chinese literature reached its high point during the ______________________ dynasty.

7. The Mongol conquest of China was completed under a great general named ______________________.

8. The ______________________ religion helped to unify Japan, in part because early emperors may have also served as priests.

9. Mongol armies led by ______________________ swept west across Europe to the outskirts of the city of Vienna in present-day Austria.

10. During the ______________________ dynasty, Chinese artisans perfected the art of making porcelain and produced delicate porcelain vases for export.

UNDERSTANDING IDEAS *(3 points each)* For each of the following, write the letter of the best choice in the space provided.

_______ **1.** The *Diamond Sutra* is the name of
- **a.** the world's first novel.
- **b.** the first known printed book.
- **c.** an early Noh play.
- **d.** an Indian literary classic.

_______ **2.** One element of Japanese culture that did NOT grow out of Chinese influences was
- **a.** early government.
- **b.** art.
- **c.** science.
- **d.** Bushido.

_______ **3.** Which society most influenced the development of other civilizations in Asia?
- **a.** Japanese
- **b.** Mongol
- **c.** Chinese
- **d.** Korean

_______ **4.** Who held most of the power during Japan's 250-year Ashikaga shogunate?
- **a.** the emperor
- **b.** the shogun
- **c.** Zen Buddhists
- **d.** the daimyo and samurai

_______ **5.** Which of the following was NOT true of China during the Sung dynasty?
- **a.** The status of women began to change.
- **b.** Foreign trade grew.
- **c.** Poverty was nearly eliminated.
- **d.** Cities and towns grew.

_______ **6.** How did China change during the Tang and Sung dynasties?
- **a.** Food production increased.
- **b.** Chinese culture flourished.
- **c.** Government became corrupt.
- **d.** No invaders threatened.

_______ **7.** A "golden age" of Chinese civilization developed during which two dynasties?
- **a.** Tang and Sung
- **b.** Sung and Sui
- **c.** Sui and Yuan
- **d.** Yuan and Tang

_______ **8.** Which society in Asia was most influenced by Indian culture?
- **a.** Siamese (Thai)
- **b.** Vietnamese
- **c.** Korean
- **d.** Khmer (Cambodian)

_______ **9.** Which was NOT a way in which Indian and Chinese cultures both influenced the rest of Asia?
- **a.** religious beliefs
- **b.** conquest
- **c.** written language
- **d.** art and architecture

_______ **10.** What change did Mongol rule bring to China?
- **a.** increased contact with the rest of the world
- **b.** more political power for average Chinese
- **c.** local governments less responsible to central government
- **d.** lower taxes and reduced trade

TRUE/FALSE *(2 points each)* Mark each statement *T* if it is true or *F* if it is false.

_______ **1.** The strength of Mongol armies was built around their heavily armed foot soldiers.

_______ **2.** Because Japan is an island nation, the Japanese people could choose whether or not they wanted contact with other peoples.

_______ **3.** Early writing systems in both Korea and Japan were based on the Chinese language.

Name ______________________ Class ______________ Date ____________

______ **4.** Lady Murasaki Shikibu became the Empress Wu and was one of only two women to rule China in her own name.

______ **5.** Much of what Europeans learned about China in the 1200s came from the writings of Kublai Khan.

PRACTICING SKILLS *(5 points each)* Study the map and answer the questions that follow.

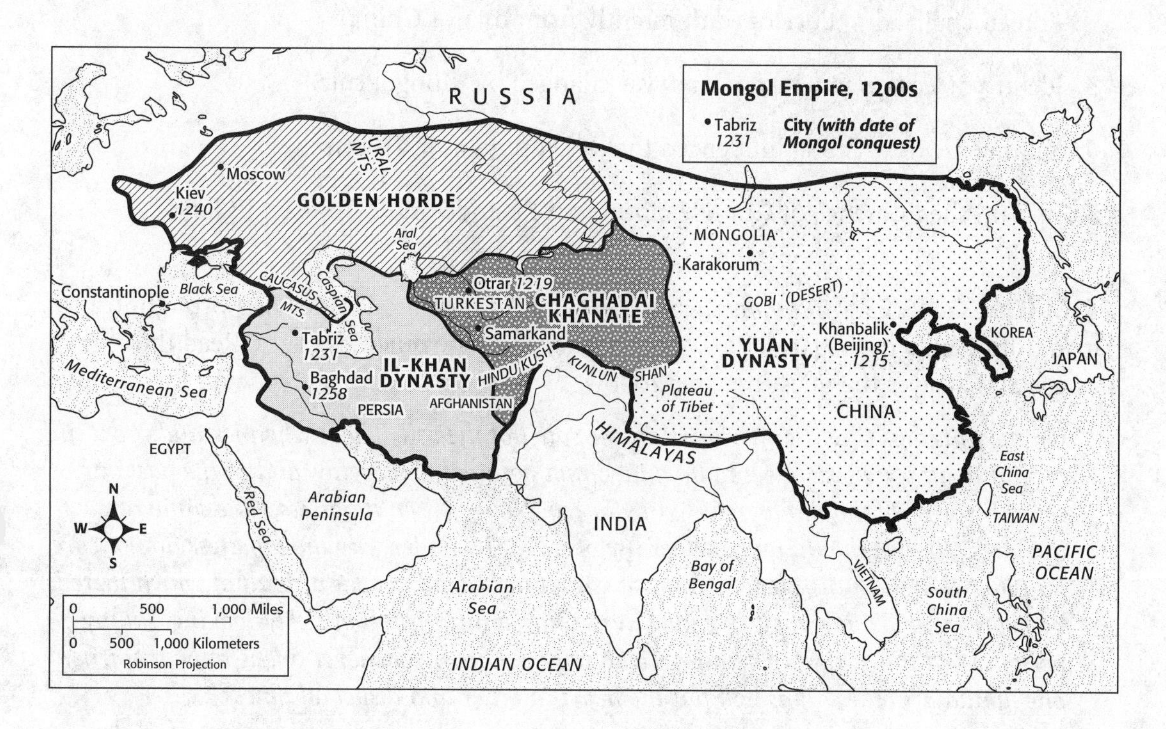

1. Which city on the map is within the Mongols' homeland?

____

2. Korea was a part of which dynasty?

____

COMPOSING AN ESSAY *(20 points)* On a separate sheet of paper, write a brief essay in response to one of the following.

1. Describe changes in agriculture that took place during the Tang and Sung dynasties.

2. Compare and contrast the office of emperor in China and Japan.

Name ______________________ Class ______________ Date ____________

Chapter Test Form B

Modern Chapter **3**

The Civilizations of East Asia

SHORT ANSWER *(10 points each)* Provide brief answers for each of the following.

1. Explain how Ghengis Khan and his successors were able to conquer such a vast empire.

2. Name two ways Chinese culture shaped Korean civilization and two ways in which Korean civilization developed differently from that of China.

3. Identify five ways in which China was changed by Mongol rule.

4. Summarize how China influenced the development of Vietnam.

5. Explain the influence of Chinese culture on Bushido and Noh plays in Japan.

PRIMARY SOURCES *(10 points each)* The Zen Buddhist monk Eisai first brought tea to Japan from China in the late 1100s. Here he discusses the qualities of tea. Read the passage and answer the questions that follow.

> *On the hillsides it [tea] grows up as in the spirit of the soil. Those who pick and use it are certain to attain a great age. India and China both value it highly, and in the past our country too once showed a great liking for tea. Now as then it possesses the same rare qualities, and we should make wider use of it. . . . I wonder why the Japanese do not care for bitter things. In the great country of China they drink tea, as a result of which there is no heart trouble and people live long lives. Our country is full of sickly-looking, skinny persons, and this is simply because we do not drink tea. Whenever one is in poor spirits, one should drink tea. This will put the heart in order and dispel all illness. . . .*
>
> From *Sources of the Japanese Tradition.* edited by Wm Theodore de Bary. Copyright © 1958 by **Columbia University Press.** Reprinted by permission of the publisher.

1. Why does Eisai think the Japanese are unwilling to drink tea?

2. What reasoning does Eisai offer to explain why drinking tea promotes long life?

COMPOSING AN ESSAY *(30 points)* Write an essay on one of the following subjects. Remember to use examples to support your essay.

1. Summarize the major achievements made under the Tang and Sung emperors and decide which dynasty was a greater period in Chinese history.

2. Describe the structure of society in feudal Japan and compare the power structure that developed during the Ashikaga shogunate with the power structure that existed before.

Name ______________________ Class ______________ Date ____________

Chapter Test Form A

Modern Chapter **4**

The Rise of the Middle Ages

MATCHING *(3 points each)* In the space provided, write the letter of the name or term that matches each description. Some answers will not be used.

_____ **1.** an effort to strengthen the church by stamping out practices and teachings that opposed church doctrines

_____ **2.** strong ruler who unified England

_____ **3.** practice of buying high positions in the church

_____ **4.** land granted by a lord in return for loyalty and service

_____ **5.** king whose rule restored order, learning, and unity to western Europe during the 800s

_____ **6.** person who received a grant of land from a lord

_____ **7.** knights were expected to live by this code of conduct

_____ **8.** protected nobles' freedoms and outlined basic rights of all English people

_____ **9.** created a set of rules that were adopted throughout Europe to govern monks' lives

_____ **10.** peasant who could not leave the land without the lord's permission

a. Thomas Becket
b. Saint Benedict
c. Charlemagne
d. chivalry
e. Eleanor of Aquitaine
f. fief
g. Inquisition
h. Magna Carta
i. serf
j. simony
k. vassal
l. William the Conqueror

UNDERSTANDING IDEAS *(3 points each)* For each of the following, write the letter of the best choice in the space provided.

_____ **1.** The pilgrimage of Henry IV to Canossa symbolized the
a. power of kings during the Middle Ages.
b. power of the pope during the Middle Ages.
c. cooperation that existed between popes and kings.
d. weakness of the Holy Roman Empire.

_____ **2.** Charlemagne's empire broke up after his death because of
a. feuds and internal wars among his successors.
b. financial problems faced by the government.
c. a series of corrupt mayors of the palace.
d. quarrels between church and government leaders.

_____ **3.** The church operated like a government during the Middle Ages, except that it did NOT
- **a.** collect taxes.
- **b.** have laws.
- **c.** rule land.
- **d.** regulate trade.

_____ **4.** Most of the power in the feudal system was held by
- **a.** the king.
- **b.** knights.
- **c.** local lords.
- **d.** burghers.

_____ **5.** The major reason for the development of feudalism was
- **a.** the need for an army to protect the church.
- **b.** the need for protection in the absence of central government.
- **c.** the need to protect trade routes across Europe.
- **d.** the need to preserve the farming system on which Europe depended for food.

_____ **6.** Which was NOT a problem the church had to deal with during the Middle Ages?
- **a.** kings appointing people to positions in the church
- **b.** corrupt church officials who charged high fees to perform religious services
- **c.** insufficient wealth to carry out its religious functions
- **d.** kings trying to gain control over the church in their countries

_____ **7.** Which type of people were LEAST likely to hold land in medieval society?
- **a.** nobles
- **b.** knights
- **c.** bishops
- **d.** peasants

_____ **8.** Which system is characterized by estates containing villages in which peasants farmed the lord's lands and provided other services to the lord?
- **a.** manorialism
- **b.** monasticism
- **c.** feudalism
- **d.** the medieval system

_____ **9.** The conflict between popes and kings that existed during much of the Middle Ages was mainly over
- **a.** ownership of land.
- **b.** the loyalty of nobles.
- **c.** differing religious beliefs.
- **d.** power and authority.

_____ **10.** How did the practice of primogeniture affect feudalism?
- **a.** strengthened it by keeping nobles' landholdings intact after they died
- **b.** weakened it by keeping nobles' landholdings intact after they died
- **c.** strengthened it by dividing nobles' lands among their heirs when they died
- **d.** weakened it by dividing nobles' lands among their heirs when they died

Name ______________________ Class ______________ Date ______________

TRUE/FALSE *(2 points each)* Mark each statement *T* if it is true or *F* if it is false.

_______ **1.** The Anglo-Saxons divided their kingdoms into districts called shires.

_______ **2.** In medieval society, a vassal had more loyalty to his lord than to his king.

_______ **3.** Otto the Great tried to establish a strong kingdom in Germany.

_______ **4.** A pope's most important advisors were the archbishops.

_______ **5.** The Concordat of Worms ended the struggles between popes and emperors.

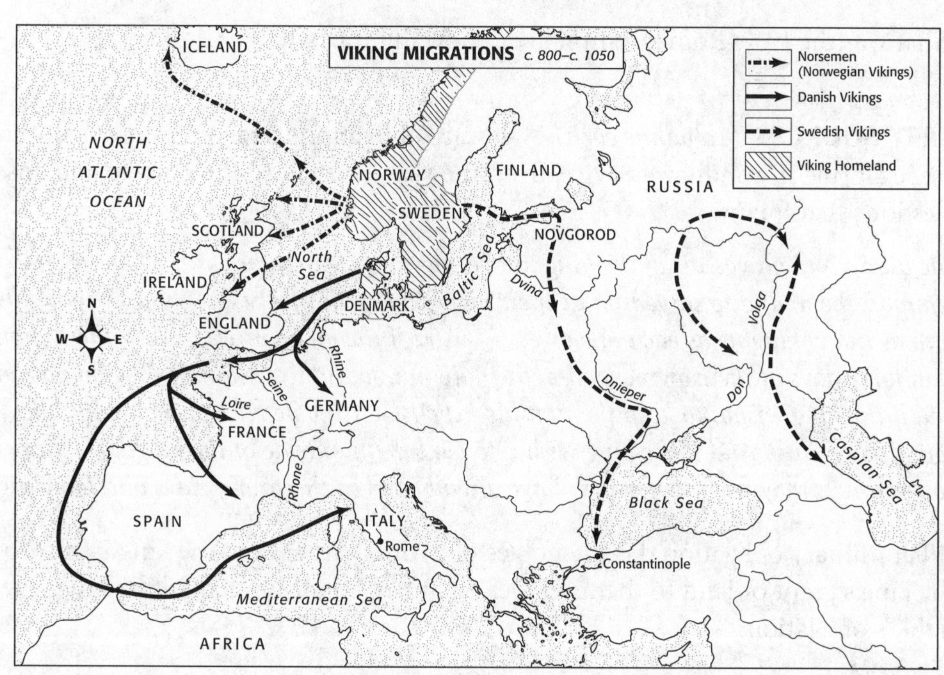

From *The Encylopedia of The Middle Ages,* edited by Norman F. Cantor. Copyright © 1999 by The Reference Works. Reprinted by permission of **Viking Penguin, a division of Penguin Putnam Inc.**

PRACTICING SKILLS *(5 points each)* Study the map and answer the questions that follow.

1. Where did the Vikings who settled in England come from?

____

2. Which Vikings migrated farthest from their homeland?

____

COMPOSING AN ESSAY *(20 points)* On a separate sheet of paper, write a brief essay in response to one of the following.

1. Explain how William I, Henry I, and Henry II increased royal power in England.

2. Describe how the Capetians expanded the power of French kings.

Name ______________________ Class ______________ Date ______________

Chapter Test Form B

Modern Chapter **4**

The Rise of the Middle Ages

SHORT ANSWER *(10 points each)* Provide brief answers for each of the following.

1. What were Charlemagne's main accomplishments?

2. Why did feudalism develop in Europe, and how was the system organized?

3. How was the church organized in Europe, and what role did it play in everyday life?

4. For what basic reason did kings and popes conflict during the Middle Ages?

5. What was the Holy Roman Empire, and how did it begin?

PRIMARY SOURCES *(10 points each)* A vassal's obligation to serve his lord is outlined in these legal rules for military service, from the year 1270. Read the passage and answer the questions that follow.

> *The baron and all vassals of the king are bound to appear before him when he shall summon them, and to serve him at their own expense for forty days and forty nights, with as many knights as each one owes. . . . And if the king wishes to keep them more than forty days at their own expense, they are not bound to remain if they do not wish it. And if the king wishes to keep them at his expense for the defence of the realm, they are bound to remain. And if the king wishes to lead them outside of the kingdom, they need not go unless they wish to, for they have already served their forty days and forty nights.*

1. What military obligation did the nobles of a kingdom have to the king in return for the king's grant of land to them? Under what two conditions could the king extend a noble's obligation?

2. What does the passage imply was the only time the king could require his nobles to fight outside the kingdom if they did not want to?

COMPOSING AN ESSAY *(30 points)* Write an essay on one of the following subjects. Remember to use examples to support your essay.

1. Some people believe that the most powerful rulers in Europe during the Middle Ages were not kings, but instead were the popes in Rome. Explain why you do or do not agree with this point of view.

2. Compare and contrast the methods by which the Norman kings of England and Capetian kings of France increased royal power. Also explain how this process helped to bring about the beginnings of democracy in each country.

Name ______________________ Class ______________ Date ______________

Chapter Test Form A

Modern Chapter **5**

The High Middle Ages

FILL IN THE BLANK *(3 points each)* For each of the following statements, fill in the blank with the appropriate name, term, or phrase.

1. In 1095 ______________________ called on Europe's nobles to stop fighting among themselves and join in a war to win back the Holy Land.

2. In the ______________________ of manufacturing that developed during the Middle Ages, workers performed their jobs from their homes.

3. ______________________ was a medieval philosophy that attempted to deal with conflicts existing between religious faith and human reason.

4. ______________________, who the English executed as a heretic during the Hundred Years' War, is today a Catholic saint and a symbol of French patriotism.

5. ______________________ argued that individuals should be allowed to read and interpret the Bible themselves, without the intervention of the clergy.

6. Poetry, romantic fiction, and fables became popular among medieval audiences because many of these works were written in ______________________.

7. Skilled workers in the Middle Ages formed ______________________, which set standards for quality of work and rules for wages, hours, and working conditions.

8. In a ______________________ economy, such as developed in medieval Europe, land, labor, and capital are controlled by individuals and not by government.

9. One of the greatest scholars of the Middle Ages was ______________________, a Dominican monk whose writings summarized medieval Christian thought.

10. *The Divine Comedy,* written by ______________________, is considered to be one of the greatest works of medieval literature.

UNDERSTANDING IDEAS *(3 points each)* For each of the following, write the letter of the best choice in the space provided.

______ **1.** What NEW type of business arose in Europe as an indirect result of the Crusades?
a. trade
b. banking
c. merchant
d. art

______ **2.** As European kings built strong nations, all the following lost power EXCEPT
a. the Catholic church.
b. non-Christians.
c. nobles.
d. people in towns.

_____ **3.** The purpose of the Crusades was for Christians to regain the Holy Land from the
a. Byzantines.
b. Christians.
c. Muslims.
d. Jews.

_____ **4.** The only Crusade that succeeded in capturing Jerusalem was the
a. First Crusade.
b. Second Crusade.
c. Third Crusade.
d. Fourth Crusade.

_____ **5.** Which was NOT an event that strengthened Spain?
a. the marriage of Ferdinand and Isabella
b. the capture of Grenada from the Muslims
c. the expulsion of Muslims and Jews from Spain
d. the addition of the kingdom of Navarre

_____ **6.** Which was NOT true of life in the Middle Ages?
a. Townspeople were exempt from working on the manors of local lords.
b. A serf who escaped to a town had to be returned to the manor.
c. Townspeople could freely sell goods in their town market, but outsiders had to pay a fee.
d. Towns had their own courts that were run by local citizens.

_____ **7.** One reason that trade increased in Europe by the late Middle Ages was the
a. influence of the Crusades.
b. Hundred Years' War.
c. invention of roads.
d. elimination of local taxes.

_____ **8.** The Babylonian Captivity
a. resulted in the expulsion of Muslims from Spain.
b. caused the War of the Roses.
c. led to the exile of Jan Hus.
d. weakened the authority of the pope.

_____ **9.** An indirect result of the Crusades was that commerce
a. increased, and kings were strengthened.
b. declined, and kings were weakened.
c. increased, and kings were weakened.
d. declined, and kings were strengthened.

_____ **10.** One change in education during the late Middle Ages was that
a. the church gained control over what was taught.
b. European schools became centers of Islamic science and learning.
c. schools opened in towns and admitted any male who could pay the fee.
d. students began to be taught Latin.

Name ______________________ Class ______________ Date ______________

TRUE/FALSE *(2 points each)* Mark each statement *T* if it is true or *F* if it is false.

______ **1.** During the Children's Crusade some of the crusaders were sold into slavery.

______ **2.** The division of Europe into feudal landholdings caused trade to increase.

______ **3.** Some local rulers taxed the goods sold at trade fairs on their lands and hired guards to keep the fairs safe for merchants and fairgoers.

______ **4.** Some cities formed the Hanseatic League in an attempt to manage trade.

______ **5.** The Great Schism developed when the French king seized fiefs that the king of England held in France.

PRACTICING SKILLS *(5 points each)* The time lines below show a typical day in the life of a medieval monk. Study the time lines and answer the questions that follow.

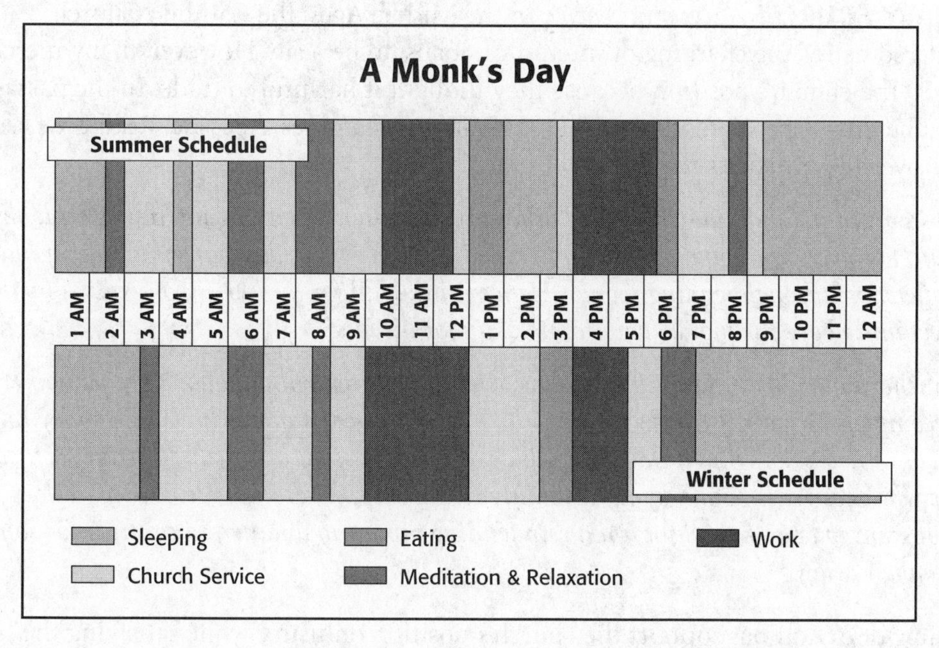

1. What activity consumed the largest number of a monk's waking hours?

____

2. How many hours a day did a monk spend at work in the summer? in winter?

____

COMPOSING AN ESSAY *(20 points)* On a separate sheet of paper, write a brief essay in response to one of the following.

1. Summarize the effects of the Hundred Years' War on England and France.

2. Explain how and why the growth of trade affected the feudal and manorial systems.

Name ______________________ Class ______________ Date ____________

Chapter Test Form B

Modern Chapter **5**

The High Middle Ages

SHORT ANSWER *(10 points each)* Provide brief answers for each of the following.

1. Explain which Crusade was the most successful and which was the biggest failure.

2. What four basic rights did townspeople gain from lords? Briefly describe each one.

3. Why did literature become more popular in the Middle Ages, and what great literary classics were produced in the Middle Ages?

4. What caused the Hundred Years' War, and how did the war strengthen representative government in England and France?

5. What was the Great Schism, and how did it affect the church's power in Europe?

PRIMARY SOURCES *(10 points each)* In the Middle Ages, the Catholic Church considered usury, the charging of interest on loans, to be a sin. However, many merchants opposed the church's position because they thought it harmful to trade. In the passage below, the great Christian scholar Thomas Aquinas examines the issue. Read the passage and answer the questions that follow.

It seems that a man may ask some other consideration [meaning interest] for money lent. For every man may lawfully provide against his own loss. But sometimes a man suffers loss through lending money. Hence it is lawful for him to ask or exact something over and above the money lent, to make up for his loss.

Furthermore, every man is bound by a kind of requirement of honor to make some recompense [reward] to one who has done him a favor. But he who lends money to a man in need, does him a favor, for which some expression of gratitude is due. Hence he who receives is bound by natural duty to make some recompense. Hence, it does not seem to be unlawful for a man, in lending money to another, to contract for some compensation.

1. How does Aquinas support the church's position on usury while satisfying the merchants at the same time?

2. What arguments does Aquinas make to support his point of view?

COMPOSING AN ESSAY *(30 points)* Write an essay on one of the following subjects. Remember to use examples to support your essay.

1. Why did Europeans join the Crusades, and what effects did the Crusades have on Europe?

2. Why did trade increase in Europe in the late Middle Ages, and how was Europe's economy affected? What factor do you think was most important in the growth of trade? Why?

Name ______________________ Class ____________ Date ____________

Unit Test Form A

Modern Unit 1

The World in Transition

UNDERSTANDING IDEAS *(3 points each)* For each of the following, write the letter of the best choice in the space provided.

______ **1.** All of the following characterized feudal Europe EXCEPT
a. the inheritance of land.
b. weak central government.
c. flourishing trade.
d. relationships between lords and serfs.

______ **2.** A major reason that the Christian church split into the Roman Catholic Church and the Eastern Orthodox Church was the
a. Great Schism.
b. Iconoclastic Controversy.
c. Haiga Sophia.
d. Magna Carta.

______ **3.** Which person does NOT belong with the others?
a. samurai
b. shogun
c. daimyo
d. caliph

______ **4.** The leaders of the Byzantine Empire wanted to
a. revive the glory of the Roman Empire.
b. do away with Roman law.
c. increase the power of the pope.
d. limit the power of wise rulers and able advisers.

______ **5.** During the Babylonian Captivity, the headquarters of the Roman Catholic Church was in
a. Moscow.
b. the Papal States.
c. Constantinople.
d. France.

______ **6.** Which association was formed by German trading cities and became a powerful commercial influence during the late Middle Ages?
a. the Concordat of Worms
b. the Holy Roman Empire
c. the Hanseatic League
d. the Lombard League

______ **7.** China's culture flourished under the rule of the
a. Ashikaga shoguns.
b. Golden Horde.
c. Sui and Yuan dynasties.
d. Tang and Sung dynasties.

______ **8.** Which group weakened the power of Muslim religious leaders by incorporating their own position of sultan into Muslim political affairs?
a. the Moors
b. the Ottoman Turks
c. the Sunni
d. the Shi'ah

______ **9.** Which of the following did NOT guide people's behavior?
a. the Donation of Pépin
b. the Pravda Russkia
c. the Justinian Code
d. the Qur'an

______ **10.** The Japanese equivalent of European chivalry was
a. Bushido.
b. Zen Buddhism.
c. Shinto.
d. seppuku.

MATCHING *(3 points each)* In the space provided, write the letter of the name or term that matches each description. Some answers will not be used.

______ **1.** prophet of Islam

______ **2.** helped to spread Buddhism in China

______ **3.** Viking leader who helped found Kievan Russia

______ **4.** Mongol leader who created a huge empire in Asia

______ **5.** unified much of Western Europe under Christian rule

______ **6.** ruled Russia as its first czar

______ **7.** led a Berber army to conquer Spain

______ **8.** powerful Mongol ruler who completed the conquest of China

______ **9.** established rules to govern monks' lives

______ **10.** great ruler of the Byzantine Empire

a. al-Rāzī
b. Charlemagne
c. Empress Wu
d. Genghis Khan
e. Ivan IV
f. Justinian
g. Kublai Khan
h. Muhammad
i. Rurik
j. Saint Benedict
k. Tāriq
l. Thomas Becket

TRUE/FALSE *(2 points each)* Mark each statement *T* if it is true or *F* if it is false.

______ **1.** Byzantine art is characterized by elaborate religious murals and icons that were intended to inspire the adoration of important figures in Christianity.

______ **2.** In the years following Muhammad's death, a split developed in Islam over whether Muslims should spread the faith through conquest or through trade.

______ **3.** Vietnam was most influenced by Chinese culture, while Indian culture had the greatest influence in what is now Cambodia.

______ **4.** Practices that brought problems and conflict to the Roman Catholic Church during the Middle Ages included simony, heresy, primogeniture, and jihad.

______ **5.** The development of banking, craft guilds, and vernacular literature in the Middle Ages were all the direct result of the growth of towns and trade.

PRACTICING SKILLS *(5 points each)* Study the map of the invasions of Europe and answer the questions that follow.

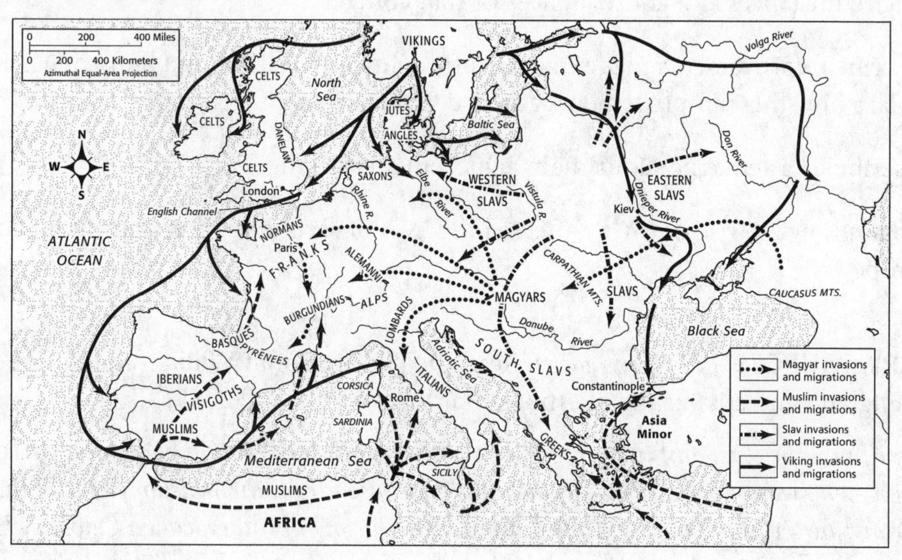

1. Where did the Slavs originally come from?

____

2. The information on this map spans a long period of time. Does the map probably depict the region before or after the Crusades? Explain how you know.

____

COMPOSING AN ESSAY *(20 points)* On a separate sheet of paper, write a brief essay in response to one of the following.

1. Discuss the relationship between religion and war in Europe and the Middle East from the A.D. 600s to the A.D. 1200s.

2. Discuss the role that the Franks, Mongols, and Turks each played in world history between the A.D. 400s and the A.D. 1400s.

Name ______________________ Class ______________ Date ____________

Unit Test Form B

Modern Unit 1

The World In Transition

SHORT ANSWER *(10 points each)* Provide brief answers for each of the following.

1. Identify five factors that helped the Byzantine Empire to exist for more than a thousand years.

2. Name one way that Europeans came into contact with Muslims and briefly describe the circumstances and consequences of that contact.

3. Describe improvements made in agriculture during the Tang and Sung dynasties and explain how these improvements affected China.

4. Describe Charlemagne's four main achievements as king.

5. Explain how the rise of towns affected the lives of serfs and other common people in Europe.

PRIMARY SOURCES *(10 points each)* Read the passage about William the Conqueror's rule in England and answer the questions that follow.

> *A hard man he was, and fierce; no man dared against his will. He had eorls [earls] in chains, who went against his will; bishops he deposed from their bishoprics and thanes [barons] he set in prison. Next, he did not spare his own brother, called Odo. . . . He had an eorldom in England, and when the king was in Normandy he was the master of this land; and him he set in prison. Among other things it is not to be forgotten, that good peace he made in this land, so that a man of any account might fare over the kingdom with a bosom full of gold unmolested; and no man dared kill another man, even if he had done much evil to him. . . .*
>
> From *The Anglo-Saxon Chronicles,* translated and conflated by Anne Savage. Published by St. Martin's Press, New York, 1983.

1. What opinion does the writer seem to have of King William? Explain.

2. What evidence from this passage illustrates the feudal system and government that William the Conqueror (King William) created in England?

COMPOSING AN ESSAY *(30 points)* Write an essay on one of the following subjects.

1. Was religion or war a greater force in shaping history in Asia, Europe, and the Middle East during the period known as Europe's Middle Ages? Explain your opinion and support it with examples.

2. Compare and contrast the feudal systems that developed in Europe and Japan. Consider religious, economic, and cultural factors, as well as each system's impact on government, when forming your response.

Name ______________________ Class ______________ Date ____________

Chapter Test Form A

Modern Chapter **6** **The Renaissance and Reformation**

MATCHING *(3 points each)* In the space provided, write the letter of the name or term that matches each description. Some answers will not be used.

______ **1.** first European to use movable type to print books

______ **2.** helped to progress the Renaissance by providing financial support to Italian artists

______ **3.** Catholic monk whose *Ninety-five Theses* helped launch the Reformation

______ **4.** perfected the technique of painting with oil on canvas

______ **5.** artist famous for painting religious scenes on the ceiling of the Sistine Chapel in the Vatican

______ **6.** Catholic Church leaders who helped lead the Counter-Reformation

______ **7.** religious order that strengthened the Catholic Church and slowed the spread of Protestantism

______ **8.** popular playwright of the northern Renaissance

______ **9.** writer who argued that rulers should be concerned only with power and political success

______ **10.** founded a Protestant church in Switzerland that attracted a strong following throughout Europe

______ **11.** writer whose book *Utopia* described what an ideal society should be like

______ **12.** great Renaissance scientist, engineer, sculptor, and painter

a. John Calvin
b. Council of Trent
c. Leonardo da Vinci
d. Isabella d'Este
e. Edict of Nantes
f. Flemish school
g. Johannes Gutenberg
h. Huguenots
i. Jesuits
j. Martin Luther
k. Niccolò Machiavelli
l. Michelangelo
m. Thomas More
n. William Shakespeare

UNDERSTANDING IDEAS *(3 points each)* For each of the following, write the letter of the best choice in the space provided.

______ **1.** Protestants are to the Reformation as ______ are to the Renaissance.
a. Catholics
b. Christians
c. monks
d. humanists

______ **2.** Which of the following was NOT characteristic of Italian Renaissance art?
a. lifelike figures
b. religious themes
c. geometric designs
d. perspective

______ **3.** The Italian humanists emphasized
a. the need to retain Roman law.
b. a renewed interest in classical learning.
c. reform of the Roman Catholic Church.
d. the need for more religion in daily life.

______ **4.** The main factor in the decline of traditional culture in the 1500s was
a. people moving from the countryside to cities.
b. the invention of the printing press.
c. the Protestant Reformation.
d. the Black Death.

______ **5.** Supporters of the Reformation objected to the selling of indulgences, which allowed
a. wealthy people to buy official positions in the Catholic Church.
b. merchants to open businesses in the Vatican in Rome.
c. people to buy pardons from punishment for their sins.
d. forgiveness of heretics who had been excommunicated from the church.

______ **6.** All of the following helped Protestantism spread in Europe EXCEPT the
a. Peace of Augsburg.
b. divorce of King Henry VIII of England.
c. conversion of French nobles to Calvinism.
d. campaigns of Holy Roman Emperor Charles V.

______ **7.** The ideas of the Italian Renaissance were spread to northern Europe by
a. Martin Luther and John Calvin.
b. merchants and northern European students who had studied in Italy.
c. sects that developed throughout Germany and Switzerland.
d. John Calvin and Thomas More.

______ **8.** The printing press contributed to all of the following EXCEPT
a. understanding and tolerance between Catholics and Protestants.
b. an interest in the outside world among residents of villages and towns.
c. the founding of schools in villages and towns.
d. making medical advice more available to people in rural areas.

TRUE/FALSE *(2 points each)* Mark each statement *T* if it is true or *F* if it is false.

______ **1.** Humanist scholars studied ancient Greek and Roman writings.

______ **2.** A government that is ruled by religious leaders is called an aristocracy.

_____ **3.** The Reformation and the Counter-Reformation both began as efforts to reform the Catholic Church.

_____ **4.** Many Europeans believed in spirits because they did not accept their priests' explanations that misfortunes were God's will or a punishment for sin.

_____ **5.** The early Renaissance began in Greece, where the religious fervor of the crusaders came into contact with Byzantine culture and technology.

PRACTICING SKILLS *(5 points each)* Study the graph and answer the questions that follow.

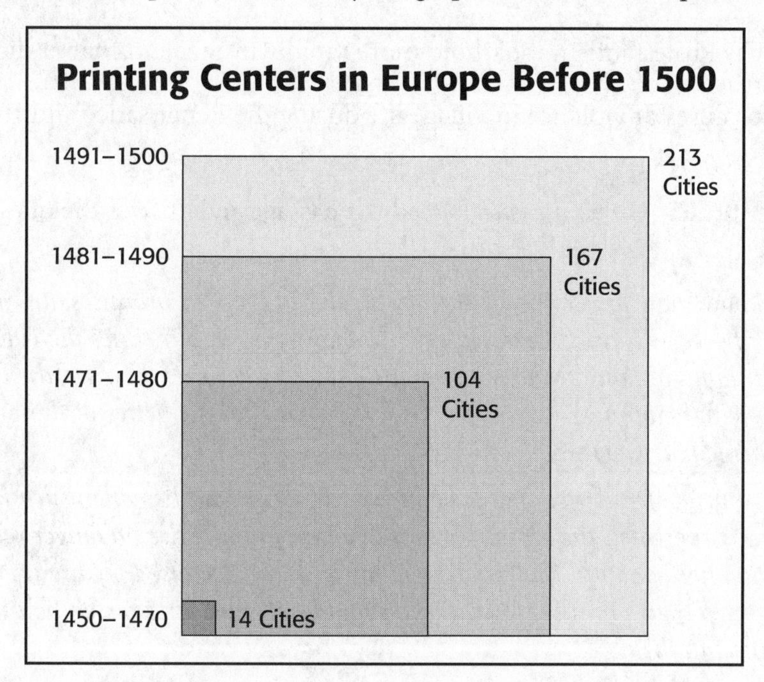

1. During which 10-year period was the spread of printing technology the greatest?

____

2. Did the spread of printing technology speed up or slow down after 1490? Explain how you know.

____

COMPOSING AN ESSAY *(20 points)* On a separate sheet of paper, write a brief essay in response to one of the following.

1. Describe the humanists' outlook on life and how they believed people should live.

2. Explain how Martin Luther's beliefs differed from those of the Catholic Church.

Name ______________________ Class ____________ Date ____________

Chapter Test Form B

Modern Chapter **6**

The Renaissance and Reformation

SHORT ANSWER *(10 points each)* Provide brief answers for each of the following.

1. Name one artist and one writer of the Italian Renaissance and explain each person's significance. Do the same for an artist and writer of the northern Renaissance.

2. Identify the three ways the Renaissance was spread from Italy into northern Europe.

3. Describe the punishments imposed on Martin Luther for his challenge of Catholic teachings and practices.

4. Explain why Protestantism took hold more rapidly in England than it did in France.

5. Name two causes of violence in village life during the Renaissance and Reformation.

PRIMARY SOURCES *(10 points each)* Read the passage and answer the questions that follow.

> *Everyone knows how praiseworthy it is for a ruler to keep his promises, and live uprightly and not by trickery. Nevertheless, experience shows that in our times the rulers who have done great things are those who have set little store by keeping their word, being skilful rather in [being] cunningly confusing men; they have got the better of those who have relied on being trustworthy. . . .*
>
> *Therefore, a prudent ruler cannot keep his word, nor should he, when such fidelity would damage him, and when the reasons that made him promise are no longer relevant. This advice would not be sound if all men were upright; but because they are treacherous and would not keep their promises to you, you should not consider yourself bound to keep your promises to them.*
>
> From *The Prince* by Niccolo Machiavelli, edited by Quentin Skinner and Russell Price. Copyright © 1988 by **Cambridge University Press.** Reprinted by permission of the publisher.

1. According to the author, for what reasons and under what circumstances should a ruler not keep his word?

2. Which of the writers you studied in this chapter most likely wrote this passage? Explain how you know.

COMPOSING AN ESSAY *(30 points)* Write an essay on one of the following subjects. Remember to use examples to support your essay.

1. Summarize the objections to the Catholic Church held by reformers during the 1500s and describe the effects of the religious upheaval that resulted.

2. Compare and contrast the background and world view of Europe's humanists in the 1300s and European villagers in the 1500s.

Name ______________________ Class ______________ Date ______________

Chapter Test Form A

Modern Chapter **7**

Exploration and Expansion

FILL IN THE BLANK *(3 points each)* For each of the following statements, fill in the blank with the appropriate name, term, or phrase.

1. ______________________ used mathematics to prove the theories of Copernicus.

2. The explorer and conqueror ______________________ seized control of the Aztec empire for Spain.

3. The Europeans' belief in ______________________ included the idea that colonies could provide raw materials for a nation and be a market for its products.

4. The philosopher ______________________ argued that all assumptions had to be proven on the basis of known facts.

5. The voyages of ______________________ explorers around the southern tip of Africa and on to Asia encouraged other nations to look for sea routes to the East.

6. A favorable ______________________ was an important part of mercantilism.

7. ______________________ found a sea route from Europe to the Pacific Ocean.

8. The transporting of African slaves across the Atlantic to the Americas was called the

______________________.

9. Direct overseas trade between Asia and Europe began when the explorer

______________________ sailed around Africa to reach India.

10. The failed policies of King ______________________ were partly responsible for weakening Spain as a world power.

UNDERSTANDING IDEAS *(3 points each)* For each of the following, write the letter of the best choice in the space provided.

______ **1.** Advances of the Scientific Revolution included all of the following EXCEPT
- **a.** the heliocentric theory of Copernicus.
- **b.** the geocentric theory of Ptolemy.
- **c.** Galileo's discovery of rings around Saturn.
- **d.** Newton's laws of motion and gravitation.

______ **2.** The rise in the use of slaves during the 1500s and 1600s was caused by the
- **a.** spread of plantation agriculture.
- **b.** rivalry between Portugal and the Netherlands.
- **c.** creation of a Middle Passage.
- **d.** increased consumption of sugar.

_____ **3.** The most important change made in science during the Scientific Revolution was the practice of forming conclusions based on
a. religious teachings.
b. earlier science.
c. recorded observations.
d. tradition.

_____ **4.** Why is the period from the 1400s to the 1700s called the Commercial Revolution?
a. Traders began using advertising to convince people to buy goods.
b. Peasants revolted and demanded factory work.
c. The European economy underwent great changes in basic economic practices.
d. Improvements in ships allowed traders to travel greater distances.

_____ **5.** When tariffs are placed on goods,
a. those goods become less expensive.
b. people are discouraged from buying the goods.
c. trade with other countries increases.
d. the value of exports increases.

_____ **6.** A major change in Europe's economy during the Commercial Revolution was the development of a standard
a. tax on trade goods.
b. trade route.
c. system of weights and measures.
d. system of money.

_____ **7.** The Portuguese established colonies or trade in every place EXCEPT
a. North America.
b. South America.
c. Africa.
d. China and Japan.

_____ **8.** All of the following factors contributed to Spain's decline EXCEPT
a. inflation that resulted from the gold that came from its colonies.
b. a culture that valued military service more than business.
c. the Protestant Reformation's weakening of the Catholic Church.
d. the persecution and expulsion of Jews and Moors.

_____ **9.** Which was NOT a result of the Columbian Exchange?
a. Corn and potatoes were introduced into Europe.
b. Native Americans began riding horses.
c. Europeans brought their diseases to the Americas.
d. The enslavement of Africans began.

_____ **10.** The Dutch became great explorers and colonizers
a. after gaining independence from Spain.
b. because of their Calvinist religious beliefs.
c. in order to convert other peoples to Christianity.
d. to gain a share of the Americas' gold.

TRUE/FALSE *(2 points each)* Mark each statement *T* if it is true or *F* if it is false.

______ **1.** The balance of trade centered around the exchange of slaves, molasses, sugar, rum, cotton, and liquor among the continents.

______ **2.** The Spaniards' desire for Inca and Aztec gold and silver in the Americas was partly due to their belief in mercantilism.

______ **3.** In the 1600s scientists turned to alchemy as the way to knowledge.

______ **4.** Joint-stock companies helped make exploration more financially practical.

______ **5.** Christopher Columbus never realized that his voyages had not reached Asia.

PRACTICING SKILLS *(5 points each)* The map below shows French and Dutch imports from their colonies in the 1770s. Study the map and answer the questions that follow.

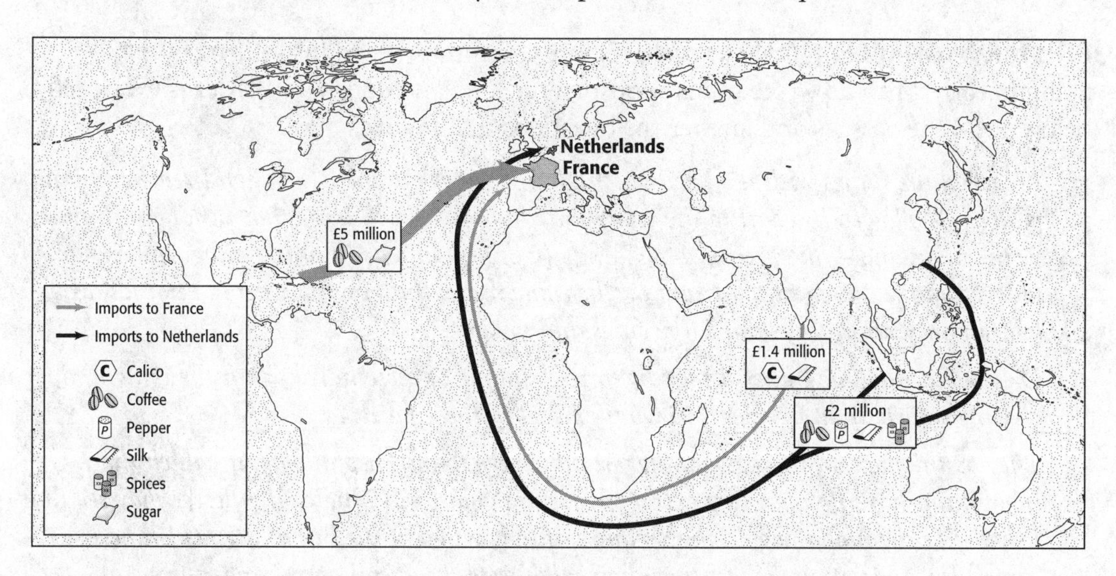

1. What products came to France from the Americas? from Asia?

____

2. What product on the map provides evidence of the Columbian Exchange? How do you know?

____

COMPOSING AN ESSAY *(20 points)* On a separate sheet of paper, write a brief essay in response to one of the following.

1. Explain how technological improvements in the 1400s made exploration possible.

2. Compare and contrast Spanish, Portuguese, and Dutch colonial policies.

Name ______________________ Class ______________ Date ______________

Chapter Test Form B

Modern Chapter **7**

Exploration and Expansion

SHORT ANSWER *(10 points each)* Provide brief answers for each of the following.

1. Explain how the way in which scientists learned about and understood the world around them changed during the era of the Scientific Revolution.

2. Identify the important advances in navigation and shipbuilding in the 1400s and explain how they encouraged exploration.

3. Describe a joint-stock company and explain how it made exploration and colonization more financially practical.

4. Explain why enslaved Africans were brought to the Americas.

5. Summarize the factors that led to the rise of the Dutch colonial empire.

PRIMARY SOURCES *(10 points each)* Before Columbus began his return voyage to Spain in early 1493, he wrote to his sponsors, the king and queen. His letter is excerpted below. Read the passage and answer the questions that follow.

I reached the Indies with the fleet which [you] . . . gave to me. . . . When I reached Juana [Cuba], I followed its coast to the westward, and found it so large that I thought it must be the mainland,—the province of Cathay [China]; and, as I found neither towns nor villages on the sea-coast . . . I kept on the same route, thinking that I could not fail to light upon [encounter] some large cities and towns. . . .

On my reaching the Indies, I took by force . . . some of these natives that they might . . . give me information in regard to what existed in these parts. . . .

They assure me that there is another island larger than [Hispaniola], in which the inhabitants have no hair. It is extremely rich in gold. . . . [T]heir Highnesses may see that I shall give them all the gold they require, if they will give me but a little assistance; spices also, and cotton, as much as their Highnesses shall command to be shipped; and . . . slaves, as many of these idolators as their Highnesses shall command to be shipped.

1. Where does Columbus think he is as he writes this letter? What evidence from the passage suggests this?

2. What request does Columbus make of the king and queen, and what does he promise them in return?

COMPOSING AN ESSAY *(30 points)* Write an essay on one of the following subjects.

1. Explain whether Spanish, Portuguese, or Dutch colonization was more damaging to non-European peoples. Provide reasons and examples to support your opinion.

2. Define the economic theory of mercantilism and explain how it influenced trade policy and shaped the role of colonies in a nation's empire.

Name ______________________ Class ______________ Date ____________

Chapter Test Form A

Modern Chapter **8** **Asia in Transition**

MATCHING *(3 points each)* In the space provided, write the letter of the name or term that matches each description. Some answers will not be used.

_____ **1.** ruler who opened Chinese ports to foreign trade

_____ **2.** gained special trading rights for Great Britain in China

_____ **3.** caused widespread destruction in southern China and weakened the Qing dynasty

_____ **4.** disarmed peasants and tried to establish a Japanese empire by invading Korea

_____ **5.** resulted from peasant discontent over tax increases and growing inefficiency of the Qing government

_____ **6.** granted the United States limited trading rights with Japan

_____ **7.** a Western reaction to mercantilism

_____ **8.** allows foreigners to follow the laws of their home country instead of those of the country in which they live

_____ **9.** agreement that weakened China and benefited foreign powers

_____ **10.** established the Qing dynasty in China

a. extraterritoriality
b. free trade
c. Hsüan-yeh
d. Manchu
e. Matthew Perry
f. Taiping Rebellion
g. Tokugawa Ieyasu
h. Toyotomi Hideyoshi
i. Treaty of Kanagawa
j. Treaty of Nanjing
k. "unequal" treaty
l. White Lotus Rebellion

UNDERSTANDING IDEAS *(3 points each)* For each of the following, write the letter of the best choice in the space provided.

_____ **1.** How did Jesuit missionaries first gain influence with China's Ming emperor?
- **a.** They used their knowledge of astronomy.
- **b.** They offered him Western trade goods.
- **c.** They took his side in a dispute with the British.
- **d.** They sought the support of Buddhist leaders.

_____ **2.** The Tokugawa shoguns weakened the power of the daimyo in Japan by doing all of the following EXCEPT
- **a.** paying salaries to the samurai.
- **b.** keeping daimyo families in the capital as hostages.
- **c.** requiring daimyo to maintain two residences.
- **d.** directly taxing peasants who lived under daimyo rule.

______ **3.** Economic changes in China during Qing rule included all of the following EXCEPT
a. an increase in farming.
b. urban growth and an increase in internal trade.
c. the end of overseas trade.
d. specialized manufacturing in parts of China.

______ **4.** What effect did losing the Opium War have on China?
a. Thousands of Chinese became drug addicts.
b. China had to give the island of Hong Kong to Britain.
c. The Chinese emperor was overthrown.
d. China became weak and was invaded by Japan.

______ **5.** Why did Japan open its ports to American ships in 1854?
a. The United States desired a United States military base in Japan.
b. Japanese leaders wanted more trade with the West.
c. The shogun feared United States military power.
d. Japan's leaders were tired of their nation's isolation.

______ **6.** What caused the Opium War that broke out in 1839?
a. British merchants insisted on selling opium to the Chinese.
b. The Chinese refused to stop selling opium to the British.
c. Drug addicts attacked British traders in China.
d. Chinese merchants stopped shipping tea to Britain.

______ **7.** Which rulers felt threatened by the presence of Jesuit priests in their nation?
a. Japan's Tokugawa shoguns
b. China's Qing and Ming rulers
c. the Tokugawa and the Qing
d. the Tokugawa and the Ming

______ **8.** What did Japan's Tokugawa shogunate and China's Ming dynasty have in common?
a. They ruled military-based feudal societies.
b. Confucianism was a strong force in their governments.
c. Disloyal Buddhist monks stirred up rebellions.
d. Western nations pressured them to allow foreign trade.

______ **9.** The Taiping Rebellion in China was led by a
a. Christian Chinese.
b. Jesuit missionary.
c. Buddhist monk.
d. Manchu noble.

______ **10.** Which is NOT a reason China abandoned overseas expansion during the Ming Dynasty?
a. Ming rulers wanted China to be self-sufficient.
b. Nomadic tribes to the north were threatening China.
c. The Ming lacked the money to defend China and also engage in sea travel.
d. The Portuguese and British navies threatened Chinese merchant ships at sea.

Name ______________________ Class ______________ Date ____________

TRUE/FALSE *(2 points each)* Mark each statement *T* if it is true or *F* if it is false.

______ **1.** Qing emperors required Chinese men to wear their hair in a tail, or queue, as a sign of Chinese submission to Manchu rule.

______ **2.** Japanese rulers feared that Christians would be less loyal than other Japanese subjects.

______ **3.** British actions in China showed little concern for China's culture and people.

______ **4.** The Portuguese introduction of muskets into Japan strengthened the samurai.

______ **5.** The failure of the Taiping Rebellion led to stronger government in China.

PRACTICING SKILLS *(5 points each)* Study the graph of peasant revolts during the Tokugawa shogunate in Japan and answer the questions that follow.

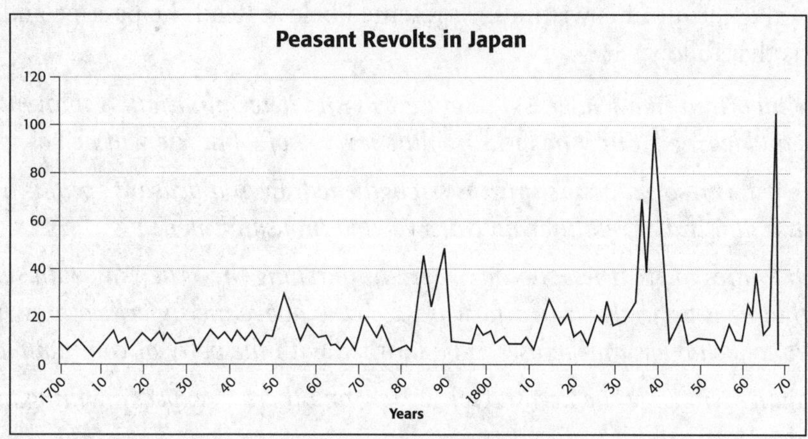

From *Hammond Atlas of World History,* Fifth Edition, edited by Richard Overy. Published by Times Books, a division of HarperCollins Publishers, Inc., London, 1999.

1. During which decade was peasant unrest in Japan the greatest?

____

2. How does Matthew Perry's opening of Japan to foreign trade in 1854 seem to have affected the stability of Japanese society? Explain how you arrived at your conclusion.

____

COMPOSING AN ESSAY *(20 points)* On a separate sheet of paper, write a brief essay in response to one of the following.

1. Compare and contrast the reasons for the collapse of the Qing Dynasty in China and the Tokugawa shogunate in Japan.

2. Explain why Japanese and Chinese rulers failed to keep their countries isolated.

Name ______________________ Class ______________ Date ____________

Chapter Test Form B

Modern Chapter **8**

Asia in Transition

SHORT ANSWER *(10 points each)* Provide brief answers for each of the following.

1. Explain why the Opium War occurred and summarize its consequences.

2. Describe two reasons for the decline of the Qing dynasty.

3. Describe the methods by which the Tokugawa shoguns brought the daimyo under control.

4. Explain why Japan's shoguns and China's emperors opposed the presence of Jesuit priests in their nations.

5. Describe how American foreign policy contributed to the fall of the Tokugawa shogunate.

PRIMARY SOURCES *(10 points each)* Yoshida Shoin was a Japanese philosopher in the mid-1800s. An excerpt of his writings is presented below. Read the passage and answer the questions that follow.

> *What is important in a leader is a resolute will and determination. A man may be versatile and learned, but if he lacks resoluteness . . . of what use will he be?*
>
> *Once the will is resolved, one's spirit is strengthened. Even a peasant's will is hard to deny, but a samurai of resolute will can sway ten thousand men.*
>
> *One who aspires to greatness should . . . study, pursuing the True Way with such a firm resolve that he is perfectly straightforward . . . rises above the superficialities of conventional behavior, and refuses to be satisfied with the petty or commonplace.*
>
> *Once a man's will is set, he need no longer rely on others or expect anything from the world. . . .*
>
> *To consider oneself different from ordinary men is wrong, but it is right to hope that one will not remain like ordinary men.*

1. What does Shoin believe a strong, determined will enables a person to do?

2. What should a strong leader think about following conventional rules of behavior?

COMPOSING AN ESSAY *(30 points)* Write an essay on one of the following subjects. Remember to use examples to support your essay.

1. How might China's history have been different if the Qing had reacted toward the West in the same way that Japan's rulers did? Could the Qing have pursued the same foreign policies as Tokugawa shoguns? Explain why or why not.

2. Describe the system of social controls the Qing rulers introduced to China. Why do you think they adopted such strict policies?

Name ______________________ Class ______________ Date ____________

Chapter Test Form A

Modern Chapter **9**

Islamic Empires in Asia

FILL IN THE BLANK *(3 points each)* For each of the following statements, fill in the blank with the appropriate name, term, or phrase.

1. The warrior princes of India in the 1300s were called ______________________.

2. Much of the Ottoman sultan's power came from a personal army of highly trained slave soldiers called ______________________, who served him for life.

3. The Sikh religion developed in today's nation of ______________________.

4. The Mughal ruler ______________________ introduced a new tax system and improved the empire's economy, which helped attract European traders to India.

5. The Safavid Empire was centered in what is today ______________________.

6. The greatest Ottoman sultan was ______________________, who is known as "the Magnificent" in Europe because he brought the Ottoman empire to its height.

7. In the 1500s a Mongol leader named ______________________ drove out the Turkish rulers of northern India and organized the Mughal Empire there.

8. A Persian military leader named ______________________ founded the Safavid Empire in the early 1500s and took the ancient Persian title of shah.

9. The political and cultural heart of the Ottoman Empire was in the present-day nation of ______________________.

10. Aurangzeb gained control of the ______________________ Empire in the mid-1600s by killing his older brother and imprisoning the emperor, who was his father.

UNDERSTANDING IDEAS *(3 points each)* For each of the following, write the letter of the best choice in the space provided.

______ **1.** To strengthen control over his empire, the Mughal emperor Akbar
- **a.** required all his subjects to convert to Islam.
- **b.** gave Rajputs positions in his government.
- **c.** increased taxes to pay for a larger army.
- **d.** formed a private army of slaves loyal only to him.

______ **2.** The actions which earned the Safavid shah ʿAbbās the title "the Great" included all of the following EXCEPT
- **a.** founding the kizilbash.
- **b.** recapturing territory lost to the Ottomans and Uzbeks.
- **c.** building a new capital.
- **d.** reforming the military by copying the Ottoman army.

______ **3.** Which of the following is NOT true of the Persians' conversion to the Shi'ah branch of Islam?
a. They were forced to convert by their rulers.
b. Shi'ah made them feel distinct from the Turks and Arabs around them.
c. Prior to converting, the Persians had persecuted Shi'ah Muslims.
d. Before becoming Shi'ah, they had been Sikhs.

______ **4.** In which empires did religious freedom exist at some time?
a. Ottoman and Safavid
b. Safavid and Mughal
c. Mughal and Ottoman
d. in none of the empires

______ **5.** The Sikh religion that was founded by Nānak blended the beliefs of
a. Buddhism and Hinduism.
b. Hinduism and Islam.
c. Islam and Buddhism.
d. Christianity and Islam.

______ **6.** The Taj Mahal is a symbol of the greatness of the
a. Mongol Empire.
b. Mughal Empire.
c. Ottoman Empire.
d. Safavid Empire.

______ **7.** The Mongol leader who stopped the Ottoman Empire's expansion into Asia in the 1400s was
a. Bābur.
b. Genghis Khan.
c. Süleyman.
d. Timur.

______ **8.** The high point of the Mughal Empire was reached during the rule of
a. Akbar.
b. Bābur.
c. Shah Jahān.
d. Timur.

______ **9.** The self-governing religious communities that the sultan set up in the Ottoman Empire were called
a. ghazis.
b. kizilbash.
c. millets.
d. reaya.

______ **10.** Which was NOT a common characteristic of the Ottoman, Safavid, and Mughal empires?
a. a rigid class structure
b. leaders who were Muslims
c. thriving trade
d. a strong military

TRUE/FALSE *(2 points each)* Mark each statement *T* if it is true or *F* if it is false.

______ **1.** Mughal ruler Shah Jahān took half the crops his subjects raised to pay the expenses of his empire.

______ **2.** After the Ottomans captured the Byzantine capital of Constantinople, they made it the capital of the Ottoman Empire.

______ **3.** Aurangzeb brought unrest to the Ottoman Empire when he restored a hated tax on Muslims.

______ **4.** Polish troops stopped the Ottomans' advance into Europe outside Vienna in the 1600s.

______ **5.** The title of "shah," which was taken by the Safavid rulers, was the ancient Persian word for "caesar."

PRACTICING SKILLS *(5 points each)* The chart below shows the basic organization of government in the Ottoman Empire. Study the chart and answer the questions that follow.

Government of the Ottoman Empire

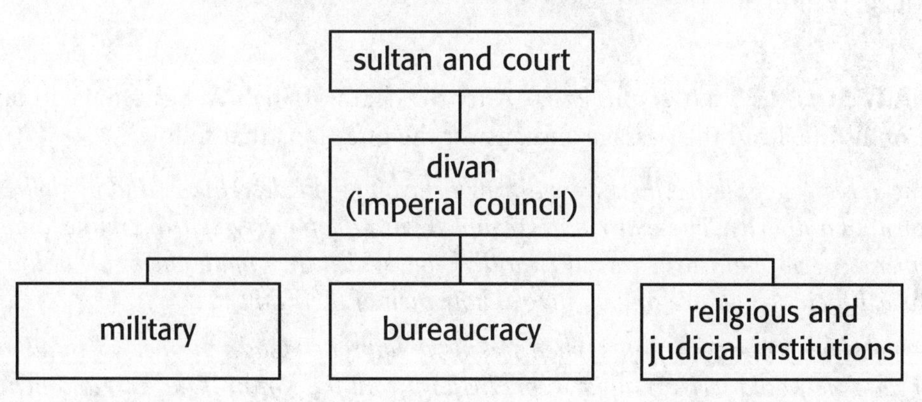

1. Who oversaw the military and the government bureaucracy in the Ottoman Empire?

____

2. In which two divisions of Ottoman government would members of the reaya be LEAST likely to be found?

____

COMPOSING AN ESSAY *(20 points)* On a separate sheet of paper, write a brief essay in response to one of the following.

1. Explain how the Ottoman, Safavid, and Mughal dynasties each used religious policy to maintain stability in and control over their empires.

2. Compare and contrast the reasons for the decline of the Ottoman, Safavid, and Mughal empires.

Name ______________________ Class ______________ Date ____________

Chapter Test Form B

Modern Chapter **9**

Islamic Empires in Asia

SHORT ANSWER *(10 points each)* Provide brief answers for each of the following

1. How was government in the Ottoman Empire organized?

2. For what reasons did the Ottoman Empire decline?

3. What Safavid ruler was known as "the Great," and what did he do to earn this designation?

4. What methods did Akbar use to unify and control the Mughal Empire?

5. What objects today are the best-known examples of the grandeur of Safavid and Mughal culture?

PRIMARY SOURCES *(10 points each)* After the death of Shah 'Abbās, a Safavid official wrote of his life. Read the passage and answer the questions that follow.

> *The ancestors of Shah Ábbās were distinguished by their descent . . . and by their spiritual authority. These attributes, coupled with the poverty, self-discipline, and the inner struggle against the carnal [worldly] soul which they made their rule of life earned their acceptance among the . . . holy men of their day. . . .*
>
> *Shah 'Abbās was never remiss when seeking to approach God's throne. . . . In all affairs of state, he would seek an augury [prediction] from the Koran [Qur'an], and he would take no action in the realm of government without asking God's advice. If the text of the Koran expressly forbade something, he would respect God's wise counsel and refrain from taking that action, even though it was desirable in order to gain some material advantage.*
>
> From *History of Shah Ábbas the Great,* vol. 1, by Eskander Beg Monshi, translated by Roger M. Savory. Published by Westview Press, Boulder, CO, 1978.

1. How did Shah Ábbās use the Qur'an in governing?

2. Whom does the writer imply was responsible for the success of the Safavid Empire and through what governing process was it successful?

COMPOSING AN ESSAY *(30 points)* Write an essay on one of the following subjects. Remember to use examples to support your essay.

1. Would you have preferred to live in the Ottoman Empire, the Safavid Empire, or the Mughal Empire at its height? Weigh cultural, economic, and political factors in considering the three alternatives. Then explain your decision, the criteria on which you based it, and the reasoning behind your choice.

2. Explain and compare how the Ottomans, Safavids, and Mughals were each able to gain and maintain control of vast, multicultural empires for hundreds of years.

Unit Test Form A

Modern Unit **2**

The Age of Exploration and Expansion

UNDERSTANDING IDEAS *(3 points each)* For each of the following, write the letter of the best choice in the space provided.

______ **1.** Merchants and traders were LEAST important in the society of
a. the Safavid Empire.
b. Qing China.
c. Renaissance Europe.
d. Tokugawa Japan.

______ **2.** The earliest beginnings of the Renaissance were in
a. the Byzantine Empire.
b. Italy.
c. Germany.
d. China.

______ **3.** European nations played a major role in the weakening or collapse of all of the following dynasties or empires EXCEPT the
a. Aztec Empire.
b. Ottoman Empire.
c. Safavid Empire.
d. Qing dynasty.

______ **4.** The basic reason for the Reformation was
a. disagreements with the practices of the Catholic Church.
b. the desire of Catholic heretics to start new religions.
c. efforts of Catholic Church leaders to reform the Church practices.
d. persecution by Catholic kings of Protestants who lived in their countries.

______ **5.** Who or what was MOST responsible for opening China to foreign trade?
a. the Taiping Rebellion
b. Matthew Perry
c. the Opium War
d. the Dutch

______ **6.** Which group did NOT make an important contribution to the Renaissance?
a. artists
b. humanists
c. merchants
d. priests

______ **7.** A belief in the economic theory of mercantilism was a major reason for
a. the growth of trade in the Safavid empire.
b. European colonization of the Americas.
c. British foreign policies toward China.
d. the United States' plan to open Japan to U.S. trade.

______ **8.** Which of the following did NOT occur at about the same time as the others?
a. the decline of the Qing dynasty in China
b. the Reformation in Europe
c. Spanish exploration of the Americas
d. the founding of the Mughal Empire in India

______ **9.** Which people first undertook voyages of exploration to connect with distant lands by sea?
a. the Chinese
b. the Dutch
c. the Portuguese
d. the Spanish

______ **10.** The Jesuits played an important role in all of the following EXCEPT
a. China during the Qing dynasty.
b. the Counter-Reformation.
c. the Safavid Empire.
d. Japan in the mid-1500s and early 1600s.

MATCHING *(3 points each)* In the space provided, write the letter of the name or term that matches each description. Some answers will not be used.

______ **1.** pressured Japan to trade with the West
______ **2.** brought the feudal daimyo under control in Japan
______ **3.** great shah of the Safavid Empire
______ **4.** weakened Qing rule in China
______ **5.** conquered the Aztec in Mexico
______ **6.** brought enslaved Africans to the Americas
______ **7.** Renaissance inventor, scientist, and artist
______ **8.** pioneered a water route from Europe to India
______ **9.** great sultan of the Ottoman Empire
______ **10.** denounced for challenging church practices

a. ʻAbbās
b. Christopher Columbus
c. Hernán Cortés
d. Galileo Galilei
e. Johannes Gutenberg
f. Vasco da Gama
g. Martin Luther
h. Middle Passage
i. Matthew Perry
j. Shah Jahan
k. Süleyman
l. Tokugawa
m. Leonardo da Vinci
n. White Lotus Rebellion

TRUE/FALSE *(2 points each)* Mark each statement *T* if it is true or *F* if it is false.

______ **1.** One result of the Reformation in Europe was the development of what is now known as the "scientific method" of learning about the natural world.

______ **2.** Of the three Islamic empires in Asia in the 1500s, the LEAST religious freedom existed in the Ottoman Empire.

______ **3.** The Renaissance and the Commercial Revolution in Europe helped to stimulate the European voyages of exploration.

______ **4.** Two of the key goods in the triangular trade were gold and African slaves.

______ **5.** The two peoples most involved in world trade in the 1600s were the Spanish and Portuguese.

PRACTICING SKILLS *(5 points each)* The map below shows the spread of the Black Death that struck Europe during the first years of the Renaissance. Study the map and answer the questions that follow.

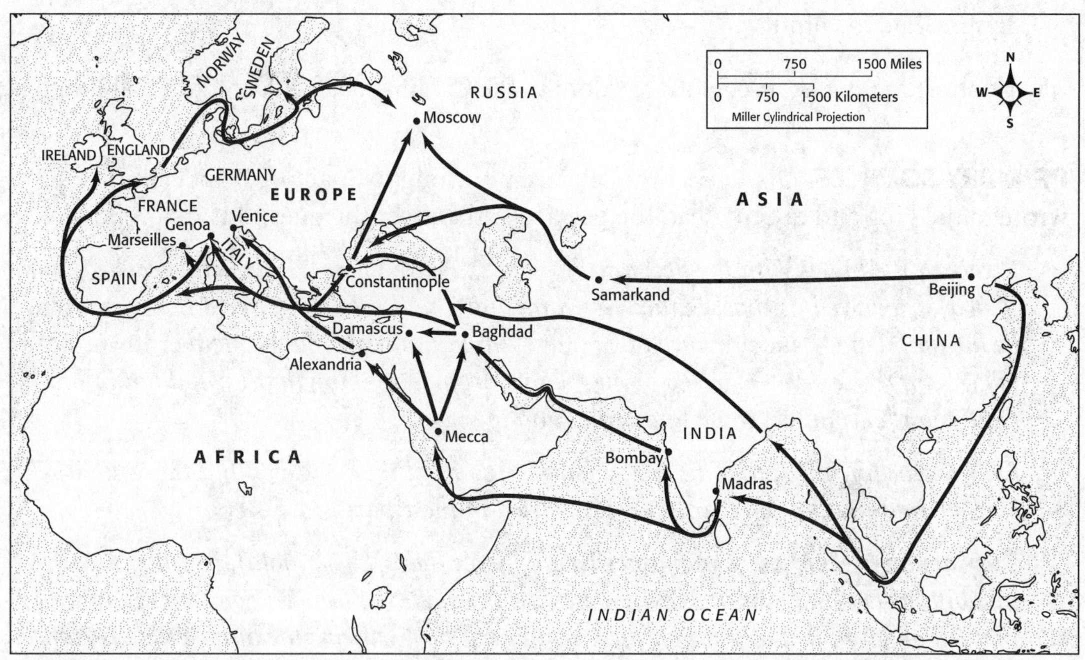

From *Encyclopedia of World History,* compiled by Market House Books Ltd. Copyright © 1998 by **Oxford University Press.** Reprinted by permission of the publisher.

1. From where did the Black Death originate?

____

2. The Black Death reached England in 1348, but not Moscow until after 1350. What likely explains this difference?

____

COMPOSING AN ESSAY *(20 points)* On a separate sheet of paper, write a brief essay in response to one of the following.

1. Compare the reasons for the decline of the Qing dynasty and the Ottoman Empire.

2. Explain how the Scientific Revolution changed the way scientists learned about the world, and cite some examples of how they applied their new methods.

Name ______________________ Class ______________ Date ____________

Unit Test Form B

Modern Unit 2 — The Age of Exploration and Expansion

SHORT ANSWER *(10 points each)* Provide brief answers for each of the following.

1. Name two Renaissance artists and two writers and explain their contributions.
2. Explain how the way scientists gathered knowledge changed during the Scientific Revolution.
3. Explain the main economic reasons behind European exploration and colonization.
4. Identify and describe two reasons for decline that the Qing dynasty and the Ottoman Empire had in common.
5. Contrast the status of religious freedom in the Ottoman, Safavid, and Mughal Empires.

PRIMARY SOURCES *(10 points each)* Before returning to Spain in 1493, Columbus wrote to the king and queen. Read the passage and answer the questions that follow.

> *I reached the Indies with the fleet which [you] . . . gave to me. . . . When I reached Juana [Cuba], I followed its coast to the westward, and found it so large that I thought it must be the mainland,—the province of Cathay [China]; and, as I found neither towns nor villages on the sea-coast . . . I kept on the same route, thinking that I could not fail to light upon [encounter] some large cities and towns. . . .*
>
> *On my reaching the Indies, I took by force . . . some of these natives that they might . . . give me information in regard to what existed in these parts. . . .*
>
> *They assure me that there is another island larger than [Hispaniola], in which the inhabitants have no hair. It is extremely rich in gold. . . . [T]heir Highnesses may see that I shall give them all the gold they require, if they will give me but a little assistance; spices also, and cotton, as much as their Highnesses shall command to be shipped; and . . . slaves, as many of these idolators as their Highnesses shall command to be shipped.*

1. Of the things he had heard about, in what did Columbus seem most interested? Explain how you know.
2. On what basis does Columbus seem to justify the enslavement of the people he has met? Explain how you know.

COMPOSING AN ESSAY *(30 points)* Write an essay on one of the following subjects.

1. Explain why the Renaissance, the Reformation, and European exploration and colonization were interrelated.
2. Think about the leadership and the fundamental ideas behind the Reformation and the Scientific Revolution. What characteristics did the two movements share? In what respects were their basic ways of thinking different?

Name ______________________ Class ______________ Date ____________

Chapter Test Form A

Modern Chapter **10**

Monarchs of Europe

FILL IN THE BLANK *(3 points each)* For each of the following statements, fill in the blank with the appropriate name, term, or phrase.

1. The Hohenzollern ruler ______________________ strengthened his small state of Brandenburg-Prussia by improving its tax system, industry, and transportation.

2. King ______________________ unified all the Hohenzollern lands in northern Germany under Prussian rule and became the first King of Prussia.

3. King ______________________ reformed the Prussian army, doubled its size, and made it one of the most powerful military forces in Europe.

4. Prussia's King ______________________ spent the first 23 years of his reign at war and the next 23 years rebuilding and strengthening his kingdom.

5. The French king ______________________, who was called the Sun King, believed that he ruled by the grace of God.

6. Philip II of Spain sent ______________________ to remove Queen Elizabeth I from power and to restore Catholic rule to England.

7. Queen Mary I wanted the ______________________ faith to be the official religion of England.

8. Russia, Prussia, and Austria divided ______________________ among themselves.

9. Catherine the Great gained access for Russia to the Black Sea by seizing its north shore from the ______________________.

10. James I was king of England and ______________________.

UNDERSTANDING IDEAS *(3 points each)* For each of the following, write the letter of the best choice in the space provided.

______ **1.** All of the following strained the French economy by the early 1700s EXCEPT
a. construction of the palace at Versailles.
b. the policies of Jean-Baptiste Colbert.
c. King Louis XIV's foreign policies.
d. four wars between 1667 and 1713.

______ **2.** Which was NOT a reason that King James I and Parliament clashed?
a. He tried to form an alliance with Spain.
b. He believed in the divine right of kings.
c. He authorized a new translation of the Bible.
d. He was a strong supporter of the Anglican Church.

_______ **3.** One aim of Cardinal Richelieu was to strengthen France by
- **a.** making Louis XIII emperor of the Holy Roman Empire.
- **b.** rejecting the Treaty of Westphalia.
- **c.** placing a Protestant French ruler on the Spanish throne.
- **d.** weakening the Holy Roman Empire.

_______ **4.** To reduce the nobles' power in France, Cardinal Richelieu
- **a.** increased the authority of the regional intendants.
- **b.** supported Protestants against Catholics.
- **c.** encouraged the growth of industry and trade.
- **d.** revoked the Edict of Nantes.

_______ **5.** By the end of the 1600s, the most powerful ruler in Europe was the
- **a.** czar of Russia.
- **b.** king of England.
- **c.** king of France.
- **d.** Holy Roman Emperor.

_______ **6.** Which practice of Czar Peter I was LEAST like those of rulers in western Europe at the time?
- **a.** his centralized system of government with control over local governments
- **b.** basing a noble's rank on the government service he performed
- **c.** his encouragement of growth in manufacturing and trade
- **d.** seeking to expand his nation by seizing new territory

_______ **7.** Russia's foreign policy under Peter the Great and Catherine the Great differed from most western European nations of the time because it focused on
- **a.** expanding Russia's national borders.
- **b.** strengthening the military.
- **c.** increasing Russia's international trade.
- **d.** colonizing lands overseas.

_______ **8.** Prussia's seizure of Silesia from Habsburg Empress Maria Theresa started the
- **a.** War of the Spanish Succession.
- **b.** War of the Austrian Succession.
- **c.** Seven Years' War.
- **d.** Thirty Years' War.

_______ **9.** In the Seven Years' War, the British and French fought each other everywhere EXCEPT
- **a.** North America.
- **b.** India.
- **c.** Europe.
- **d.** North Africa.

_______ **10.** All of the following actions of Peter the Great helped to westernize Russia EXCEPT
- **a.** building St. Petersburg and making it Russia's new capital.
- **b.** forcing his nobles to shave off their long beards and dress in European styles.
- **c.** visiting Western countries in disguise and learning more about the Western way of life.
- **d.** granting Russian nobles large estates with thousands of serfs.

TRUE/FALSE *(2 points each)* Mark each statement *T* if it is true or *F* if it is false.

______ **1.** The belief of some European kings in the 1600s and 1700s that they had a God-given right to rule was called the "Mandate of Heaven."

______ **2.** One way that some monarchs controlled their nobles was by requiring them to live near the palace so they could be watched.

______ **3.** In a move called the Pragmatic Sanction, Britain and France exchanged allies in Europe.

______ **4.** Habsburg and Hohenzollern were rival ruling families in Europe.

______ **5.** England's Queen Elizabeth I arrested and beheaded Mary, Queen of Scots.

PRACTICING SKILLS *(5 points each)* Study the chart of English, Spanish, and Scottish royal families and answer the questions that follow.

The English Succession to 1603

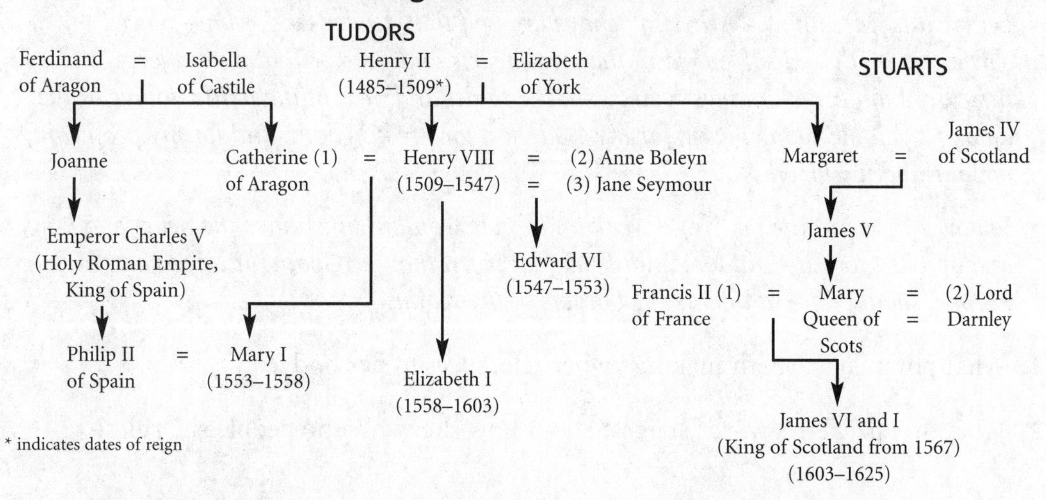

1. Which two monarchs were related by both blood and marriage? Explain.

____

2. Which king of England was a son of a king of France? Explain.

____

COMPOSING AN ESSAY *(20 points)* On a separate sheet of paper, write a brief essay in response to one of the following.

1. Describe the factors that isolated Russia from the rest of Europe before the 1700s.

2. Explain the role of religion in England's troubles in the late 1500s and early 1600s.

Name ______________________ Class ______________ Date ____________

Chapter Test Form B

Modern Chapter **10**

Monarchs of Europe

SHORT ANSWER *(10 points each)* Provide brief answers for each of the following

1. How did Cardinal Richelieu and Louis XIV strengthen the power of the French central government over the nobility and religious interests?

2. Why might the Seven Years' War be considered a "world war"?

3. How did the actions of Louis XIV affect the economy of France?

4. What steps did Prussia's Hohenzollern rulers Frederick William, Frederick I, and Frederick William I take to launch its rise to power?

5. For what reasons did England's King James I and Parliament clash?

PRIMARY SOURCES *(10 points each)* In August 1588, Queen Elizabeth I addressed her troops as England awaited the invasion of the Spanish Armada. Read the passage and answer the questions that follow.

> *Let tyrants fear; I have always so behaved myself that, under God, I have placed my chiefest strength and safeguard in the loyal hearts and good will of my subjects. And therefore I am come amongst you . . . in the midst and heat of the battle, to live or die amongst you all; to lay down, for my God, and for my kingdom, and for my people, my honour and my blood . . .*
>
> *I know I have but the body of a weak and feeble woman; but I have the heart of a king, and of a king of England too; and think foul scorn that . . . Spain, or any prince of Europe, should dare to invade the borders of my realms. . . .*

1. What point is Elizabeth making by her references to her body?

2. What do Elizabeth's words suggest about how she views the people she rules?

COMPOSING AN ESSAY *(30 points)* Write an essay on one of the following subjects. Remember to use examples to support your essay.

1. Compare and contrast the goals and accomplishments of Peter the Great and Catherine the Great in Russia.

2. Explain how the Thirty Years' War, which began in 1618, and its outcome affected the balance of power in Europe for the next 150 years.

Name ______________________ Class ______________ Date ______________

Chapter Test Form A

Modern Chapter 11 Enlightenment and Revolution in England and America

MATCHING *(3 points each)* In the space provided, write the letter of the name or term that matches each description. Some answers will not be used.

_____ **1.** placed a tax on documents such as wills, mortgages, and contracts

_____ **2.** overthrew the monarch in a bloodless transfer of power

_____ **3.** the first written constitution of any major European nation

_____ **4.** barred Catholics from becoming rulers of England

_____ **5.** overthrew the rule of King George III and Parliament

_____ **6.** abolished the monarchy and set up a commonwealth

_____ **7.** established the first government of the United States

_____ **8.** refusal of Scots to make changes in their religious practices

_____ **9.** protected English people against unfair arrest and imprisonment

_____ **10.** joined England and Scotland to form the nation of Great Britain

a. Act of Settlement
b. Act of Union
c. American Revolution
d. Articles of Confederation
e. English Revolution
f. Glorious Revolution
g. Habeas Corpus Act
h. Instrument of Government of 1653
i. National Covenant
j. Navigation Act of 1651
k. Rump Parliament
l. Stamp Act

UNDERSTANDING IDEAS *(3 points each)* For each of the following, write the letter of the best choice in the space provided.

_____ **1.** The philosophes based their ideas about government on
a. classical Greece and Rome.
b. Thomas More's ideal government in *Utopia.*
c. the commonwealth set up under Oliver Cromwell.
d. the ideals of the American Revolution.

_____ **2.** Britain's policy toward its American colonies changed after 1763 in all of the following ways EXCEPT
a. the levying of new taxes.
b. a ban on settlement west of the Appalachians.
c. limiting the colonies' power in Parliament.
d. enforcing its trade laws.

______ **3.** Parliament's selection of Mary and her Dutch husband William of Orange to be the king and queen of England is called the
a. Restoration.
b. Glorious Revolution.
c. Act of Settlement.
d. Act of Union.

______ **4.** Which is LEAST like the others in its content and purpose?
a. Declaration of Independence
b. English Bill of Rights
c. Petition of Right
d. U.S. Bill of Rights

______ **5.** The Baron de Montesquieu believed the best government would have
a. a very powerful leader.
b. religious freedom for all.
c. a system of checks and balances.
d. a separation of church and state.

______ **6.** The American Constitution
a. is based on the British system of government.
b. set up a government with three branches.
c. gave the most governing power to the states.
d. declares that all people have a right to "life, liberty, and the pursuit of happiness."

______ **7.** All of the following were factors in causing England's civil war EXCEPT
a. a rebellion in Scotland.
b. the policies of the Long Parliament.
c. a rebellion in Ireland.
d. the execution of King Charles I.

______ **8.** Thomas Jefferson based the Declaration of Independence largely on the ideas of
a. John Locke.
b. George Washington.
c. Baron de Montesquieu.
d. King George III.

______ **9.** Colonists who supported Britain in the American Revolution were called
a. Dissenters.
b. Patriots.
c. Tories.
d. Whigs.

______ **10.** Parliament's passage of the Toleration Act in 1689
a. allowed the king to avoid execution and go into exile in France.
b. granted some religious freedom to Protestants who were not Anglicans.
c. brought Charles II to the throne.
d. required the king to call Parliament into session once every three years.

TRUE/FALSE *(2 points each)* Mark each statement *T* if it is true or *F* if it is false.

______ **1.** The sea dogs were pirates and traders who helped England expand overseas.

______ **2.** Most of the major thinkers of the Enlightenment were British.

______ **3.** The Whigs and Tories were English political parties that formed during the Restoration.

______ **4.** The Parliamentary government that was set up in England following the overthrow of Charles I gained the widespread support of the English people.

______ **5.** The ideas of the Enlightenment encouraged the American Revolution.

PRACTICING SKILLS *(5 points each)* Study the graph and answer the questions that follow.

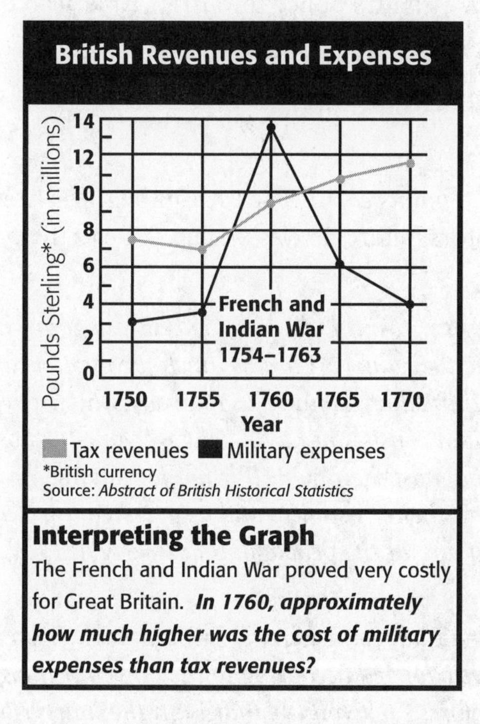

1. What effect did the French and Indian War have on the British government's budget?

____

2. What clues does the graph provide to suggest why Britain continued to increase taxes after the war?

____

COMPOSING AN ESSAY *(20 points)* On a separate sheet of paper, write a brief essay in response to one of the following.

1. What support could the English Parliament have found in the writings of John Locke to justify its actions in the English Revolution and the Glorious Revolution?

2. In what ways were Britain's colonial policies in India both similar to and different from its policies in North America?

Name ______________________ Class ______________ Date ____________

Chapter Test Form B

Modern Chapter 11 **Enlightenment and Revolution in England and America**

SHORT ANSWER *(10 points each)* Provide brief answers for each of the following.

1. Briefly describe the sequence of events that led to the English civil war.

2. Explain the religious factors behind the Glorious Revolution.

3. Describe how mercantilism affected Britain's colonies in India and North America.

4. Explain how and why Britain's policy toward its American colonies changed.

5. Summarize the reasons the United States had for replacing the Articles of Confederation with the Constitution.

PRIMARY SOURCES *(10 points each)* The excerpt below is from the final statement of King Charles I to his captors before he was executed. Read the passage and answer the questions that follow.

> *[Y]ou will never do right . . . until you give God his due, the King his due (that is, my successors) and the people their due[.] I am as much for them as any of you. . . . And truly I desire their liberty and freedom as much as anybody whomsoever. But I must tell you that their liberty and freedom consists in having of government; those laws by which their life and their goods may be most their own. It is not for having share in government . . . that is nothing pertaining to them. A subject and a sovereign are clean different things, and therefore until . . . you do put the people in that liberty as I say, certainly they will never enjoy themselves.*
>
> *It was for this that now I am come here. If I would have given way to an arbitrary way, for to have all the laws changed according to the power of the sword I needed not to have come here. And, therefore, I tell you . . . that I am the martyr of the people.*

1. From Charles' point of view expressed in this statement, why is he being executed?

2. What evidence does Charles' statement provide of his belief in absolute monarchy?

COMPOSING AN ESSAY *(30 points)* Write an essay on one of the following subjects. Remember to use examples to support your answer.

1. Explain how the ideas of Thomas Hobbes and John Locke are expressed in the Declaration of Independence. In what ways were their ideas modified in the Declaration?

2. The government that emerged out of the struggles in Britain in the 1600s and 1700s was a "limited constitutional monarchy." Explain the meaning of each word in that description as it applies to British government. Then discuss three political developments during that period which contributed to the process of creating this form of government.

Name ____________________ Class ____________ Date ____________

Chapter Test Form A

Modern Chapter 12 **The French Revolution and Napoléon**

FILL IN THE BLANK *(3 points each)* For each of the following statements, fill in the blank with the appropriate name, term, or phrase.

1. The Second Estate in the Old Regime consisted of ____________________.

2. The French people resented the wild spending, Austrian heritage, and political influence of Louis XVI's wife, Queen ____________________.

3. The group in the Legislative Assembly that wanted to get rid of the king and set up a republic became known as the ____________________.

4. The ____________________ replaced the National Assembly in ruling France.

5. The First Estate in the Old Regime was the ____________________.

6. The five-person government that ruled France after the National Convention was called the ____________________.

7. The agreement that Napoléon reached with the pope to allow religious freedom in France was called the ____________________.

8. The ____________________ replaced the Legislative Assembly in ruling France as the Revolution took a radical turn.

9. The first five years of Napoléon's rule was called the ____________________.

10. The largest and poorest group in France was ____________________.

UNDERSTANDING IDEAS *(3 points each)* For each of the following, write the letter of the best choice in the space provided.

______ **1.** In the 1700s the French people were discontented for all of the following reasons EXCEPT
- **a.** the clergy and nobles had gained more power.
- **b.** families were larger and needed more food.
- **c.** food prices rose faster than wages.
- **d.** common people paid high taxes, while clergy and nobles paid none.

______ **2.** The Congress of Vienna met
- **a.** to punish Napoléon for his wars.
- **b.** to settle religious disputes in Europe.
- **c.** to settle issues about the future of Europe.
- **d.** to elect a new Holy Roman Emperor.

______ **3.** The National Assembly accomplished all of the following EXCEPT
a. adopt the Declaration of the Rights of Man and of the Citizen.
b. write a constitution that greatly limited the power of the king.
c. bring an end to the Reign of Terror.
d. seize lands of the Catholic Church and sell them to French peasants.

______ **4.** The Declaration of the Rights of Man and of the Citizen
a. granted basic rights to all French men and women.
b. stated the human rights of French men.
c. limited the power and privileges of the nobles.
d. restored the freedom and power of the Huguenots.

______ **5.** One reason for Napoléon's rise to power in France was
a. his commanding physical appearance.
b. his marriage to Joséphine de Beauharnais.
c. his family's titles.
d. Louis XVI's support.

______ **6.** Napoléon's final defeat occurred at
a. Vienna.
b. Moscow.
c. Wellington.
d. Waterloo.

______ **7.** Napoléon made all the following changes in Europe EXCEPT
a. force Austria and Prussia to sign treaties.
b. unite some German states into a confederation.
c. claim the title of Holy Roman Emperor.
d. create the Kingdom of Italy.

______ **8.** The most radical of the legislative bodies that governed France during the revolution was the
a. National Assembly.
b. National Convention.
c. Legislative Assembly.
d. the Directory.

______ **9.** What was the most important reason for Napoléon's failure to conquer Russia?
a. the skill of Russian generals
b. British aid to Russia
c. a poor French navy
d. Russia's climate and size

______ **10.** After Napoléon's defeat, Europe was governed by a system called the
a. Concert of Europe.
b. Concordat.
c. Continental System.
d. Directory.

Name ______________________ Class ______________ Date ____________

TRUE/FALSE *(2 points each)* Mark each statement *T* if it is true or *F* if it is false.

_______ **1.** The French Revolution began when the Third Estate of the Estates General declared itself to be the National Assembly of France.

_______ **2.** The French Revolution had been under way for more than three years before the king was arrested and executed.

_______ **3.** France was forced into war when outsiders tried to restore the monarchy.

_______ **4.** The Duke of Wellington defeated Napoléon's attempt to invade Britain.

_______ **5.** Another name for the poor rural peasants in France was the bourgeoisie.

PRACTICING SKILLS *(5 points each)* Study the map of Napoléon's Empire between 1805 and 1815 and answer the questions that follow.

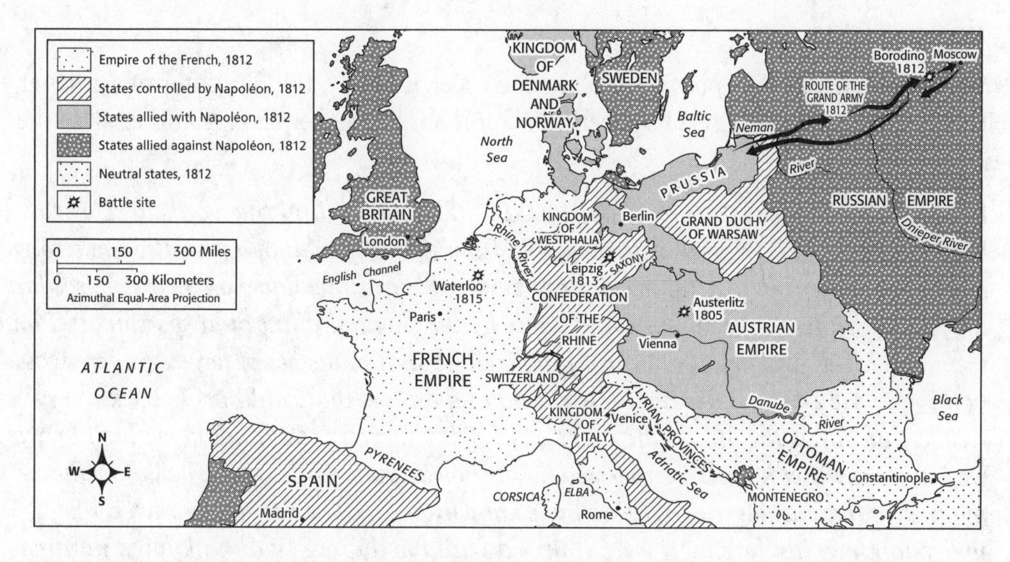

1. Why was Napoléon's alliance with Prussia so important to his war plans?

____

2. In what country did Napoléon's final defeat take place?

____

COMPOSING AN ESSAY *(20 points)* On a separate sheet of paper, write a brief essay in response to one of the following.

1. Discuss the Reign of Terror, including its purpose, its victims, and how it concluded.

2. Describe Napoléon's reforms of French government and explain how they affected the rest of Europe.

Name ______________________ Class ______________ Date ______________

Chapter Test Form B

Modern Chapter **12** **The French Revolution and Napoléon**

SHORT ANSWER *(10 points each)* Provide brief answers for each of the following.

1. What political and social reforms did the National Assembly make during the French Revolution? What purpose did it have in taking these actions?

2. Which of the three legislatures that governed France between 1789 and 1795 was the most radical? Explain why.

3. What changes did Napoléon make in the political organization of Europe?

4. How did the Russians use geography to defeat Napoléon? What was the effect of that defeat?

5. What problems did the nations of Europe face after Napoléon, and how did they attempt to keep the peace?

PRIMARY SOURCES *(10 points each)* In the excerpt below, the daughter of a former advisor to King Louis XVI recalls meeting Napoléon. Read the passage and answer the questions that follow.

> *I saw him for the first time at Paris [in 1797]. I could not find the words to reply to him. . . . But, when I was a little recovered from the confusion of admiration, a strongly marked sentiment of fear followed. Bonaparte, at that time, had no power; . . . so that the fear which he inspired was caused only by the singular effect of his person . . . I had seen men highly worthy of esteem; I had likewise seen monsters of ferocity: there was nothing in the effect which Bonaparte produced on me, that could bring back to my recollection either the one or the other. . . . [H]is character could not be defined by words we commonly use; he was neither good, nor violent, nor gentle, nor cruel, after the manner of individuals of whom we have knowledge. . . . His cast of character, his understanding, his language, were stamped with the impress of an unknown nature.*
>
> From "By an 'Ideologue'" by Madame Germaine de Staël from *Napoleon,* edited by Maurice Hutt. Published by Prentice-Hall, Inc., Englewood Cliffs, NJ, 1972.

1. How does the writer describe her reaction upon meeting Napoléon?

2. To what does the writer attribute her reaction? What reasons for it does she dismiss?

COMPOSING AN ESSAY *(30 points)* Write an essay on one of the following subjects.

1. Summarize the social, political, and cultural effects of the French Revolution. Based on these consequences, do you think it can be considered a success? Explain why or why not.

2. Were social, political, or economic factors more important as causes for the French Revolution? Explain and support your answer.

Name ______________________ Class ______________ Date ____________

Unit Test Form A

Modern Unit **3**

From Absolutism to Revolution

UNDERSTANDING IDEAS *(3 points each)* For each of the following, write the letter of the best choice in the space provided.

______ **1.** The Enlightenment's most important thinkers were
a. American.
b. British.
c. French.
d. German.

______ **2.** Which revolution involved the LEAST amount of change?
a. the American Revolution
b. the English Revolution
c. the French Revolution
d. the Glorious Revolution

______ **3.** The first European nation to end the absolute power of its monarchs was
a. Austria.
b. England.
c. France.
d. Prussia.

______ **4.** All of the following were important steps in German unification EXCEPT
a. the Napoléonic Wars
b. the Act of Union
c. the Thirty Years' War
d. Hohenzollern rule.

______ **5.** Which pair of rulers were husband and wife?
a. Mary I of England and Philip II of Spain
b. Catherine the Great and Peter the Great of Russia
c. Maria Theresa of Austria and Frederick I of Prussia
d. Mary Queen of Scots and James I of England

______ **6.** Which European rulers lost their heads?
a. Charles I and Napoléon
b. Napoléon and James II
c. James II and Louis XVI
d. Louis XVI and Charles I

______ **7.** Who was NOT a military leader before becoming a government leader?
a. Oliver Cromwell
b. Napoléon Bonaparte
c. Frederick the Great
d. George Washington

______ **8.** Jacobin is to the French Revolution as ______ is to the English civil war.
a. Roundhead
b. Tory
c. Cavalier
d. Whig

______ **9.** Religious freedom and toleration were political issues in the 1600s and 1700s everywhere EXCEPT in
a. France.
b. North America.
c. Russia.
d. Great Britain.

______ **10.** All of the following ruled as absolute monarchs EXCEPT
a. King Louis XIV of France.
b. King William III of England.
c. Czar Peter I of Russia.
d. King Charles I of England.

_______ **11.** The ideas of which two thinkers can be found in the Declaration of Independence and the U.S. Constitution?
a. Locke and Montesquieu
b. Montesquieu and Voltaire
c. Voltaire and Rousseau
d. Rousseau and Locke

_______ **12.** The nation LEAST interested in overseas colonization and trade in the 1600s and 1700s was
a. France.
b. Great Britain.
c. the Netherlands.
d. Russia.

MATCHING *(3 points each)* In the space provided, write the letter of the name that matches each description. Some answers will not be used.

_______ **1.** made Prussia a military power in Europe in the 1700s by doubling the size of its army

_______ **2.** Netherlands prince who became king of England in the Glorious Revolution of 1689

_______ **3.** His conflict with the Long Parliament in the 1640s launched the English civil war.

_______ **4.** ruled over or otherwise controlled most of Europe in the early 1800s

_______ **5.** secured Protestant rule in England by defeating the Spanish Armada in 1588 and by beheading her Catholic rival for the throne

_______ **6.** the "Sun King" who ruled for 72 years in the 1600s and early 1700s and built the spectacular palace of Versailles outside of Paris

_______ **7.** secured Russia's first warm-water sea ports in the 1700s by seizing the north shore of the Black Sea from the Turks

_______ **8.** His coronation as king in 1660 marked the beginning of the Restoration in England.

a. Catherine the Great
b. Charles I
c. Charles II
d. Elizabeth I
e. Frederick the Great
f. Frederick William I
g. Louis XIV
h. Louis XVI
i. Maria Theresa
j. Napoléon
k. Peter the Great
l. William III

TRUE/FALSE *(2 points each)* Mark each statement *T* if it is true or *F* if it is false.

_______ **1.** Of all the wars fought in Europe in the 1600s and 1700s, the only conflict that involved creation or protection of an empire was the Seven Years' War.

_______ **2.** Remnants of the feudal society that characterized Europe's Middle Ages still existed in both Russia and France in the 1700s.

_______ **3.** In both Russia and France, one way that rulers tried to keep their important nobles under control was by requiring them to live in the capital.

_______ **4.** The English Bill of Rights, the French Declaration of the Rights of Man and of the Citizen, and the American Bill of Rights all guaranteed basic rights to the nation's citizens.

_______ **5.** The Napoléonic Wars destroyed Europe's systems of alliances.

PRACTICING SKILLS *(5 points each)* The chart below compares the system of government that developed in Great Britain with the system that developed in the United States. Study the chart and answer the questions that follow.

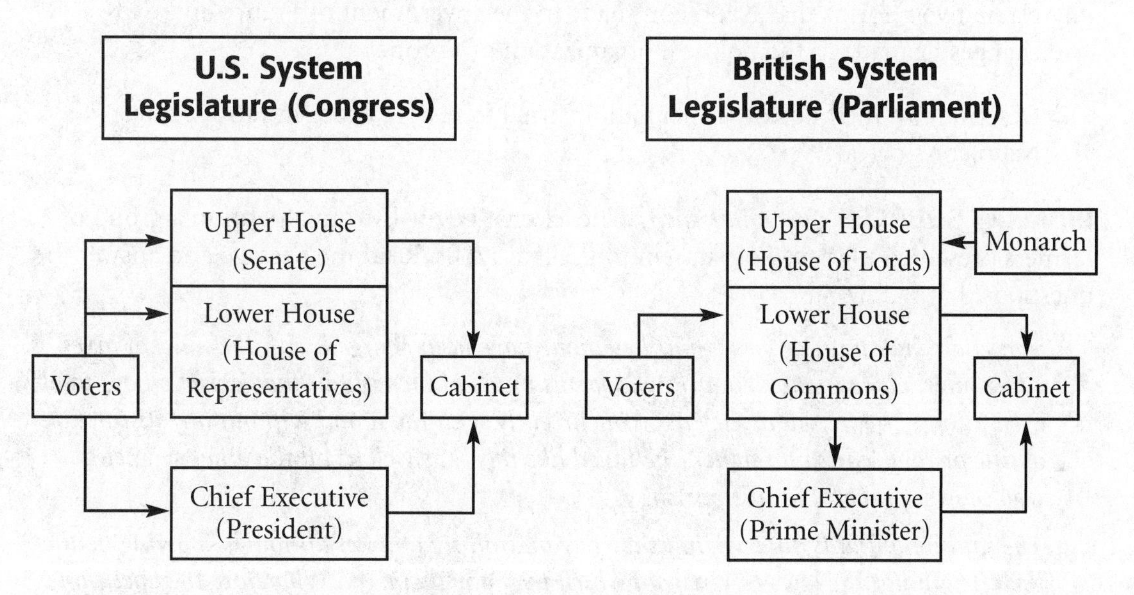

1. In which system do the people have the most influence on government? Explain why.

____

2. What differences exist between the powers of the legislature in the United States system and Britain?

____

COMPOSING AN ESSAY *(20 points)* On a separate sheet of paper, write a brief essay in response to one of the following.

1. Summarize the causes of the English civil war, the American Revolution, and the French Revolution. Point out similarities where they exist.

2. Discuss the role of religion and religious conflict in the governing of England and France in the 1600s.

Name ______________________ Class ______________ Date ____________

Unit Test Form B

Modern Unit 3 — From Absolutism to Revolution

SHORT ANSWER *(10 points each)* Provide brief answers for each of the following.

1. Compare how Cardinal Richelieu in France and Czar Peter I of Russia gained royal control over government from the nobles.
2. Summarize the steps by which the Hohenzollerns unified Prussia and made it one of the most powerful nations in Europe.
3. State the ideas of John Locke and Baron de Montesquieu that influenced the writing of the Declaration of Independence and the United States Constitution.
4. Name two reforms that Napoléon made in the government of France and two changes he made in the political organization of Europe.
5. Describe two methods by which nations tried to restore order in Europe after Napoléon's defeat.

PRIMARY SOURCES *(10 points each)* The excerpt below is from a petition a group of farmers presented to their government in the late 1700s. Read the passage and answer the questions that follow.

> *The said inhabitants observe that they alone have been charged with the mass of taxes, while their seigneur [nobleman], who farms much of the land in the parish, enjoys total exemption. . . . Wherefore they ask, concurrently with them and without any distinction of title or rank, the said seigneur be taxed like them, as well as all the other seigneurs who possess property in this parish. . . .*
>
> *The said inhabitants observe that they pay an infinity of taxes although knowing neither their origin nor the laws in virtue of which they pay them. . . . Wherefore they petition that all taxes be abolished which presently exist and were not consented to by the Nation assembled. . . .*
>
> From *The French Revolution,* edited by Philip Dawson. Copyright © 1967 by Prentice-Hall, Inc. Reprinted by permission of **Simon & Schuster Adult Publishing Group.**

1. What two complaints are the petitioners making, and what is their demand?
2. Judging from the content of this petition, from which country in Europe did the petition likely come? Explain.

COMPOSING AN ESSAY *(30 points)* Write an essay on one of the following subjects. Remember to use examples to support your essay.

1. Compare the English civil war, the American Revolution, and the French Revolution. Consider similarities and differences in their causes and goals, in their nature and course, and in their outcomes when you construct your answer.
2. Compare and contrast the foreign policies of Britain, France, and Russia as they applied to territorial expansion before 1800.

Name ______________________ Class ______________ Date ____________

Chapter Test Form A

Modern Chapter **13**

The Industrial Revolution

MATCHING *(3 points each)* In the space provided, write the letter of the name or term that matches each description. Some answers will not be used.

_____ **1.** believed that a capitalist society would split into two economic classes

_____ **2.** Scottish economist who wrote *The Wealth of Nations*

_____ **3.** system of producing large numbers of identical items

_____ **4.** American inventor of the cotton gin

_____ **5.** process by which common lands were fenced off into individual holdings

_____ **6.** process of producing steel by forcing air through molten metal to burn out impurities

_____ **7.** English landowner who invented a seed drill that made it possible to plant seeds in straight rows

_____ **8.** era of rapid industrial development that began in Great Britain

_____ **9.** American engineer who was the first to build a profitable steamboat

_____ **10.** American who invented the telegraph and a system for encoding the alphabet

a. Adam Smith
b. Bessemer process
c. Eli Whitney
d. enclosure movement
e. Industrial Revolution
f. Jethro Tull
g. Karl Marx
h. mass production
i. Richard Arkwright
j. Robert Fulton
k. Samuel Morse
l. socialism

UNDERSTANDING IDEAS *(3 points each)* For each of the following, write the letter of the best choice in the space provided.

_____ **1.** In a capitalist system, the means of production is
a. publicly owned.
b. privately owned.
c. owned by labor unions.
d. owned by workers.

_____ **2.** A corporation that controls every stage of an entire industry is a
a. cartel.
b. combine.
c. conglomerate.
d. commune.

______ **3.** At the beginning of the Industrial Revolution, Great Britain had land, capital, and labor conditions called the
a. domestic system.
b. factory system.
c. factors of production.
d. business cycle.

______ **4.** According to people who are in favor of the idea of laissez-faire, government should
a. stay out of business.
b. regulate business.
c. hire the unemployed.
d. not be an employer.

______ **5.** The use of automatic machinery to increase production is called
a. mass production.
b. vulcanization.
c. mechanization.
d. utilitarianism.

______ **6.** The last stage of socialism, which is characterized by a classless society, is called
a. democratic socialism.
b. regulated anarchy.
c. proletarianism.
d. pure communism.

______ **7.** Which did NOT help determine workers' wages under the factory system?
a. other costs of production
b. whether workers owned their own tools
c. the number of workers available
d. wages for other kinds of work

______ **8.** Alternating periods of prosperity and economic decline are known as the
a. supply and demand curve.
b. natural law of economics.
c. free enterprise system.
d. business cycle.

______ **9.** Negotiation between labor unions and employers is called
a. going on strike.
b. collective bargaining.
c. free enterprise.
d. utopian socialism.

______ **10.** Who patented the modern steam engine?
a. James Watt
b. Andrew Carnegie
c. John Stuart Mill
d. Henry Bessemer

TRUE/FALSE *(2 points each)* Mark each statement *T* if it is true or *F* if it is false.

______ **1.** Women and children received the same pay for their work that men did.

______ **2.** France, Germany, and other European countries were slower to industrialize than Great Britain was because the wars following the French Revolution had disrupted their economies.

______ **3.** A corporation that almost completely controls the production or sale of a single good or service is called a monopoly.

______ **4.** By the end of the Middle Ages, transportation in Europe was greatly improved.

______ **5.** According to the law of supply and demand, when there is not enough of an item to meet the demand, the manufacturer can charge more for the item, and the manufacturer's profits rise.

PRACTICING SKILLS *(5 points each)* Study the map and answer the questions that follow.

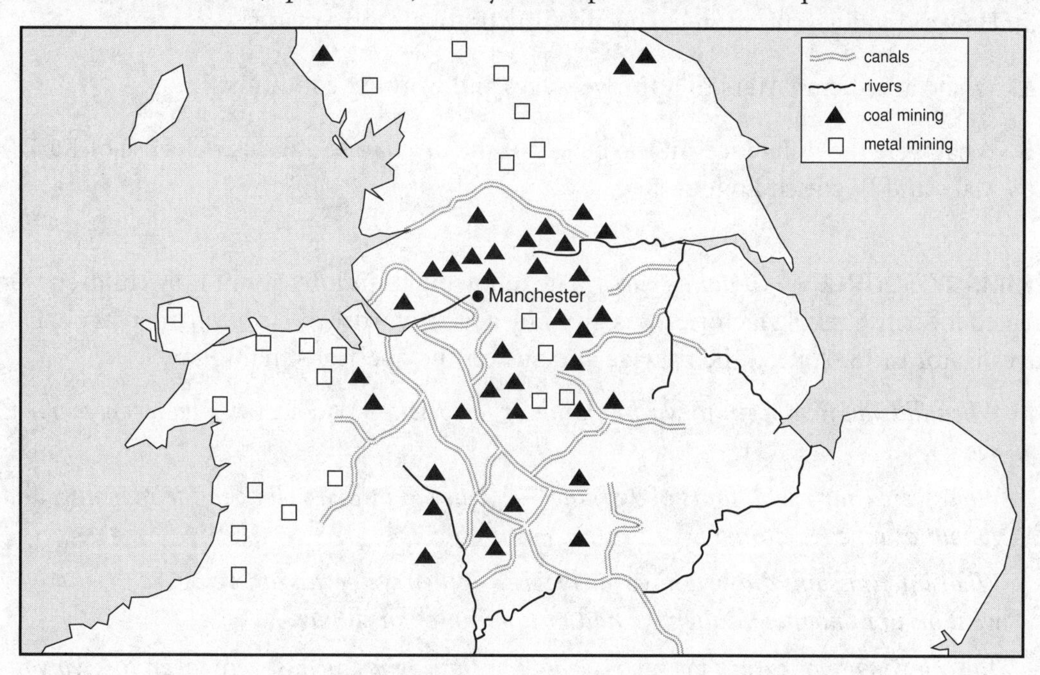

1. What raw materials were available in the area around Manchester?

____

2. How did the geography of the area around Manchester affect its industrial development?

____

COMPOSING AN ESSAY *(20 points)* On a separate sheet of paper, write a brief essay in response to one of the following.

1. Compare and contrast the elements of capitalism and socialism.

2. Explain the relationship between the Industrial Revolution and the increase in the size and importance of the middle class.

Name ______________________ Class ______________ Date ____________

Chapter Test Form B

Modern Chapter **13**

The Industrial Revolution

SHORT ANSWER *(10 points each)* Provide brief answers for each of the following.

1. What factors made Great Britain a favorable site for rapid industrial development in the 1700s and 1800s?

2. What effect did industrialization have on the lives of women?

3. How did industrialization change the way products were made?

4. What caused employers to improve wages and working conditions?

5. What were the differences in the beliefs of the utopian socialists and those of Karl Marx and Friedrich Engels?

PRIMARY SOURCES *(10 points each)* The following testimony about how children were treated in British textile factories was given by a factory worker to a parliamentary investigator in 1832. Read the passage and answer the questions that follow.

> *When did you first begin to work in mills or factories?—When I was about ten years of age.*
>
> *What were your usual hours of working?—We began at five o'clock in the morning, and got out at nine . . . at night.*
>
> *What intermissions did you have for meals?—When we began at five in the morning, we went on until noon, and then we had forty minutes for dinner. . . .*
>
> *To keep you at your work for such a length of time, what means were taken to keep you awake and attentive?—They whipped us at times.*
>
> *Were any of the female children whipped?—Yes, they were whipped in the same way as the younger boys.*

1. How long was a normal workday for a child who worked in a textile factory?

2. Besides working long hours, what other treatment did child workers experience?

COMPOSING AN ESSAY *(30 points)* Write an essay on one of the following subjects. Remember to use examples to support your answer.

1. Summarize the ways industrialization changed British society. Discuss changes in agriculture, manufacturing, work, and the organization of business.

2. Compare and contrast the views of different groups in society—such as industrialists, workers, economists, reformers, and socialists—about the effects of industrialization.

Name ______________________ Class ______________ Date ____________

Chapter Test Form A

Modern Chapter **14**

Life in the Industrial Age

FILL IN THE BLANK *(3 points each)* For each of the following statements, fill in the blank with the appropriate name, term, or phrase.

1. The process of heating liquids to kill bacteria and prevent fermentation is known as ______________________.

2. ______________________ was the Austrian doctor who introduced the idea that the unconscious mind helps determine human behavior.

3. ______________________ was the American inventor who improved the electric lightbulb and developed a system for transmitting electricity.

4. The artistic movement of the early 1800s that appealed to individuality and imagination, and valued emotion and instinct above reason, was called ______________________.

5. The movement of people away from the countries in which they were born is known as ______________________.

6. ______________________, the use of chemicals to kill disease-causing germs, was developed by the English surgeon Joseph Lister.

7. ______________________ adapted rugby into the game that became known as football in the United States.

8. ______________________ was a painter of landscapes and still lifes whose work influenced the postimpressionists.

9. The American inventor who transmitted the human voice over distance through a wire was ______________________.

10. Social Darwinism, the theory that wealthy and powerful people have superior abilities, was developed by ______________________.

UNDERSTANDING IDEAS *(3 points each)* For each of the following, write the letter of the best choice in the space provided.

______ **1.** The Wright brothers' airplane flew successfully because they
- **a.** used gasoline as a fuel.
- **b.** used a dynamo.
- **c.** combined science with technology.
- **d.** combined quantum theory with relativity.

______ **2.** Which social science compares different societies?
- **a.** sociology
- **b.** political science
- **c.** archaeology
- **d.** anthropology

______ **3.** The process of radioactivity was discovered by
a. Max Planck.
b. Sigmund Freud.
c. Albert Einstein.
d. Pierre and Marie Curie.

______ **4.** Advances in medicine in the 1800s
a. helped prolong life.
b. put an end to epidemics.
c. cut the cost of surgery.
d. all of the above.

______ **5.** The MOST important cause of the growth of cities was
a. the development of suburbs.
b. the growth of the factory system.
c. improvements in law enforcement.
d. laws requiring education for all children.

______ **6.** Writers and artists who take the approach called realism deal with
a. everyday life.
b. emotion and instinct.
c. love of nature.
d. the solar system.

______ **7.** Which was NOT an advance in biology in the 1800s?
a. the role of cells in cloning
b. the role of cells in disease
c. the discovery that all living things are made up of cells
d. the knowledge that all cells divide and multiply

______ **8.** The process of revealing and analyzing unconscious motivations is known as
a. evolution.
b. psychoanalysis.
c. social Darwinism.
d. psychosis.

______ **9.** Which was NOT a goal of public education in the 1800s?
a. educated soldiers
b. patriotic citizens
c. workers who could appreciate culture
d. workers who could read and write

______ **10.** People's diets were improved by new knowledge about pasteurization, refrigeration, and the use of
a. the five food groups.
b. low-calorie foods.
c. vitamins and minerals.
d. low-fat foods.

TRUE/FALSE *(2 points each)* Mark each statement *T* if it is true or *F* if it is false.

______ **1.** Guglielmo Marconi developed a way to send messages through underground cables.

______ **2.** Michael Faraday's discovery that magnetism can generate electricity led to the development of the first dynamo.

______ **3.** The subject of politics was not studied until the 1600s, when French philosophers created political science.

______ **4.** The largest emigrations during the 1800s were from Central and South America, Africa, Australia, and New Zealand to Europe.

______ **5.** Louis Pasteur made a vaccine from weakened anthrax germs that prevented animals from catching the disease.

PRACTICING SKILLS *(5 points each)* The following chart shows population changes from 1650 to 1950. Study the chart and answer the questions that follow.

Estimated Population (in millions) 1650–1950

	1650	1700	1750	1800	1850	1900	1950
World	545	623	728	906	1,171	1,608	2,400
North America	1	1	1	6	26	81	166
Central America	6	6	5	10	13	25	51
South America	6	6	6	9	20	38	111
Europe	100	110	140	187	266	401	559
Asia	330	400	479	602	749	937	1,302
Africa	100	98	95	90	95	120	198
Pacific Islands	2	2	2	2	2	6	13

1. By about how many times did the population of Europe change during the industrial age of the 1800s?

____

2. Did Asia and Africa appear to benefit as much as Europe from industrialization during the 1800s? Explain how you arrived at your conclusion.

____

COMPOSING AN ESSAY *(20 points)* On a separate sheet of paper, write a brief essay in response to one of the following.

1. How did Darwin's theory of evolution influence the field of sociology?

2. How did education change during the 1800s?

Name ______________________ Class ______________ Date ____________

Chapter Test Form B

Modern Chapter **14**

Life in the Industrial Age

SHORT ANSWER *(10 points each)* Provide brief answers for each of the following

1. What was the effect of the development of electrical power on communications?

2. How did advances in medicine during the 1800s affect people's lives?

3. What is sociology, and how did it develop?

4. In what ways did cities change during the 1800s?

5. In what ways are realism and naturalism similar and different?

PRIMARY SOURCES *(10 points each)* Read this passage from William Wordsworth's "Preface to *Lyrical Ballads*" and answer the questions that follow.

The principal object, then, proposed in these poems was to choose incidents and situations from common life, and to relate or describe them, throughout, as far as was possible in a selection of language really used by men, and at the same time to throw over them a certain coloring of imagination, whereby ordinary things should be presented to the mind in an unusual aspect. . . . Humble and rustic life was generally chosen, because, in that condition, the essential passions of the heart find a better soil in which they can attain their maturity, are under less restraint, and speak a plainer and more emphatic language; because in that condition of life our elementary feelings coexist in a state of greater simplicity, and, consequently, may be more accurately contemplated, and more forcibly communicated. . . .

1. Why did Wordsworth chose to write about the lives of humble country people in most of his poems?

2. Which characteristics of romanticism does Wordsworth mention in this passage?

COMPOSING AN ESSAY *(30 points)* Write an essay on one of the following subjects. Remember to give examples to support your essay.

1. Do you think that the scientific and technological advances of the 1800s improved people's lives? Explain and support your answer with information about the changes in electricity, communications, transportation, and medicine. Explain also the response to the Industrial Age by artists, writers, and musicians.

2. How would life in the industrial age have been different without the intellectual developments in such areas as the social sciences and public education?

Name ______________________ Class ______________ Date ____________

Chapter Test Form A

Modern Chapter **15**

The Age of Reform

MATCHING *(3 points each)* In the space provided, write the letter of the name or term that matches each description. Some answers will not be used.

_____ **1.** member of the British Liberal Party who was sent to Canada to reform the government in 1838

_____ **2.** white people born in the Latin American colonies of Spain and Portugal

_____ **3.** law governing the area bordered by the Appalachian Mountains, Ohio and Mississippi rivers, and Great Lakes

_____ **4.** members of the council set up by socialists and radical republicans to rule Paris in 1871

_____ **5.** Conservative prime minister of Great Britain when Queen Victoria became the Empress of India

_____ **6.** Liberal prime minister of Great Britain who passed the Education Act of 1870

_____ **7.** leader of the 1791 revolt by mulattoes and slaves in Saint Domingue

_____ **8.** leader whose coup d'état marked the start of the Second French Empire

_____ **9.** document that freed the slaves in the parts of the United States that were rebelling against the Union

_____ **10.** leader of Latin American revolutions known as *El Libertador* (The Liberator)

a. Benjamin Disraeli
b. Communards
c. creoles
d. Emancipation Proclamation
e. Toussaint-Louverture
f. José de San Martin
g. Lord Durham
h. Louis-Napoléon
i. Monroe Doctrine
j. Northwest Ordinance
k. Simón Bolívar
l. William Gladstone

UNDERSTANDING IDEAS *(3 points each)* For each of the following, write the letter of the best choice in the space provided.

______ **1.** The goal of some reforms enacted by British liberals was to
a. protect slave traders.
b. abolish the monarchy.
c. reduce suffrage.
d. extend suffrage.

______ **2.** Under British rule, the Maori in New Zealand
a. got rich from mining gold.
b. fought wars over land.
c. were protected from disease.
d. were sold as slaves.

______ **3.** The desire of most Irish people to have home rule was known as the
a. Irish freedom policy.
b. representation doctrine.
c. Irish question.
d. problem of Ireland.

______ **4.** Targeting both military and civilian resources in war is known as
a. modern war.
b. civil war.
c. guerilla war.
d. total war.

______ **5.** The event that started the French revolution of 1848 was
a. a decree restricting free speech.
b. widespread support for a republican government.
c. the abdication of Louis Philippe.
d. support for a descendant of Charles X.

______ **6.** Alfred Dreyfus was
a. guilty of bribery.
b. guilty of adultery.
c. falsely accused of spying for Germany.
d. falsely accused of covering up a scandal.

______ **7.** Which is NOT a way in which the United States gained territory in the 1800s?
a. war with France
b. purchase from France
c. war with Mexico
d. purchase from Spain

______ **8.** Disputes among which nations led to the Crimean War?
a. Palestine, Great Britain, and Russia
b. Russia, Great Britain, and Germany
c. Russia, the Ottoman Empire, and France
d. France, Germany, and the Ottoman Empire

______ **9.** When Spain tried to regain its Latin American colonies, the United States responded with
a. the Northwest Ordinance.
b. a declaration of war.
c. an offer to help.
d. the Monroe Doctrine.

______ **10.** Ambitious mestizo military leaders in Latin America were known as
a. peninsulares.
b. caudillos.
c. creoles.
d. intendants.

Name _________________________ Class ______________ Date ____________

TRUE/FALSE *(2 points each)* Mark each statement *T* if it is true or *F* if it is false.

_______ **1.** According to the philosophy called liberalism, the government should protect the rights and civil liberties of individuals.

_______ **2.** The U.S. Civil War broke out because President Lincoln signed a law making slavery illegal.

_______ **3.** After the defeat of Napoléon in 1815, France set up a republic and elected Louis Philippe to head it.

_______ **4.** After the Spanish king was stripped of some powers, upper-class creoles in Mexico staged an independence movement.

_______ **5.** Great Britain developed a single, unified colony in Australia.

PRACTICING SKILLS *(5 points each)* Study the map and answer the questions that follow.

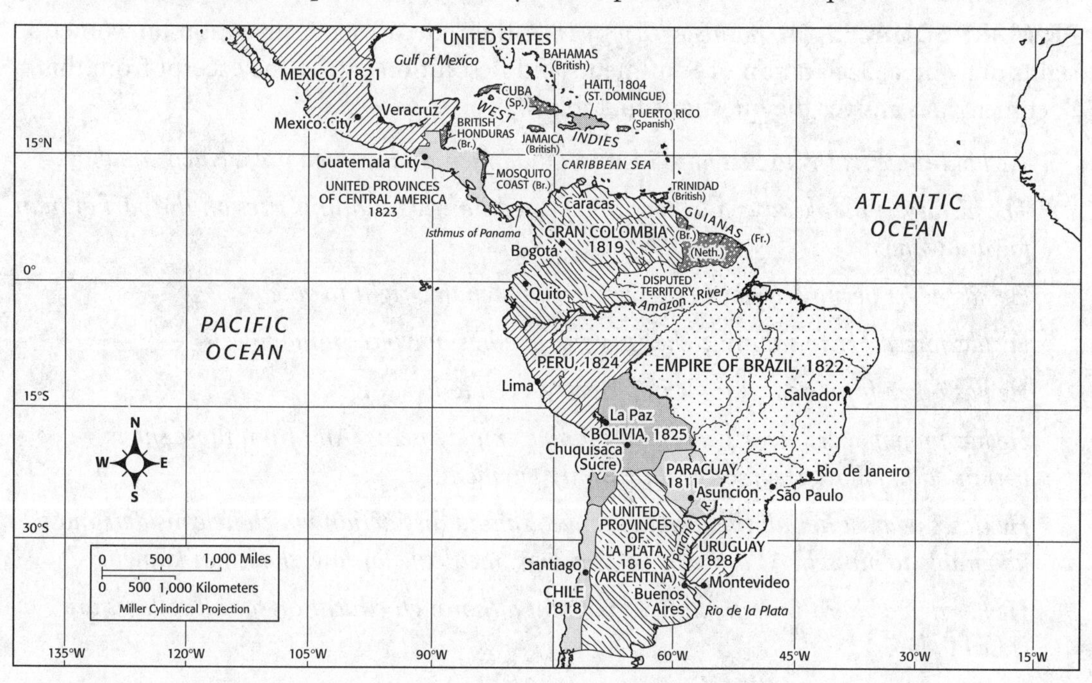

1. Which nations gained their independence before 1820?

____

2. Which nations gained their independence after 1820?

____

COMPOSING AN ESSAY *(20 points)* On a separate sheet of paper, write a brief essay in response to one of the following.

1. Describe the factors that led to the U.S. Civil War.

2. Explain how the American Indians were treated on haciendas.

Name ______________________ Class ______________ Date ____________

Chapter Test Form B

Modern Chapter **15**

The Age of Reform

SHORT ANSWER *(10 points each)* Provide brief answers for each of the following.

1. In what ways was the response of the British government to uprisings in Canada different from its response to the American colonies?

2. What were the causes of the French revolution of 1848?

3. What led the people of Paris to set up the Commune?

4. How did the policies of Charles III lead to revolution in Latin America?

5. What problems did Latin America encounter after independence?

PRIMARY SOURCES *(10 points each)* In 1848 the Seneca Falls Convention on women's rights drew up a Declaration of Sentiments and Resolutions. Read the excerpt from this document and answer the questions that follow.

We hold these truths to be self-evident: that all men and women are created equal . . .

The history of mankind is a history of repeated injuries and injustices on the part of man toward women. . . .

He has never permitted her to exercise her inalienable right to vote.

He has forced her to submit to laws, which she has no voice in making.

He has taken from her all right in property, even to her wages.

He has monopolized nearly all the profitable employments. And from those she is permitted to follow, she receives but scanty payment.

He closes against her all the avenues to wealth and distinction which he considers most honorable to himself. As a teacher of theology, medicine, or law, she is not known.

He has denied her the opportunity to obtain a thorough education for all colleges are closed to her.

1. What injustices does the declaration list?

2. This declaration follows the same format as the Declaration of Independence. Why do you think the delegates to the Seneca Falls Convention used this format?

COMPOSING AN ESSAY *(30 points)* Write an essay in response to one of the following subjects. Remember to use examples to support your essay.

1. Explain why this chapter is titled "The Age of Reform." Use examples from Great Britain, the United States, France, and Latin America.

2. Compare and contrast the ways Great Britain and Spain treated their colonies and the other countries they ruled.

Name ______________________ Class ______________ Date ____________

Chapter Test Form A

Modern Chapter **16** **Nationalism in Europe**

FILL IN THE BLANK *(3 points each)* For each of the following statements, fill in the blank with the appropriate name, term, or phrase.

1. The customs union called the ______________________ made industrialization possible by making prices lower and more uniform.

2. Czar Nicholas I instituted a program called ______________________ to force non-Russian peoples to adopt the Russian language, religion, and customs.

3. The coalition of Bulgaria, Serbia, Greece, and Montenegro that won a war against the Ottoman Empire was known as the ______________________.

4. Giuseppe Mazzini's ______________________ was dedicated to spreading the ideas of the risorgimento, or resurgence.

5. The assassination of ______________________ ended the period of liberal reform in Russia.

6. After the king of Denmark tried to annex ______________________ in 1863, Prussia and Austria went to war against Denmark.

7. ______________________ and his "Expedition of the Thousand" captured Sicily and Naples.

8. ______________________ reduced Bismarck's power and forced his resignation in 1890.

9. ______________________ was Emperor of Austria and King of Hungary.

10. ______________________, or "culture struggle," was an anti-Catholic program initiated by Bismarck.

UNDERSTANDING IDEAS *(3 points each)* For each of the following, write the letter of the best choice in the space provided.

______ **1.** The upper house of the German legislature was called the
a. Reichstag.
b. Zollverein.
c. Senate.
d. Bundesrat.

______ **2.** The Prussian king who became emperor of the German Empire was
a. William I.
b. William II.
c. Francis I.
d. Francis II.

_____ **3.** The early Italian nationalist movement was the
a. Carbonari.
b. risorgimento.
c. Young Italy movement.
d. brown shirts.

_____ **4.** The emancipation of the serfs
a. kept them in farming.
b. led to economic security.
c. did not solve all problems.
d. increased factory wages.

_____ **5.** When 1913 ended, the Ottoman Empire's presence in Europe included
a. Bulgaria and Greece.
b. Constantinople, Bosnia, and Herzegovina.
c. only the city of Constantinople.
d. Serbia and Bosnia.

_____ **6.** The fact that Germany's industrialization came later than that of Britain and France
a. was a result of a lack of natural resources.
b. was a result of government disinterest.
c. let the Germans use the best methods and machinery available.
d. kept Germany from becoming a great industrial power.

_____ **7.** One problem Italy faced after unification was
a. Austria's refusal to give up Venice.
b. Sicily's refusal to become part of the new nation.
c. lack of a leader accepted by the people of all states.
d. tension between the north and the south.

_____ **8.** Terrorism was used by the
a. People's Will group.
b. Populists.
c. czar.
d. serfs.

_____ **9.** Serbia became independent as a result of
a. a revolt led by Kossuth.
b. the Treaty of San Stefano.
c. the Dual Monarchy.
d. the Seven Weeks' War.

_____ **10.** The Social Democratic Party
a. had many members elected to the Reichstag.
b. never achieved much representation.
c. supported private ownership of industry.
d. supported the actions of the cartels

TRUE/FALSE *(2 points each)* Mark each statement *T* if it is true or *F* if it is false.

_____ **1.** Industrialization lagged in Russia because of a lack of natural resources.

_____ **2.** The Ottoman Empire granted social and political equality as well as religious and cultural freedom to non-Muslim minorities.

______ **3.** Camillo Benso di Cavour, who was chief minister of Sardinia, was a republican and supported the goals of the liberals.

______ **4.** Otto von Bismarck opposed democracy and the establishment of a parliament.

______ **5.** In 1883 Bismarck began instituting reforms the socialists had proposed, so that fewer people would have reason to support the socialists.

PRACTICING SKILLS *(5 points each)* The following map shows how the Ottoman Empire was broken apart in the 19th and early 20th centuries. Study the map and answer the questions that follow.

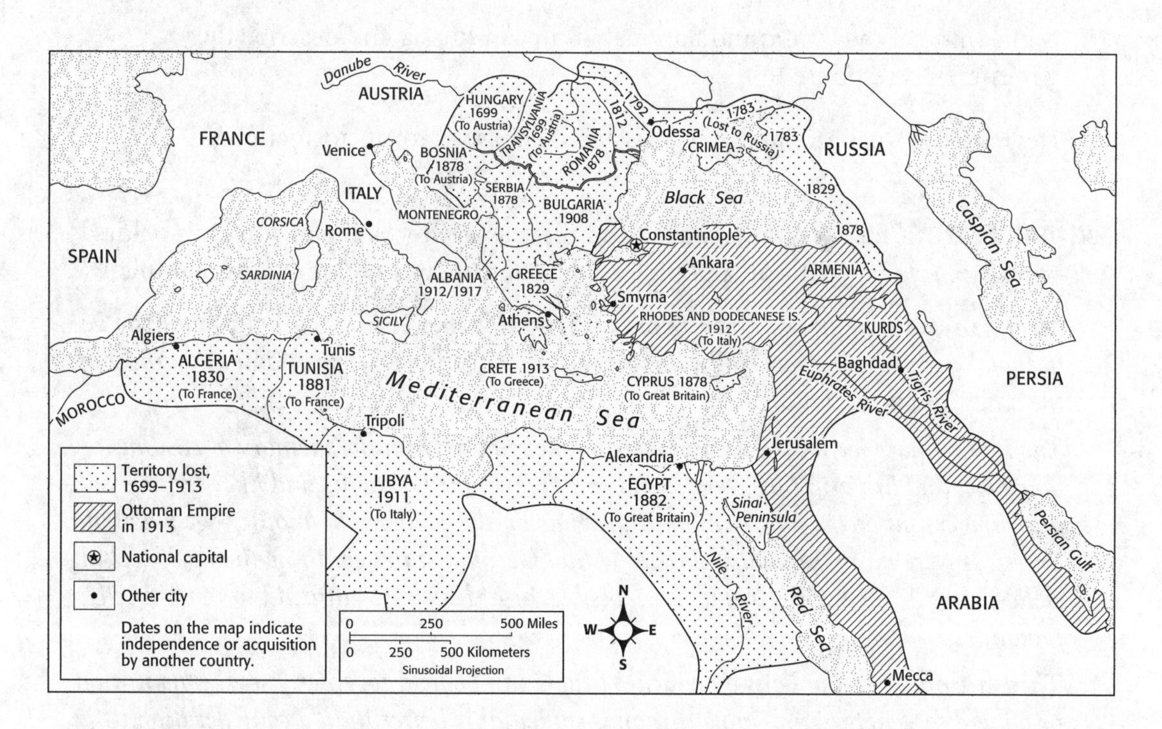

1. According to the map, which were the first countries to be taken over by another country? What year and by what country were they taken over?

____

2. According to the map, which was the first country to become independent?

____

COMPOSING AN ESSAY *(20 points)* On a separate sheet of paper, write a brief essay in response to one of the following.

1. Describe the ways Otto von Bismarck maintained his power when faced with opposition.

2. Explain why attempts to liberalize the Russian government failed.

Name ______________________ Class ______________ Date ______________

Chapter Test Form B

Modern Chapter **16**

Nationalism in Europe

SHORT ANSWER *(10 points each)* Provide brief answers for each of the following.

1. Name two of the important leaders in Italy's unification movement and describe what each did to further his cause.

2. Describe some of the changes that the German states had to make to come together as a single nation.

3. Discuss some of the problems Bismarck faced as chancellor of the German Empire.

4. Name some of the ethnic and national groups in Russia and describe the government's response to them.

5. Describe the Dual Monarchy and discuss the reasons for its formation.

PRIMARY SOURCES *(10 points each)* Read this passage by Wilhelm von Humboldt, a 19th-century German politician and philosopher, and answer the questions that follow.

> *[A nation] must be strong and free to build up self-reliance in the people, to pursue its national development peacefully, and to keep an advantageous position in the midst of the other European nations.*
>
> *The feeling that Germany is a unit does not depend only on the memory of customs, language, and literature. It also depends on the memory of rights and liberties enjoyed—and dangers suffered—in common. It depends on the memory of another age when our ancestors were more unified. If the individual German states continue their self-seeking, isolated status, they will learn it is impossible, or at least very difficult, to remain self-reliant. . . .*
>
> *There are only two methods by which a people can be held together: a real constitution or a mere confederation. A constitution is undeniably better than a confederation. It is more impressive, more binding, more lasting.*

1. According to von Humboldt, what is the main reason the German states should unify?

2. Which method does von Humboldt favor for unifying Germany and why?

COMPOSING AN ESSAY *(30 points)* Write an essay on one of the following subjects. Remember to give examples to support your essay.

1. Compare and contrast the different ways nationalism was manifested in Italy, Germany, Russia, Austria-Hungary, and the Ottoman Empire.

2. Discuss the effects of nationalism in Italy, Germany, Russia, Austria-Hungary, and the Ottoman Empire on the peace and security of the world.

Name ______________________ Class ______________ Date ____________

Chapter Test Form A

Modern Chapter **17**

The Age of Imperialism

MATCHING *(3 points each)* In the space provided, write the letter of the name or term that matches each description. Some answers will not be used.

_____ **1.** Dutch settlers in South Africa

_____ **2.** Muslim leader who led a revolt against Egyptian rule in the Sudan

_____ **3.** queen who tried to keep foreigners out of Hawaii

_____ **4.** leader of a revolt against Huerta in Mexico

_____ **5.** colonies in which a small number of officials rule the native people

_____ **6.** colonies in which local rulers keep their titles but a foreign power really controls the area

_____ **7.** Belgian ruler who ruled the Congo as a private colony

_____ **8.** Siamese ruler who played the British and French against each other to keep his country independent

a. Afrikaans
b. Boers
c. dependent colonies
d. Leopold II
e. Liliuokalani
f. al-Mahdī
g. Mongkut
h. protectorates
i. spheres of influence
j. Venustiano Carranza

UNDERSTANDING IDEAS *(3 points each)* For each of the following, write the letter of the best choice in the space provided.

_____ **1.** Which was NOT a reason for imperialism in the 19th century?
a. respect from other countries
b. source of troops for armies
c. source of finished products
d. places for ships to refuel

_____ **2.** The phrase "the White Man's Burden" refers to
a. the idea that white people stayed in the sun too long.
b. the idea that non-Western people needed help from Westerners.
c. the amount of luggage that the Europeans brought with them.
d. the amount of raw materials that the Europeans sent back.

______ **3.** The Fashoda crisis was a dispute between
a. France and the Ottoman Empire over Tunis.
b. Belgium and France over the Congo.
c. the Netherlands and Britain over South Africa.
d. Britain and France over the Sudan.

______ **4.** Egypt came under British rule in part because of the
a. Suez Canal.
b. Strait of Gibraltar.
c. pyramids.
d. diamond trade.

______ **5.** Which West African state remained independent?
a. Ghana
b. Liberia
c. Senegal
d. French West Africa

______ **6.** Cecil Rhodes controlled
a. the Suez Canal.
b. game hunting in Kenya.
c. trade in ivory, rubber, and palm oil.
d. South African diamond production.

______ **7.** The British government took control of India when
a. the Suez Canal was built.
b. Hindus and Muslims began fighting.
c. soldiers rebelled against the British East India Company.
d. European princes asked the British to keep order.

______ **8.** The Meiji Restoration was the return of the
a. shogunate to power.
b. emperor to power.
c. old social class system.
d. old constitution.

______ **9.** The United States declared war on Spain after
a. the *Maine* exploded in the Havana harbor.
b. the Treaty of Paris was broken.
c. Spain crushed the Guam independence movement.
d. Cuba refused to allow a U.S. naval base on the island.

______ **10.** The United States decision to force Latin American countries to repay their loans was called the
a. Monroe Doctrine Extension.
b. Veracruz Proclamation.
c. Roosevelt Corollary.
d. Platt Amendment.

TRUE/FALSE *(2 points each)* Mark each statement *T* if it is true or *F* if it is false.

______ **1.** The term imperialism refers to one country's taking control of another country's government, trade, or culture.

______ **2.** Europeans ruled the people in their colonies paternalistically, as if they were children.

_____ **3.** The Algerians resisted French colonization for 40 years.

_____ **4.** Japan cut itself off from Western influences and resisted industrialization.

_____ **5.** Imperialism contributed to rapid worldwide growth.

_____ **6.** President Wilson sent troops into Mexico to capture Pancho Villa.

_____ **7.** Indians who attended British schools learned about democracy and socialism, and some favored a gradual movement to self-rule.

_____ **8.** The Platt Amendment allowed United States officials to take over the Panama Canal.

PRACTICING SKILLS *(5 points each)* This graph shows foreign export by Great Britain and Germany in 1898 and 1913. Study the graph and answer the questions that follow.

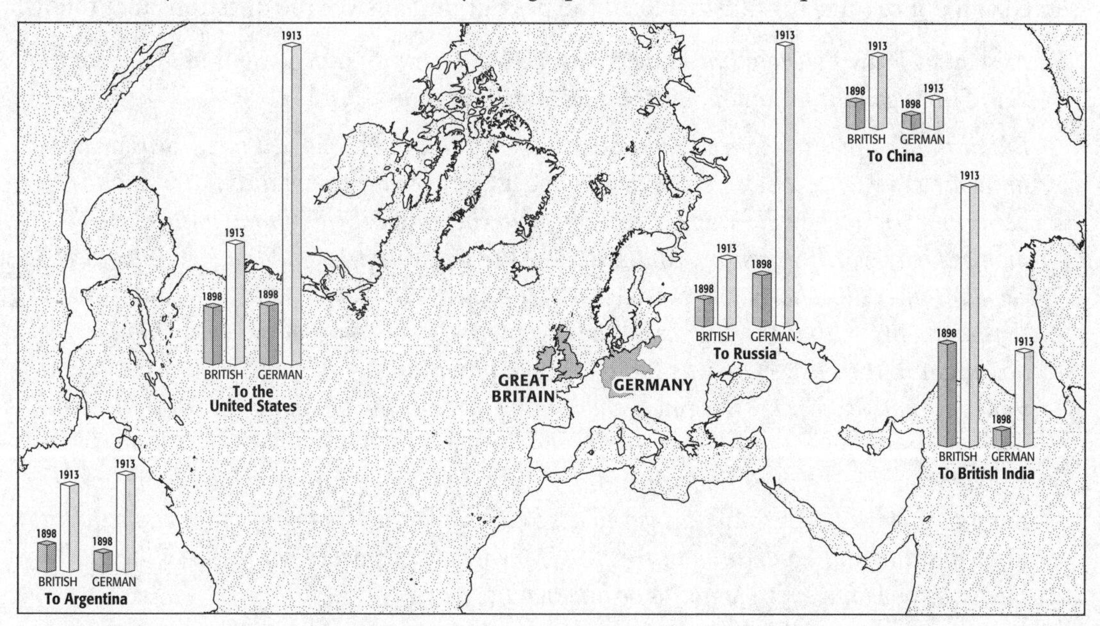

1. To which countries did Germany export more than Great Britain in 1898? In 1913?

____

2. To which country did British exports increase the most between 1898 and 1913?

____

COMPOSING AN ESSAY *(20 points)* On a separate sheet of paper, write a brief essay in response to one of the following.

1. Discuss the economic causes of imperialism.

2. Compare and contrast the Platt Amendment and the Roosevelt Corollary.

Name ______________________ Class ______________ Date ____________

Chapter Test Form B

Modern Chapter **17**

The Age of Imperialism

SHORT ANSWER *(10 points each)* Provide brief answers for each of the following.

1. What role did Christian missionaries play in imperialism?
2. How did the financing of the Suez Canal allow Great Britain to take control of it?
3. Who lived in South Africa, and how did the British come to control the area in the 19th century?
4. What colonies did Great Britain control in Southeast Asia, and why did it want them?
5. Why did the United States want a canal in Panama, and how did it get the right to build it?

PRIMARY SOURCES *(10 points each)* The following was written by an Englishman who served as a police officer in Burma. Read the passage and answer the questions that follow.

> *As soon as I saw the elephant I knew with perfect certainty that I ought not to shoot him. . . . [T]he elephant looked no more dangerous than a cow. . . .*
>
> *But at that moment I glanced round at the crowd that had followed me. It was an immense crowd. . . . They were watching me as they would watch a conjurer about to perform a trick. They did not like me, but with the magical rifle in my hands I was momentarily worth watching. And suddenly I realized that I should have to shoot the elephant after all. The people expected it of me and I had got to do it . . . . And it was at that moment . . . that I first grasped the hollowness, the futility of the white man's dominion in the East. Here was I, the white man with his gun, standing in front of the unarmed native crowd—seemingly the leading actor of the piece; but in reality I was only an absurd puppet pushed to and fro by the will of those yellow faces behind. I perceived in this moment that when the white man turns tyrant it is his own freedom that he destroys. . . . A sahib has got to act like a sahib; he has to appear resolute, to know his own mind and do definite things. . . . [M]y whole life, every white man's life in the East, was one long struggle not to be laughed at.*
>
> From *Shooting an Elephant and Other Essays* by George Orwell. Copyright© 1936 by George Orwell. Reprinted by permission of **Bill Hamilton as the Literary Executor of the Estate of the Late Sonia Brownell Orwell and Secker & Warburg Ltd.**

1. What point is the author making about the authority of European colonizers in Asia?
2. What point is the author making about the effect on a European of acting as a colonizer?

COMPOSING AN ESSAY *(30 points)* Write an essay on one of the following subjects. Remember to use examples to support your answer.

1. How did imperialism benefit the European nations? Were there benefits for the colonized regions? Provide evidence supporting both sides of the question.
2. In what ways would life have been different for the original residents of settlement colonies, dependent colonies, protectorates, and spheres of influence? Provide examples from Africa, Asia, and Latin America.

Name ______________________ Class ______________ Date ____________

Unit Test Form A

Modern Unit **4**

Industrialization and Nationalism

UNDERSTANDING IDEAS *(3 points each)* For each of the following, write the letter of the best choice in the space provided.

______ **1.** Industrialization required a combination of
a. factories, communications, and agriculture.
b. workers, agriculture, and energy.
c. workers, resources, and money.
d. mass production, energy, and communications.

______ **2.** The development of electricity as a power source
a. led to advances in communications.
b. led to the colonization of island nations.
c. led to advances in the social sciences.
d. led to population increases in industrialized nations.

______ **3.** Industrialization did NOT have an effect on
a. the world of work.
b. international relations.
c. the laws of nature.
d. music and art.

______ **4.** Which countries had a large presence in North Africa?
a. United States and Russia
b. France and Great Britain
c. Belgium and Germany
d. Italy and Germany

______ **5.** Benjamin Disraeli wanted to
a. pass an education act.
b. pass a bill on home rule for Ireland.
c. advance the causes of the Liberal Party.
d. expand the British empire.

______ **6.** In the Balkans, nationalism led to
a. an independent Balkan state.
b. division into independent nations.
c. the Crimean War.
d. nihilism.

______ **7.** Improvements in medicine, sanitation, and food distribution helped bring about
a. the eradication of bacterial infections.
b. the eradication of unsanitary conditions.
c. a growth in population and mass culture.
d. a growth in population and emigration.

______ **8.** What resource spurred competition for control of South Africa?
a. diamonds
b. oil
c. rubber
d. tea

______ **9.** European revolts in the mid-19th century were a result of
a. Austria-Hungary's failure.
b. uprisings in France.
c. rebellion in Russia.
d. Germany's foreign policy.

______ **10.** Which is NOT a reform based on 19th-century liberalism?
a. availability of medical care
b. abolition of slavery
c. extension of suffrage
d. protection of civil rights

FILL IN THE BLANK *(3 points each)* For each of the following statements, fill in the blank with the appropriate name, term, or phrase.

1. The first president of Gran Columbia was ______________________.

2. The czar of Russia was an ______________________, which means he held absolute power over his subjects.

3. ______________________ is an economic system in which the means of production are owned by individuals and groups, rather than by the government.

4. ______________________ is an economic system in which the means of production are owned by the government and operated for the benefit of all people.

5. The British wanted control of the ______________________ because they wanted a more direct route to their colonies in India, Australia, and New Zealand.

6. The ______________________ gave notice to European nations not to interfere in the independent governments in the Western Hemisphere.

7. When he became king of Prussia, ______________________ appointed Otto von Bismarck to head the Prussian cabinet.

8. ______________________ occurs when people give up their own culture and adopt another culture.

9. The theory that creatures whose characteristics are best adapted to their environment will survive was advanced by ______________________.

10. ______________________ made the everyday lives of ordinary people into the subjects of art and literature.

TRUE/FALSE *(2 points each)* Mark each statement *T* if it is true or *F* if it is false.

______ **1.** Free public education was an outgrowth of ideas about liberty, equality, and representative government from the American and French revolutions.

Name ______________________ Class ______________ Date ____________

Unit 6, Unit Test Form A, continued

_______ **2.** After Napoleon was defeated, the government of France remained stable throughout the rest of the 19th century.

_______ **3.** The Dual Monarchy was headed by one ruler and had two separate parliaments.

_______ **4.** Because more people were needed to work on farms, 19th century capitalists moved their factories to the colonies in search of cheap labor.

_______ **5.** Most Europeans believed that they could learn from the valuable ancient knowledge of non-Western peoples.

PRACTICING SKILLS *(5 points each)* The following chart shows population changes from 1800 to 1910. Study the chart and answer the questions that follow.

Population (in millions)					
	1800	**1850**	**1880**	**1900**	**1910**
Great Britain	16.1	27.5	35.1	41.8	45.0
France	27.3	35.8	37.7	39.0	39.6
Germany	24.6	35.9	45.2	56.4	64.9
Italy	18.1	24.3	28.5	32.5	34.7

(From *World Population and Production: Trends and Outlooks* by W. S. Woytinsky and E. S. Woytinsky. Copyright © 1953 by the Twentieth Century Fund. Reprinted by permission of the Twentieth Century Fund.)

1. Based on this chart, which two countries experienced the greatest pressures to reduce their burgeoning populations through emigration or colonization between 1800 and 1880?

____

2. Based on this chart, which country had the least need for its citizens to emigrate?

____

COMPOSING AN ESSAY *(20 points)* On a separate sheet of paper, write a brief essay in response to one of the following.

1. What was the effect of the European Industrial Revolution on the nations of Asia?

2. How did advances in technology during the period of industrialization make 19th century imperialism possible?

Name ______________________ Class ______________ Date ____________

Unit Test Form B

Modern Unit **4**

Industrialization and Nationalism

SHORT ANSWER *(10 points each)* Provide brief answers for each of the following.

1. How did the British treat the native peoples who lived in the countries they colonized?

2. What aspects of industrialization did the British reformers object to and what changes did they propose?

3. What were coaling stations, and why were they important to imperialists?

4. What were the goals of the Italian nationalists of the 19th century?

5. How did the growth of cities change the number and types of entertainment activities?

PRIMARY SOURCES *(10 points each)* Read this justification of colonialism by a British colonial administrator and answer the questions that follow.

Let it be admitted at the outset that European brains, capital, and energy have not been, and never will be, expended in developing the resources of Africa from motives of pure philanthropy; that Europe is in Africa for the mutual benefit of her own industrial classes, and of the native races in their progress to a higher plane; that the benefit can be made reciprocal, and that it is the aim and desire of civilised administrators to fulfill this dual mandate.

By railways and roads, by reclamation of swamps and irrigation of deserts, and by a system of fair trade and competition, we have added to the prosperity and wealth of these lands, and checked famine and disease. We have put an end to the awful misery of the slave-trade and inter-tribal war, to human sacrifice and the ordeals of the witch-doctor. Where these things survive they are severely suppressed. We are endeavouring to teach the native races to conduct their own affairs with justice and humanity, and to educate them alike in letters and in industry. . . .

From *The Dual Mandate in Tropical Africa* by Lord Frederick Lugard. First published in 1922. Reprinted by permission of **Frank Cass & Co. Ltd.**

1. What does the author mean by "this dual mandate" at the end of the first paragraph?

2. According to the author, how have Europeans fulfilled the second part of the mandate?

COMPOSING AN ESSAY *(30 points)* Write an essay on one of the following subjects. Remember to give examples to support your answer.

1. Describe the opinions that a 19th century socialist would hold of imperialism in Asia or in South Africa.

2. Describe how the unification of Germany shows the relationship between industrialization, nationalism, and imperialism.

Chapter Test Form A

Modern Chapter **18** **World War I and the Russian Revolution**

MATCHING *(3 points each)* In the space provided, write the letter of the name or term that matches each description. Some answers will not be used.

_____ **1.** Great Britain, France, Russia, and others

_____ **2.** Germany, Austria-Hungary, Bulgaria, and the Ottoman Empire

_____ **3.** the proposals for a more just world that Woodrow Wilson presented to Congress in 1918

_____ **4.** systematic extermination of a people

_____ **5.** a colony set aside by the League of Nations to be ruled by the government of an "advanced" nation

_____ **6.** the glorification of armed strength

_____ **7.** moderate faction in the fight for control of the soviets

_____ **8.** radical faction in the fight for control of the soviets

_____ **9.** warring nations

_____ **10.** an agreement to stop fighting

a. Allied Powers
b. armistice
c. atrocity
d. belligerents
e. Bolsheviks
f. Central Powers
g. Fourteen Points
h. genocide
i. League of Nations
j. mandate
k. Mensheviks
l. militarism

UNDERSTANDING IDEAS *(3 points each)* For each of the following, write the letter of the best choice in the space provided.

_____ **1.** The Paris Peace Conference was attended by
a. all of the countries involved in World War I except Bulgaria.
b. all of the countries involved in World War I except Italy.
c. all of the countries involved in World War I.
d. only some of the countries involved in World War I.

_____ **2.** The terms of the armistice included
a. replacing the kaiser with a new government.
b. canceling the Treaty of Brest Litovsk.
c. withdrawing troops from Russia.
d. withdrawing troops from Paris.

______ **3.** The MAIN purpose of propaganda in the war was to
a. frighten the enemy.
b. sway world opinion.
c. stir up patriotism.
d. sell more papers.

______ **4.** Great Britain's and France's purpose in attacking Gallipoli was to
a. remove Russia from the war.
b. remove the Ottoman Empire from the war.
c. attack Bulgaria from the east.
d. attack Greece from the northeast.

______ **5.** Which nation was NOT a member of the Triple Entente?
a. Belgium
b. Great Britain
c. Russia
d. France

______ **6.** The League of Nations could enforce decisions by
a. stripping countries of their colonies.
b. refusing to seat a nation's representatives.
c. imposing economic sanctions.
d. using military force as a first resort.

______ **7.** When the czar dissolved the Duma,
a. it gave up its power.
b. it refused to disband.
c. the army sided with the czar.
d. the people sided with the czar.

______ **8.** Bolshevik leader Vladimir Lenin believed that social reforms in Russia might not move as fast as Karl Marx predicted, so Lenin's leaders
a. trained Russian workers to become a revolutionary force.
b. supported the Mensheviks.
c. planned for a Russian government with a czar and parliament.
d. continued the war against Germany.

______ **9.** Which country gained land after the war?
a. Russia
b. Bulgaria
c. Belgium
d. the Ottoman Empire

______ **10.** Which member of the Triple Alliance fought on the side of the Triple Entente?
a. the Ottoman Empire
b. Bulgaria
c. Austria-Hungary
d. Italy

TRUE/FALSE *(2 points each)* Mark each statement *T* if it is true or *F* if it is false.

______ **1.** The assassination of the heir to the Austro-Hungarian throne by Serbian nationalists set off World War I.

_____ **2.** President Woodrow Wilson applauded the sinking of the *Lusitania* as a great Allied victory.

_____ **3.** The Bolsheviks named themselves the Communist Party in 1918.

_____ **4.** As a result of the Treaty of Versailles, the Polish Corridor divided Germany, and Danzig became a free city under the League of Nations.

_____ **5.** The countries that made up the Central Powers surrendered at the same time and asked for peace as a group.

PRACTICING SKILLS *(5 points each)* Study the maps and answer the questions that follow.

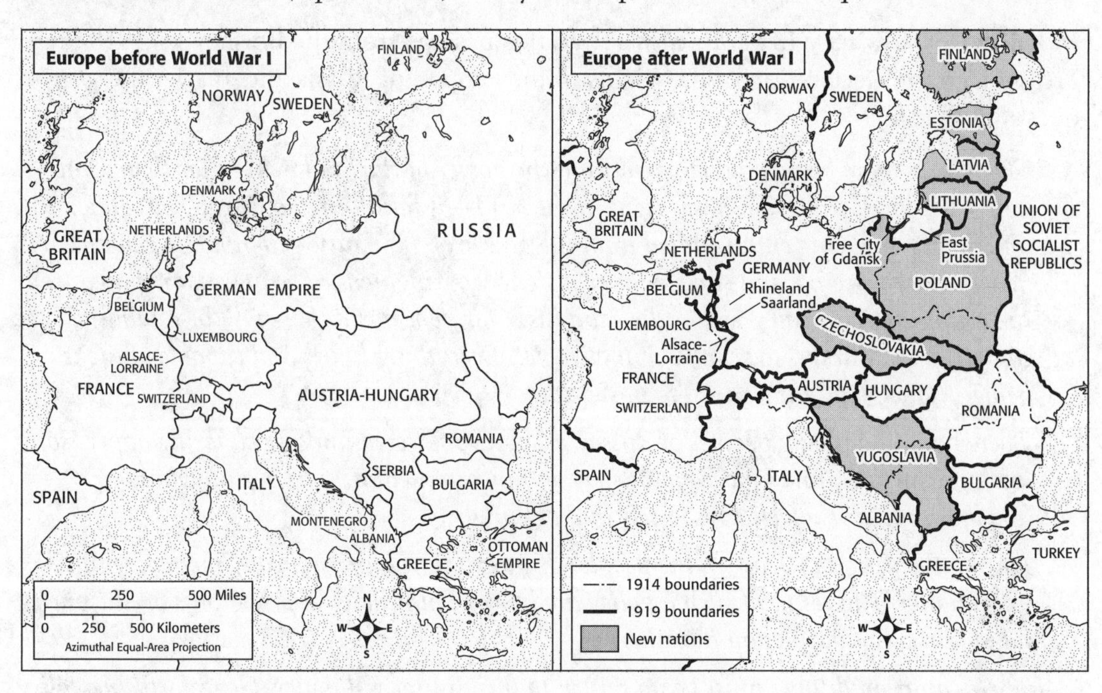

1. Name the nation that Germany shared a common border with before, but not after, the war.

____

2. Name the four nations that were created exclusively out of Russian land.

____

COMPOSING AN ESSAY *(20 points)* On a separate sheet of paper, write a brief essay in response to one of the following.

1. Describe the causes of the spring 1917 Russian Revolution.

2. Compare and contrast the attitudes of the Allies about the peace settlement at the Paris Peace Conference.

Name ______________________ Class ______________ Date ______________

Chapter Test Form B

Modern Chapter **18** **World War I and the Russian Revolution**

SHORT ANSWER *(10 points each)* Provide brief answers for each of the following.

1. Why did Bismarck form the Triple Alliance?

2. What developments caused the United States to enter the war?

3. What was the reaction of the Allies to the Treaty of Brest Litovsk?

4. What were the six general proposals in Wilson's Fourteen Points?

5. What was Germany's response to the Treaty of Versailles?

PRIMARY SOURCES *(10 points each)* Read this passage from the Bolsheviks' 1918 Preamble to the Declaration of the Rights of the Peoples of Russia and answer the questions that follow.

> *The peasants are being emancipated from the power of the landowners, for there is no longer the landowner's property right in the land—it has been abolished. The soldiers and sailors are being emancipated from the power of autocratic generals, for generals will henceforth be elective and subject to recall. The workingmen are being emancipated from the whims and arbitrary will of the capitalists, for henceforth there will be established the control of the workers over mills and factories. Everything living and capable of life is being emancipated from the hateful shackles.*
>
> *There remain only the peoples of Russia, who have suffered and are suffering oppression and arbitrariness, and whose emancipation must immediately be begun, whose liberation must be effected resolutely and definitely.*
>
> *During the period of Tsarism the peoples of Russia were systematically incited against one another. The result of such a policy are known: massacres and pogroms on the one hand, slavery of peoples on the other.*
>
> *There can be and there must be no return to this disgraceful policy. Henceforth the policy of a voluntary and honest union of the peoples of Russia must be substituted . . .*
>
> *Only as the result of such a union can the workers and peasants of the peoples of Russia be cemented into one revolutionary force able to resist all attempts on the part of the imperialist-annexationist bourgeoisie.*

1. Which groups did the Bolsheviks want to free?

2. What did the Bolsheviks believe to be the benefit of a union by the peoples of Russia?

COMPOSING AN ESSAY *(30 points)* Write an essay on one of the following subjects. Remember to use examples to support your essay.

1. What role did economic conditions play in World War I?

2. What effect did World War I have on national self-determination in Europe?

Name ______________________ Class ____________ Date ____________

Chapter Test Form A

Modern Chapter 19

The Great Depression and the Rise of Totalitarianism

FILL IN THE BLANK *(3 points each)* For each of the following statements, fill in the blank with the appropriate name, term, or phrase.

1. The worldwide economic collapse that followed World War I is known as the ______________________.

2. The purpose of the ______________________ was to protect France from another German invasion.

3. The ______________________ was a U.S. program that provided old-age benefits.

4. The system in which the government controls all economic decisions is known as the ______________________.

5. *The Rite of Spring* by Russian-born composer ______________________ shocked people because it broke with musical tradition.

6. The fascist ______________________ in Italy claimed to be defending Italy against a communist revolution.

7. Lenin formed the ______________________ to spread the Communist revolution to other countries.

8. Hitler called his regime the ______________________.

UNDERSTANDING IDEAS *(3 points each)* For each of the following, write the letter of the best choice in the space provided.

______ **1.** Cubism is
- **a.** poetry emphasizing rhyme.
- **b.** music emphasizing form.
- **c.** art emphasizing geometric designs.
- **d.** architecture based on the shape of a building.

______ **2.** A general strike by French workers resulted in the
- **a.** Maginot Line.
- **b.** Locarno Pact.
- **c.** Fascist Party.
- **d.** Popular Front government.

______ **3.** Skyscrapers were made possible by the
- **a.** use of structural steel.
- **b.** adoption of functionalism.
- **c.** change in zoning laws.
- **d.** low cost of glass.

______ **4.** Which was NOT a result of the Easter Rising?
- **a.** stronger Irish nationalism
- **b.** execution of many leaders
- **c.** intervention by the British
- **d.** independence from Britain

______ **5.** The New Deal was a
- **a.** program to rebuild Europe after the war.
- **b.** reform program instituted by Herbert Hoover.
- **c.** relief program instituted by Franklin Roosevelt.
- **d.** program to help farmers throughout the world.

______ **6.** When German troops entered the Rhineland in 1936, Germany was
- **a.** acting within international law.
- **b.** violating the Treaty of Versailles.
- **c.** responding to a request from Britain.
- **d.** working toward greater world stability.

______ **7.** Under Lenin's New Economic Policy
- **a.** some free enterprise was allowed.
- **b.** only heavy industry was nationalized.
- **c.** farming and transportation were nationalized.
- **d.** all industries were nationalized.

______ **8.** France resisted the Great Depression longer than Great Britain because
- **a.** Great Britain was less industrialized.
- **b.** France was less industrialized.
- **c.** France had a more stable government.
- **d.** Great Britain had a weaker currency.

______ **9.** Many Germans saw the Weimar Republic as
- **a.** a traitor to German interests.
- **b.** a solution to financial chaos.
- **c.** a strong and effective government.
- **d.** an efficient corporatist state.

______ **10.** The goal of the first Five-Year Plan was to
- **a.** give peasants their own land to farm.
- **b.** produce more consumer goods.
- **c.** industrialize the Soviet Union.
- **d.** reward workers and farmers.

TRUE/FALSE *(2 points each)* Mark each statement *T* if it is true or *F* if it is false.

______ **1.** James Joyce was an American-born poet who described the postwar world in *The Waste Land.*

______ **2.** At the end of World War I, European farmers were able to reestablish themselves financially and increase the growth of crops like grain.

______ **3.** France had to repay the United States and French citizens for money borrowed to obtain war materials.

______ **4.** Stalin and Trotsky agreed that only workers in the Soviet Union needed revolution.

______ **5.** The king of Italy asked Mussolini to lead a coalition government.

______ **6.** The Lost Generation refers to political dissidents imprisoned in the Soviet Union.

______ **7.** The U.S. stock market crash was the start of a worldwide economic depression.

______ **8.** Britain divided Ireland into the Irish Free State and Northern Ireland.

PRACTICING SKILLS *(5 points each)* Study the cartoon and answer the questions that follow.

From *Visualized Modern History* by Philip Dorf (Oxford Book Company, Inc.)

1. What do the ship and the waters represent?

____

2. What is the cartoon saying about international trade?

____

COMPOSING AN ESSAY *(20 points)* On a separate sheet of paper, write a brief essay in response to one of the following.

1. Describe the effect of the policy of economic nationalism after World War I.

2. Compare and contrast fascism and communism.

Name ______________________ Class ______________ Date ____________

Chapter Test Form B

Modern Chapter **19**

The Great Depression and the Rise of Totalitarianism

SHORT ANSWER *(10 points each)* Provide brief answers for each of the following.

1. What is a pandemic, and what was the effect of the influenza pandemic in 1918–1919?

2. What measures did the government of Great Britain use to protect its position after the war?

3. What happened on Black Tuesday?

4. What problems did the nations in eastern Europe face after the war?

5. What did Stalin do when a Communist Party official was assassinated in 1934?

PRIMARY SOURCES *(10 points each)* Read this excerpt from a speech given by Adolf Hitler in 1929 and answer the questions that follow.

The entire struggle for survival is a conquest of the means of existence, which in turn results in the elimination of others from these same sources of subsistence. As long as there are peoples on this earth, there will be nations against nations and they will be forced to protect their vital rights in the same way as the individual is forced to protect his rights.

One is either the hammer or the anvil. We confess that it is our purpose to prepare the German people [again] for the role of the hammer. . . . How can we achieve power? We admit freely and openly that if our movement is victorious, we will be concerned day and night with the question of how to produce the armed forces which are forbidden to us by the peace treaty [Treaty of Versailles]. We solemnly confess that we consider everyone a scoundrel who does not try day and night to figure out a way to violate this treaty, for we have never recognized this treaty. . . .

We confess further that we will dash anyone to pieces who should dare to hinder us in this undertaking . . .

1. What is Hitler's goal?

2. How does Hitler intend to achieve his goal?

COMPOSING AN ESSAY *(30 points)* Write an essay on one of the following subjects. Remember to give examples to support your essay.

1. Discuss the ways in which society during the 1920s reflected disillusionment and a focus on the present. Consider literature, popular culture, and economics in your answer.

2. Compare and contrast Mussolini's Italy, Hitler's Germany, and Stalin's Soviet Union.

Name ______________________ Class ______________ Date ______________

Chapter Test Form A

Modern Chapter 20 Nationalist Movements Around the World

MATCHING *(3 points each)* In the space provided, write the letter of the name or term that matches each description. Some answers will not be used.

_____ **1.** leader of the Indian nationalist movement

_____ **2.** leader of the Kenyan nationalist movement

_____ **3.** Egyptian nationalist group that led a revolt against the British

_____ **4.** Cuban army sergeant who overthrew the reform government

_____ **5.** policy giving all nations equal rights to engage in trade in China

_____ **6.** Mexican artist whose paintings show the plight of peasants

_____ **7.** agreement that ended the war between Russia and Japan in 1905

_____ **8.** Mexican president who nationalized the oil industry

_____ **9.** letter expressing British support for a Jewish homeland

_____ **10.** commander of the Nationalist army who led the Northern Expedition campaign against Chinese warlords

a. Balfour Declaration
b. Chiang Kai-shek
c. Diego Rivera
d. Fulgencio Batista
e. Gerardo Machado
f. Jomo Kenyatta
g. Lázaro Cárdenas
h. Mohandas Gandhi
i. Open Door Policy
j. Treaty of Portsmouth
k. Treaty of Shimonoseki
l. Wafd Party

UNDERSTANDING IDEAS *(3 points each)* For each of the following, write the letter of the best choice in the space provided.

_____ **1.** After the British declared Egypt independent in 1922,
a. there were no British left in the country.
b. the British were unable to use the Suez Canal.
c. Italy moved in to take Britain's place.
d. British military forces remained in the country.

_____ **2.** To which peoples did Great Britain promise an independent state?
a. Persians, Palestinian Arabs, and Jews
b. Palestinian Arabs and Jews only
c. Persians only
d. Jews only

______ **3.** What was the cause of Reza Shah Pahlavi's downfall?
a. a war on rebellious tribes
b. an alliance with Germany
c. the secret police
d. an opposing political party

______ **4.** The movement that attacked Chinese Christians and foreign missionaries was called the
a. Boxer Rebellion.
b. Kuomintang.
c. Meiji Restoration.
d. Old China movement.

______ **5.** What did Chiang Kai-shek's government fail to do in the 1920s?
a. construct roads
b. improve education
c. institute land reform
d. fund defense

______ **6.** Why did Chiang Kai-shek pay little attention to the growth of Japanese nationalism?
a. He was focusing on running for office.
b. He was involved in making the Long March.
c. He was establishing rural reforms.
d. He was fighting the Chinese Communists.

______ **7.** One result of industrialization in Japan was
a. that fewer children were born to Japanese families.
b. neighborhoods filled with skyscrapers.
c. emigration to Korea, Taiwan, and the United States.
d. the growth of markets abroad for Japanese goods.

______ **8.** The target of the alliance between Japan and Britain was
a. Russia.
b. Korea.
c. China.
d. Germany.

______ **9.** The Good Neighbor Policy stressed
a. political cooperation between Russia and China.
b. Japanese nonintervention in Chinese affairs.
c. economic cooperation of Latin America nations.
d. United States nonintervention in Latin American affairs.

______ **10.** Latin American labor unions tended to hold what views?
a. democratic or fascist
b. socialist or anarchist
c. fascist or socialist
d. apolitical or democratic

TRUE/FALSE *(2 points each)* Mark each statement *T* if it is true or *F* if it is false.

______ **1.** The goal of Zionism was an independent Jewish homeland in Palestine.

______ **2.** Mustafa Kemal asked the Greek government to intervene in Turkey.

______ **3.** Chinese Nationalists descended on Beijing in what is now called the Long March.

______ **4.** As a result of economic problems during the 1920s, military officers played a greater role in the government of Japan.

______ **5.** In the 1920s, Latin American nations exported agricultural products because no mining industry existed.

PRACTICING SKILLS *(5 points each)* Study the map and answer the questions that follow.

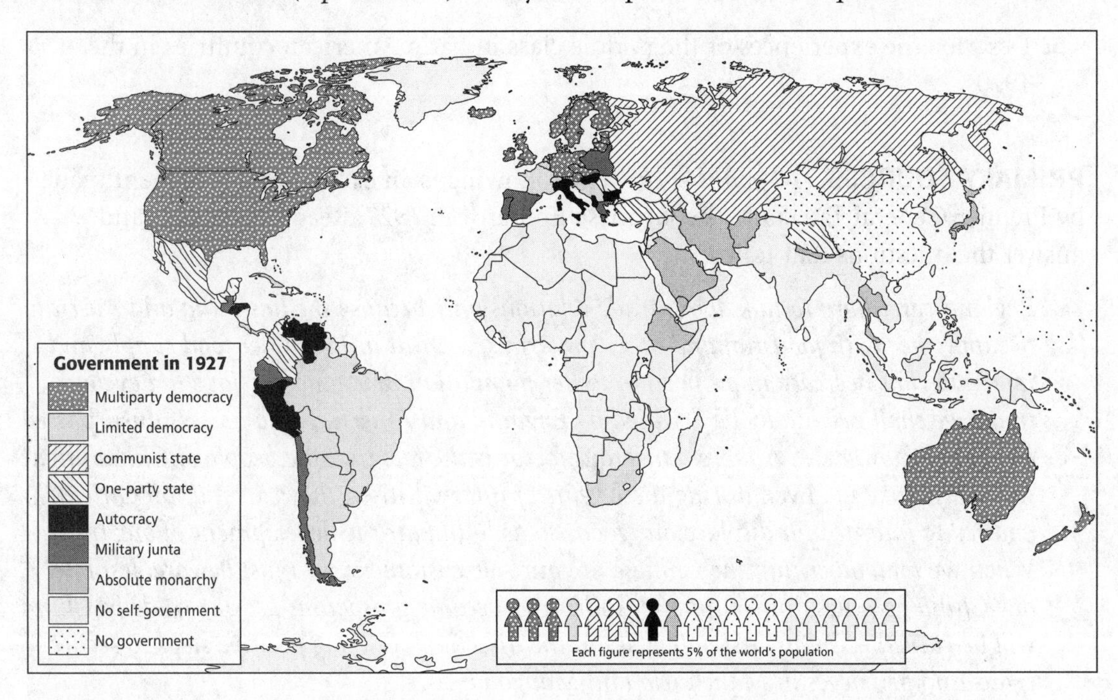

1. What percentage of the world's population lived in colonized nations in 1927?

____

2. What percentage of the world's population was ruled by a single person or party or the military?

____

COMPOSING AN ESSAY *(20 points)* On a separate sheet of paper, write a brief essay in response to one of the following.

1. What was the effect of World War I on the colonies of Africa?

2. What did Mao Zedong and his followers do in Shaanxi province, and what was the effect?

Name ______________________ Class ______________ Date ____________

Chapter Test Form B

Modern Chapter 20 Nationalist Movements Around the World

SHORT ANSWER *(10 points each)* Provide brief answers for each of the following.

1. Describe the actions involved in passive resistance against the British in India.
2. Discuss the steps Mustafa Kemal took to modernize Turkey.
3. List the "Three Principles of the People" of Sun Yixian.
4. Discuss the social tensions that arose in Japan as a result of economic development, universal education, and Western ideas.
5. Describe the experiences of the middle class in Latin American countries in the 1920s.

PRIMARY SOURCES *(10 points each)* The following is an excerpt of a statement made by Premier General Tanaka to the Japanese Emperor in 1927. Read the passage and answer the questions that follow.

England can afford to talk about trade relations only because she has India and Australia to supply her with foodstuff and other materials. . . . But in Japan her food supply and raw materials decrease in proportion to her population. If we merely hope to develop trade, we shall eventually be defeated by England and America, who possess unsurpassed capitalistic power. . . . A more dangerous factor is the fact that the people of China might some day wake up. Even during these years of internal strife, they can still toil patiently, and try to imitate and displace our goods so as to impair the development of our trade. When we remember that the Chinese are our sole customers, we must beware, lest one day China becomes unified and her industries become prosperous . . . our trade in China will be ruined. . . . Our best policy lies in the direction of taking positive steps to secure rights and privileges in Manchuria and Mongolia. . . .

The way to gain actual rights in Manchuria and Mongolia is to use this region as a base and under the pretense of trade and commerce penetrate the rest of China. . . . [and] seize the resources all over the country. Having China's entire resources at our disposal, we shall proceed to conquer India, the Archipelago, Asia Minor, Central Asia, and even Europe . . .

1. What does the prime minister see as Japan's problem regarding trade?
2. How does the prime minister suggest solving this problem?

COMPOSING AN ESSAY *(30 points)* Write an essay on one of the following subjects. Remember to use examples to support your essay.

1. Compare and contrast Great Britain's reaction to demands for independence by India to their reaction to similar demands from Canada, Australia, and New Zealand.
2. Discuss the relationship of culture and nationalist feelings.

Name ______________________ Class ______________ Date ____________

Chapter Test Form A

Modern Chapter **21** **World War II**

MATCHING *(3 points each)* In the space provided, write the letter of the name or term that matches each description. Some answers will not be used.

_____ **1.** agreement that Germany and the Soviet Union would never attack each other

_____ **2.** 1928 agreement making war illegal

_____ **3.** Hitler's plan for creating a single political and economic system for Europe

_____ **4.** law authorizing the United States president to supply war materials to Great Britain on credit

_____ **5.** systematic plan formulated in 1942 for exterminating Jews in concentration camps

_____ **6.** invasion of northwest France

_____ **7.** Spanish fascist party

_____ **8.** statement issued by Franklin Roosevelt and Winston Churchill listing shared beliefs

_____ **9.** Nazi program to destroy the entire Jewish population of Europe

_____ **10.** agreement between Japan and Germany to stop the spread of communism

a. Anti-Comintern Pact
b. Atlantic Charter
c. Falange
d. Final Solution
e. German-Soviet nonaggression pact
f. Kellogg-Briand Pact
g. Lend-Lease Act
h. Marshall Plan
i. New Order
j. Operation Overlord
k. Wannsee Conference
l. Yalta Conference

UNDERSTANDING IDEAS *(3 points each)* For each of the following, write the letter of the best choice in the space provided.

_____ **1.** Two years after Osachi Hamaguchi was shot
a. the emperor abdicated his throne.
b. the military controlled the Japanese government.
c. Japan withdrew from Manchuria.
d. Japan signed an agreement with China.

_____ **2.** Francisco Franco's government in Spain was MOST similar to
a. Tojo's government in Japan.
b. Stalin's government in Russia.
c. Hitler's government in Germany.
d. Mussolini's government in Italy.

_____ **3.** The policy of appeasement is associated with
a. Neville Chamberlain.
b. Winston Churchill.
c. Charles de Gaulle.
d. Charles Lindbergh.

_____ **4.** What effect did the Allied defeat at Dunkerque have on the British?
a. It sapped their will.
b. It raised their spirits.
c. It destroyed their army.
d. It destroyed their navy.

_____ **5.** When Jews arrived at the concentration camps
a. they were killed immediately.
b. they were immediately put to work.
c. they were divided into groups by age, sex, and health.
d. they were immediately sent to gas chambers that were disguised as showers.

_____ **6.** The commander of United States forces in Africa in 1942 was
a. Mark Clark.
b. Bernard Montgomery.
c. Harry Truman.
d. Dwight D. Eisenhower.

_____ **7.** World War II was officially started by
a. Japan's fake attack on a railway in Manchuria.
b. Japan's sneak attack on Pearl Harbor.
c. Germany's invasion of Poland.
d. Germany's invasion of Czechoslovakia.

_____ **8.** The Free French government was located in
a. London.
b. Vichy.
c. Paris.
d. Normandy.

_____ **9.** Which country remained neutral throughout World War II?
a. Russia
b. France
c. Bulgaria
d. Spain

_____ **10.** The United States strategy in the Pacific of capturing certain Japanese islands and skipping others was known as
a. island hopping.
b. blitzkrieg.
c. Potsdam.
d. Operation Overlord.

TRUE/FALSE *(2 points each)* Mark each statement *T* if it is true or *F* if it is false.

_____ **1.** The Ethiopian army held off Italy long enough for the Allies to come to its aid.

_____ **2.** In 1939 Germany's western front was the location of a "phony war."

_____ **3.** Germany and Italy declared war on France and Great Britain at the same time.

______ **4.** Erwin Rommel's troops defeated the British at the Battle of El Alamein.

______ **5.** Some Germans and other Europeans ignored what was happening to Jews in Europe.

PRACTICING SKILLS *(5 points each)* Study the following cartoon, which appeared in a British newspaper in 1939, and answer the questions that follow.

Rendezvous

Reprinted by permission of *The Standard* newspaper.

1. Whom do the two standing figures in the cartoon represent?

____

2. What does the contrast between the polite behavior and the dialogue show?

____

COMPOSING AN ESSAY *(20 points)* On a separate sheet of paper, write a brief essay in response to one of the following.

1. Describe the events leading to Hitler's annexation of Austria.

2. Explain how the feelings of Americans about the war changed between 1935 and 1941.

Chapter Test Form B

Modern Chapter **21**

World War II

SHORT ANSWER *(10 points each)* Provide brief answers for each of the following.

1. What role did the League of Nations play in the events leading up to World War II?

2. How did the German-Soviet nonaggression pact give Germany a military advantage?

3. How did the Allies respond to Hitler's invasion of Russia?

4. Why did Japan attack Pearl Harbor, and what was the result?

5. What happened in Italy after the Allies invaded Sicily?

PRIMARY SOURCES *(10 points each)* Read this passage from Winston Churchill's speech to Parliament following Dunkerque and answer the questions that follow.

I have, myself, full confidence that if all do their duty, if nothing is neglected, and if the best arrangements are made, as they are being made, we shall prove ourselves once again able to defend our Island home, to ride out the storm of war, and to outlive the menace of tyranny, if necessary for years, if necessary alone. . . . That is the will of Parliament and the nation. . . . Even though large tracts of Europe and many old and famous States have fallen or may fall into the grip of the Gestapo and all the odious apparatus of Nazi rule, we shall not flag or fail. We shall go on to the end, we shall fight in France, we shall fight on the seas and oceans, we shall fight with growing confidence and growing strength in the air, we shall defend our Island, whatever the cost may be, we shall fight on the beaches, we shall fight on the landing grounds, we shall fight in the fields and in the streets, we shall fight in the hills; we shall never surrender, and even if, which I do not for a moment believe, this Island or a large part of it were subjugated and starving, then our Empire beyond the seas, armed and guarded by the British Fleet, would carry on the struggle, until, in God's good time, the New World, with all its power and might, steps forth to the rescue and the liberation of the old.

1. What is the warning to the British government and people in this speech?

____

2. What does Churchill mean by the last part of the last sentence?

____

COMPOSING AN ESSAY *(30 points)* Write an essay on one of the following subjects. Remember to give examples to support your essay.

1. Discuss the relationship of the Spanish Civil War to World War II.

2. Discuss some of the actions and events that made World War II different from the wars that preceded it.

Name ______________________ Class ______________ Date ____________

Unit Test Form A

Modern Unit **5** **World War in the Twentieth Century**

UNDERSTANDING IDEAS *(3 points each)* For each of the following, write the letter of the best choice in the space provided.

______ **1.** Bismarck formed the Triple Alliance to prevent an alliance between
a. Austria and Russia.
b. Russia and England.
c. France and Russia.
d. France and England.

______ **2.** After signing the treaty of Brest Litovsk, Russia's leaders
a. focused on internal political problems.
b. formed a coalition government with the czar.
c. signed a nonaggression pact with Bulgaria.
d. sent the Red Army to China.

______ **3.** Sun Yixian and his followers favored
a. a communist government and economic system.
b. a constitutional government and civil liberties.
c. a dictatorship with restraints on freedom.
d. a monarchy and isolation from the West.

______ **4.** Japan went to war with Russia over
a. Cambodia.
b. Vietnam.
c. Mongolia.
d. Manchuria.

______ **5.** After World War I, the world seemed to be
a. the same as before the war.
b. much safer than before the war.
c. peaceful and easy to understand.
d. frightening and unpredictable.

______ **6.** After World War I, France tried to protect itself by
a. building the Maginot Line.
b. signing a nonaggression pact with Germany.
c. developing a new form of warfare.
d. building a large airforce.

______ **7.** The result of the Munich Conference in 1938 was
a. Hitler's invasion of the Soviet Union.
b. Hitler's invasion of Poland.
c. Hitler's annexation of the Sudetenland.
d. Hitler's annexation of Austria.

______ **8.** After V-E Day, the war in the Pacific continued for
a. a year.
b. six months.
c. three months.
d. three weeks.

_____ **9.** Under Reza Shah Pahlavi, Iran
a. had freedom of the press.
b. gave women more rights.
c. was dominated by Russia.
d. had no industry.

_____ **10.** German aggression was helped by
a. the English Channel.
b. French maquis members.
c. Norwegian collaborators.
d. the Russian winter.

FILL IN THE BLANK *(3 points each)* For each of the following statements, fill in the blank with the appropriate name, term, or phrase.

1. ______________________ used nonviolence to lead the nationalist movement in India.

2. ______________________ was president of the United States during World War I and outlined the Fourteen Points, his plan to make the world safer and more just.

3. ______________________ led the United States through the Great Depression and World War II.

4. The leader of Italy's Fascist Party who became dictator was ______________________.

5. The leader responsible for modernizing Turkey was ______________________.

6. ______________________ led the Bolshevik faction of the Communist Party and became the first leader of the Soviet Union.

7. The premier of the militaristic government in Japan that launched the attack on the United States at Pearl Harbor was ______________________.

8. ______________________ led the Falangist rebels to victory in the Spanish Civil War.

9. The military commander who led the Chinese Nationalists after the death of Sun Yixian was ______________________.

10. The leader of the Chinese Communist Party after the Long March was ______________________.

TRUE/FALSE *(2 points each)* Mark each statement *T* if it is true or *F* if it is false.

_____ **1.** When nations try to protect their own industries by placing tariffs on goods imported from other countries, they are engaging in economic nationalism.

______ **2.** Woodrow Wilson promoted the League of Nations, but the United States never became a member.

______ **3.** The Chinese group known as the Boxers rebelled against the conservative rule of the Empress Dowager Tz'u-hsi and encouraged foreign investment.

______ **4.** Africans in a number of colonies organized nationalist movements after World War I.

______ **5.** By late 1940, the tide of war had turned, and the Allies were firmly in command.

PRACTICING SKILLS *(5 points each)* The following map shows the failure of Russia to promote world revolution. Study the map and answer the questions that follow.

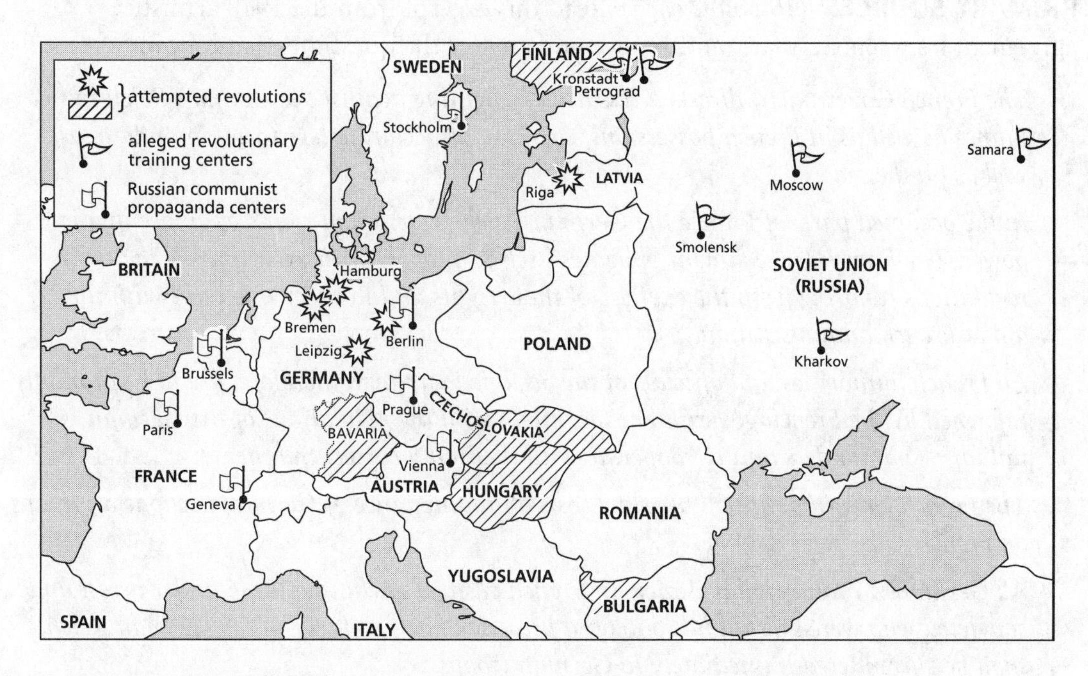

1. In what cities did communists attempt revolutions?

____

2. In what countries did communists attempt revolutions?

____

COMPOSING AN ESSAY *(20 points)* On a separate sheet of paper, write a brief essay in response to one of the following.

1. What role did nationalism play in causing World Wars I and II?

2. What effect did the Great Depression have on the nations of Latin America?

Name ______________________ Class ______________ Date ______________

Unit Test Form B

Modern Unit 5 — World War in the Twentieth Century

SHORT ANSWER *(10 points each)* Provide brief answers for each of the following.

1. How did Hitler use Germany's democratic system to gain control over the country?
2. In what way did Soviet agriculture change during the early years of the Communist regime?
3. What involvement did Great Britain have in the Middle East between the wars?
4. What caused the Spanish Civil War?
5. What was Hitler's master plan for Europe in World War II?

PRIMARY SOURCES *(10 points each)* Read this excerpt from the 1940 armistice agreement between Germany and France and answer the questions that follow.

The French Government directs a cessation of fighting against the German Reich in France as well as in French possessions, colonies, protectorate territories, mandates as well as on the seas. . . .

In the occupied parts of France the German Reich exercises all rights of an occupying power. The French Government obligates itself to support with every means the regulations resulting from the exercise of these rights and to carry them out with the aid of French administration.

All French authorities and officials of the occupied territory, therefore, are to be promptly informed by the French government to comply with the regulations of the German military commanders and to cooperate with them in a correct manner. . . .

The French Government will bear the costs of maintenance of German occupation troops on French soil.

All German war and civil prisoners in French custody, including those under arrest and convicted who were seized and sentenced because of acts in favor of the German Reich, shall be surrendered immediately to German troops. . . .

French troops in German prison camps will remain prisoners of war until conclusion of a peace.

1. What does this section of the armistice agreement obligate France to do?
2. What does this section of the armistice agreement obligate Germany to do?

COMPOSING AN ESSAY *(30 points)* Write an essay on one of the following subjects. Remember to give examples to support your answer.

1. How did the Treaty of Versailles help lead to World War II?
2. What effect did the League of Nations have during the 1920s and 1930s, and why?

Name ______________________ Class ______________ Date ____________

Chapter Test Form A

Modern Chapter **22**

Europe and North America in the Postwar Years

MATCHING *(3 points each)* In the space provided, write the letter of the name or term that matches each description. Some answers will not be used.

_____ **1.** United Nations body to which all member nations are admitted

_____ **2.** United Nations body with five permanent and ten temporary members

_____ **3.** political and military alliance among twelve Western nations

_____ **4.** anticommunist United States senator who questioned the loyalty of government officials

_____ **5.** United States president who instituted the Great Society social reform program

_____ **6.** policy statement that the United States must help prevent the spread of communism

_____ **7.** European organization that abolished import quotas and tariffs for member nations

_____ **8.** massive economic assistance by the United States to postwar Europe

a. Common Market
b. General Assembly
c. George McGovern
d. Harry Hopkins
e. Joseph McCarthy
f. Lyndon Johnson
g. Marshall Plan
h. NATO
i. Security Council
j. Truman Doctrine

UNDERSTANDING IDEAS *(3 points each)* For each of the following, write the letter of the best choice in the space provided.

_____ **1.** Stalin believed that free elections
a. should take place in all nations immediately.
b. could not take place until nations were socialist.
c. were completely unnecessary.
d. should be held under United Nations auspices.

_____ **2.** The Cuban missile crisis was
a. an attack on Cuba by the Soviet Union.
b. an attack on the United States by Cuba.
c. a standoff between the United States and Soviet Union.
d. a standoff between Cuba and the United States.

_____ **3.** At the Nürnberg trials
a. Nazi leaders were tried for crimes against humanity.
b. Germany was tried for waging war.
c. Hitler was tried for genocide.
d. Germany and Japan were tried for sneak attacks.

_____ **4.** The war of ideas between the United States and the Soviet Union was the
a. Warsaw Pact.
b. Iron Curtain.
c. Cold War.
d. Marshall Plan.

_____ **5.** The Soviet Union's response to the NATO treaty was to
a. isolate West Berlin.
b. establish the Cominform.
c. build the Berlin Wall.
d. adopt the Warsaw Pact.

_____ **6.** Charles de Gaulle was
a. a firm supporter of NATO.
b. a nationalist.
c. an autocratic leader.
d. an imperialist.

_____ **7.** East Germany tried to keep people from escaping to the West by
a. signing the Warsaw Pact.
b. blockading West Berlin.
c. making the Berlin Miracle.
d. building the Berlin Wall.

_____ **8.** Which postwar country was the MOST stable?
a. Italy
b. Greece
c. Sweden
d. France

_____ **9.** The United States policy of restricting the spread of communism was called
a. containment.
b. buffering.
c. isolationism.
d. democratization.

_____ **10.** During the 1960s, Canada was challenged by
a. NATO.
b. Quebec's separatism.
c. the DEW Line.
d. lack of natural resources.

TRUE/FALSE *(2 points each)* Mark each statement *T* if it is true or *F* if it is false.

_____ **1.** At Potsdam in 1945, the Allies agreed that Germany should be permanently divided into two nations.

_____ **2.** Eleanor Roosevelt was instrumental in persuading Americans to support the United Nations.

_____ **3.** The Soviet Union created a buffer zone of communist nations along its western borders, leading the Western powers to fear that it planned to dominate Europe.

_____ **4.** The Soviet Union respected the presence of the Western democracies in Berlin and allowed free passage through East Germany.

______ **5.** In a welfare state, the government is the main organization responsible for social welfare.

______ **6.** Yugoslavia under Tito was a loyal member of the Communist bloc.

______ **7.** Congress enthusiastically passed all of the domestic legislation introduced by John F. Kennedy.

______ **8.** Martin Luther King Jr. and his supporters held peaceful demonstrations and protests against discrimination.

PRACTICING SKILLS *(5 points each)* The following chart shows the organization of the United Nations. Study the chart and answer the questions that follow.

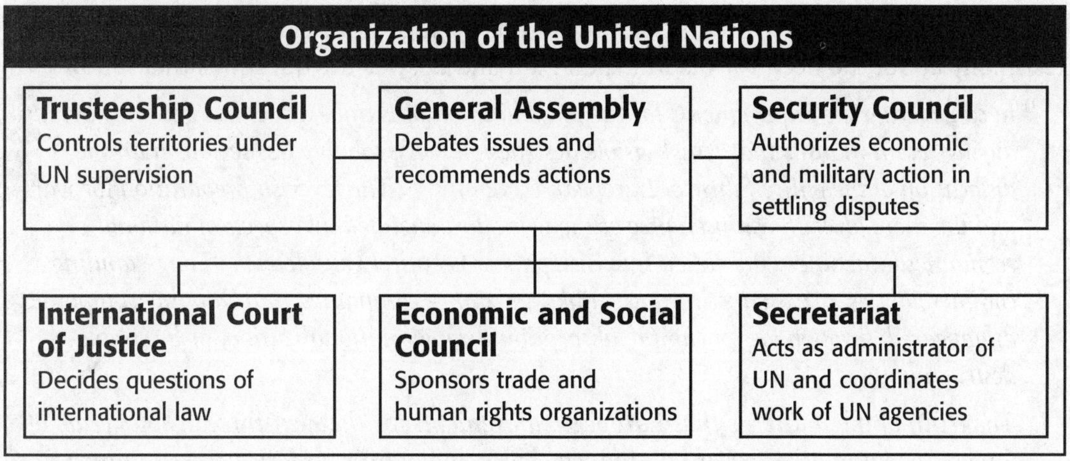

Organization of the United Nations

Trusteeship Council	Controls territories under UN supervision
General Assembly	Debates issues and recommends actions
Security Council	Authorizes economic and military action in settling disputes
International Court of Justice	Decides questions of international law
Economic and Social Council	Sponsors trade and human rights organizations
Secretariat	Acts as administrator of UN and coordinates work of UN agencies

1. If your country were engaged in a border dispute with another nation, what body of the UN would try to decide what to do about the situation?

____

2. If you were the head of an organization devoted to reforming prison conditions in nations across the world, with what body of the UN would you likely confer?

____

COMPOSING AN ESSAY *(20 points)* On a separate sheet of paper, write a brief essay in response to one of the following.

1. What were the areas of disagreement between the Western democracies and the Soviet Union at the end of the war?

2. What actions did Nikita Khrushchev take as Soviet leader, and with what results?

Name ______________________ Class ______________ Date ______________

Chapter Test Form B

Modern Chapter **22**

Europe and North America in the Postwar Years

SHORT ANSWER *(10 points each)* Provide brief answers for each of the following.

1. What agreements did Churchill, Roosevelt, and Stalin reach at the 1945 Yalta conference?
2. What role did the Soviet Union play in Europe after the war?
3. What was the West German "miracle"?
4. What role did Algeria play in postwar Europe?
5. What domestic issues caused conflicts in the United States during the postwar era?

PRIMARY SOURCES *(10 points each)* Read this passage from George Marshall's Senate testimony about the need for his Marshall Plan and answer the questions that follow.

In considering the requirements for the rehabilitation of Europe, . . . it has become obvious during recent months that [this] visible destruction was probably less serious than the dislocation of the entire fabric of European economy. . . . The feverish preparation for war and the more feverish maintenance of the war effort engulfed all aspects of national economies. Machinery has fallen into disrepair or is entirely obsolete. . . . Long-standing commercial ties, private institutions, banks, insurance companies, and shipping companies disappeared, through loss of capital, absorption through nationalization, or by simple destruction. . . .

The truth of the matter is that Europe's requirements for the next three or four years of foreign food and other essential products—principally from America—are so much greater than her present ability to pay that she must have substantial additional help or face economic, social, and political deterioration of a very grave character. . . .

It is logical that the United States should do whatever it is able to do to assist in the return of normal economic health in the world, without which there can be no political stability and no assured peace. [The purpose of our policy] should be the revival of a working economy in the world so as to permit the emergence of political and social conditions in which free institutions can exist.

1. How does Marshall characterize the state of industrialization in Europe?
2. What reason does Marshall give for United States economic aid to Europe?

COMPOSING AN ESSAY *(30 points)* Write an essay on one of the following subjects. Remember to give examples to support your essay.

1. Compare and contrast the postwar economic status of Western European nations with that of the Soviet Union and Eastern Europe.
2. Compare and contrast the way the United States treated its allies with the way the Soviet Union treated its allies.

Name ______________________ Class ______________ Date ____________

Chapter Test Form A

Modern Chapter **23**

Asia Since 1945

FILL IN THE BLANK *(3 points each)* For each of the following statements, fill in the blank with the appropriate name, term, or phrase.

1. The ______________________ was an attempt to induce social change in China by means of violence.

2. The associates of the widow of Mao Zedong who wanted to continue the Cultural Revolution were known as the ______________________.

3. India's policy toward the United States and the Soviet Union during the 1950s and 1960s was called ______________________.

4. A ______________________ like India's has some ownership of industry by government and some by private companies.

5. Douglas MacArthur's occupation government of Japan was known as ______________________.

6. The ______________________ were large industrial firms controlled by powerful Japanese families.

7. The idea that the fall of one country in Southeast Asia to communism would cause all the other countries in the area to become communist is known as the ______________________.

8. The ______________________ was signed in 1954 and ended the war between France and Vietnam.

9. ______________________ is a group devoted to promoting economic growth and social progress in Southeast Asia.

10. Cambodian Communists were called the ______________________.

UNDERSTANDING IDEAS *(3 points each)* For each of the following, write the letter of the best choice in the space provided.

______ **1.** At the time of independence, the people of India were divided by
- **a.** religion.
- **b.** geography.
- **c.** ideology.
- **d.** economic systems.

______ **2.** Indira Gandhi was the
- **a.** wife of the president of the Philippines.
- **b.** president of the Philippines.
- **c.** prime minister of Pakistan
- **d.** prime minister of India.

_____ **3.** India and Pakistan disagreed about control of
a. Bangladesh.
b. Kashmir.
c. Tibet.
d. Punjab.

_____ **4.** China's Five-Year Plan, called the Great Leap Forward, resulted in
a. lower industrial output.
b. higher industrial output.
c. privately owned farms.
d. riots in the cities.

_____ **5.** The leader of the Viet Minh who declared Vietnam independent in 1945 was
a. Pol Pot.
b. Ngo Dinh Diem.
c. Ho Chi Minh.
d. U Nu.

_____ **6.** Which of the following is NOT currently a problem in Asia?
a. lack of stability of governments
b. economic isolation from the West
c. too much population growth
d. growing gap between the rich and the poor

_____ **7.** The status of Taiwan
a. was settled by treaty shortly after the Communist revolution.
b. is as a province of the People's Republic of China.
c. is controversial because of religious differences.
d. remains a point of contention between the United States and China.

_____ **8.** A parliamentary democracy was set up in Japan as a provision of the
a. peace treaty.
b. Liberal-Democratic Party.
c. MacArthur Constitution.
d. zaibatsu.

_____ **9.** Japan and the Soviet Union disagreed about
a. Tibet.
b. Korea.
c. the Kuril Islands.
d. Hokkaido.

_____ **10.** North Vietnam's 1968 attack was called the
a. Ho Chi Minh Trail.
b. Tet Offensive.
c. Christmas War.
d. Khmer Rouge.

TRUE/FALSE *(2 points each)* Mark each statement *T* if it is true or *F* if it is false.

_____ **1.** The start of India's independence was marred by violence and massacres.

_____ **2.** Myanmar has been criticized for its human rights violations and its production of illegal narcotics.

_____ **3.** The United States backed the North Koreans after World War II, and the Soviet Union backed the South Koreans.

_______ **4.** Japan did not experience land reform after World War II.

_______ **5.** Asian nations raised money for development by exporting natural resources and agricultural goods, by borrowing money, and by encouraging foreign investment.

PRACTICING SKILLS *(5 points each)* Study this cartoon about the prodemocracy movement in China and answer the questions that follow.

Linda Boileau, *Frankfort State Journal*, Rothco Cartoon Syndicate. Reprinted by permission.

1. What does the figure on the ground represent?

____

2. What does the cartoon imply about the condition of democracy in China?

____

COMPOSING AN ESSAY *(20 points)* On a separate sheet of paper, write a brief essay in response to one of the following.

1. Discuss the reforms Deng Xiaoping instituted in China and how they related to the Tiananmen Square Massacre.

2. Discuss the attitude of the Japanese government about building up its military during the postwar years, and whether there has been any change in attitude over time.

Name ______________________ Class ______________ Date ____________

Chapter Test Form B

Modern Chapter **23**

Asia Since 1945

SHORT ANSWER *(10 points each)* Provide brief answers for each of the following.

1. What position did the Indian independence movement take in World War II?

2. Who were the Red Guards, and what did they do?

3. What was the effect of economic growth on Japanese society?

4. What effect did the Vietnam War have on Laos and Cambodia?

5. What countries are known as the "Four Tigers," and to what does the name refer?

PRIMARY SOURCES *(10 points each)* Read this passage from an article in *The New York Times* about the election of Benazir Bhutto and answer the questions that follow.

The Prime Minister . . . seems to embody all the fresh new spirit that Pakistanis hope will infuse their nation after 11 years of military rule and an "Islamization" campaign that diminished women's rights and made a rough, male-dominated frontier nation even more austere and cheerless. . . .

In developing human resources, Ms. Bhutto's gender may have the greatest psychological impact because Pakistan's women need a heightened sense of self-respect and greater involvement in national life, . . . an important adviser to Ms. Bhutto, said. . . .

Ms. Bhutto has never portrayed herself as a feminist in a nation that would be conservatively—but not radically—Islamic even without the policies of the late President. In shops, offices, houses and in crowds gathered to see the new Prime Minister, women invariably beam when asked whether it is important that their country will be run by one of them. Do they think a woman can rule a Muslim nation?

"Why not?" is the almost universal reply.

Some of Pakistan's most conservative Muslim theologians take a different view. A few days before the election, they issued a categorical ruling saying that a woman could not head an Islamic state.

From "Pakistan Is Sure of Its Leader, Less Sure of Her Plans" by Barbara Crossette from *The New York Times.* December 4, 1988. Copyright © 1988 by **The New York Times Company.** Reprinted by permission of the publisher.

1. What beliefs were in conflict as a result of the election of Benazir Bhutto?

2. What were the possible outcomes of this election? Explain what really happened.

COMPOSING AN ESSAY *(30 points)* Write an essay on one of the following subjects. Remember to give examples to support your answer.

1. Discuss the political development of Asian nations and the reasons their governments developed as they did.

2. Discuss whether the identity of the colonial powers that ruled Asian countries before World War II made a difference in their experience of gaining independence.

Name ______________________ Class ______________ Date ____________

Chapter Test Form A

Modern Chapter **24** **Africa and the Middle East Since 1945**

MATCHING *(3 points each)* In the space provided, write the letter of the name or term that matches each description. Some answers will not be used.

______ **1.** a French protectorate that became a constitutional monarchy after independence in 1956

______ **2.** a British colony of the Gold Coast, achieved full independence in 1957

______ **3.** experienced violent civil war between its two major ethnic groups, the Tutsi and the Hutu

______ **4.** formerly a Portuguese colony, one of three nations to become independent in 1974

______ **5.** a colony called the Belgian Congo, experienced years of violence after achieving independence in 1960

______ **6.** the British colony of South Rhodesia that withheld rights from the black population, became an independent nation in 1980 with free elections open to all

______ **7.** formerly part of France, granted independence by Charles de Gaulle in 1962 after a violent war

______ **8.** after independence, one region seceded from the federation and declared itself a new state called Biafra, leading to a civil war

______ **9.** a British colony, achieved independence under Jomo Kenyatta in 1963 after a long guerilla campaign

______ **10.** part of a British colony called the Federation of Rhodesia and Nyasaland, became an independent state in 1964 with majority African rule

a. Algeria
b. Angola
c. Ghana
d. Guinea
e. Kenya
f. Morocco
g. Nigeria
h. Rwanda
i. South Africa
j. Zaire
k. Zambia
l. Zimbabwe

UNDERSTANDING IDEAS *(3 points each)* For each of the following, write the letter of the best choice in the space provided.

______ **1.** What movement promoted African cultural unity?
a. Mau Mau
b. apartheid
c. Pan-Africanism
d. intifada

______ **2.** Segregation in South Africa was called
a. Mau Mau.
b. apartheid.
c. Pan-Africanism.
d. intifada.

______ **3.** The ANC leader who became the first African president of South Africa was
a. Desmond Tutu.
b. Steven Biko.
c. Nelson Mandela.
d. Robert Mugabe.

______ **4.** In many new African nations, the military stepped in when the leaders
a. did not improve conditions quickly enough.
b. sided with the Soviet Union.
c. moved too far away from Islam.
d. made too many changes too quickly.

______ **5.** Desertification was caused by
a. excessive drilling for oil.
b. strip-mining for minerals.
c. grazing too many cattle on the land.
d. overusing and overplanting the land.

______ **6.** In the 1950s, Turkey was allied with the
a. communist countries.
b. NATO countries.
c. United Arab Republic.
d. Islamic League.

______ **7.** In 1947 the United Nations voted to
a. set up a Jewish state.
b. set up an Arab state.
c. set up both a Jewish and an Arab state.
d. maintain the status quo in Palestine.

______ **8.** After Iran nationalized the Anglo-Iranian Oil Company, a coup restored power to the shah with the help of
a. Great Britain.
b. France.
c. Egypt.
d. the United States.

______ **9.** The Camp David Accords were
a. a framework for peace.
b. a peace treaty.
c. a blueprint for a Palestinian state.
d. a blueprint for an Israeli-Arab nation.

______ **10.** The conservative Islamic leader who led the overthrow of the shah of Iran was
a. Saddam Hussein.
b. the Ayatollah Khomeini.
c. Yasir Arafat.
d. Hafiz Asad.

TRUE/FALSE *(2 points each)* Mark each statement *T* if it is true or *F* if it is false.

______ **1.** All the colonized nations in Africa obtained independence by waging long wars of liberation.

______ **2.** All the new African nations were fortunate to have numerous crops and natural resources they could export.

______ **3.** French troops withdrew from Syria and Lebanon after battles with nationalists and pressure from the British.

_______ **4.** Most Middle Eastern states became independent because of the leadership of young nationalists who had been educated in the West.

_______ **5.** Iraq attacked Iran over control of a waterway between the two nations.

PRACTICING SKILLS *(5 points each)* The following graph shows land use in Africa. Study the graph and answer the questions that follow.

LAND USE IN AFRICA

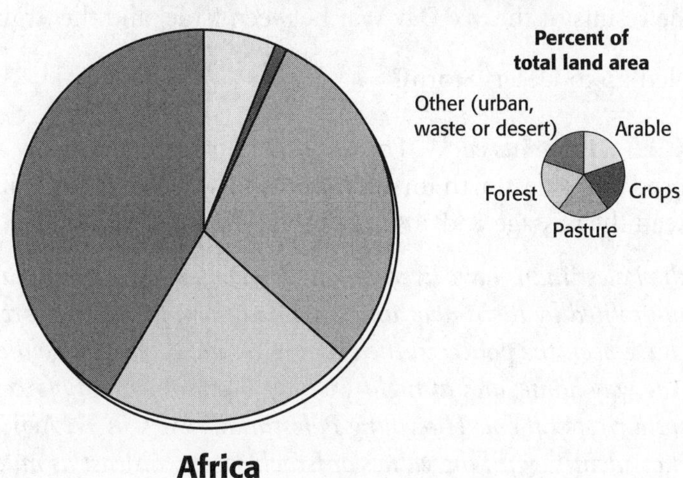

From *The Great World Atlas,* updated edition published by CLF, a division of Quadrillion Publishing Ltd., Surrey, UK, 1999.

1. Is more land used for agriculture or for grazing livestock?

____

2. Is it possible to determine how much land is used for cities? Why?

____

COMPOSING AN ESSAY *(20 points)* On a separate sheet of paper, write a brief essay in response to one of the following.

1. Discuss the effect of the Cold War on African nations.

2. Discuss the background, events, and results of the Suez Crisis.

Name ________________ Class ________ Date ________

Chapter Test Form B

Modern Chapter 24 **Africa and the Middle East Since 1945**

SHORT ANSWER *(10 points each)* Provide brief answers for each of the following.

1. Why did Charles de Gaulle change his mind about withdrawing French aid to African colonies that chose independence?
2. What role did ethnic conflicts play in the experience of some of the new African nations?
3. What Arab nation benefited from the 1948 war with Israel, and how did it benefit?
4. What were the results of the Six-Day War between Israel and the Arab nations?
5. What events led up to Desert Storm?

PRIMARY SOURCES *(10 points each)* This passage is from an article by an Israeli journalist who posed as a Palestinian for six months to see what life was like in the occupied areas. Read the passage and answer the questions that follow.

For 20 years the Palestinians have lived among us. During the day we have been the employers who profited by their labor and exploited them for all they are worth; in the afternoon we have been the police; in the evening we have been the soldiers at the roadblock on the way home; and at night we have been the security forces who entered their homes and arrested them. The young Palestinians work in Tel Aviv, Jerusalem, and other cities. They identify with the values of Israeli society at least as much as they do with their traditional backgrounds. They get a whiff of the democratic privileges that Israeli citizens enjoy, but they cannot share them. The young man who spends his work week among a people living under democratic rule returns to his home, which is only an hour away but which has (in effect, if not officially) been under curfew for 20 years. Any Arab who walks in the streets at a late hour can expect to be detained and questioned about his actions, even during periods of relative calm. He sees and recognizes the value of freedom but is accorded the kind of treatment that characterizes the most backward dictatorial regimes. How can he be anything but frustrated?

In the end, the impression I was left with formed a depressing picture of fear and mistrust on both sides.

1. According to this passage, how do Palestinians view Israelis?
2. What reasons does the passage give to explain why Palestinians are frustrated?

COMPOSING AN ESSAY *(30 points)* Write an essay on one of the following subjects. Remember to give examples to support your essay.

1. Discuss whether the identity of the colonial powers that ruled African countries before World War II made a difference in their experience of gaining independence.
2. Discuss the effectiveness of alliances among Arab nations.

Name ______________________ Class ______________ Date ____________

Chapter Test Form A

Modern Chapter **25**

Latin America Since 1945

FILL IN THE BLANK *(3 points each)* For each of the following statements, fill in the blank with the appropriate name, term, or phrase.

1. ______________________ is an economic alliance between Mexico, the United States, and Canada.

2. The alliance of 35 of the independent nations in the Western Hemisphere is known as the ______________________.

3. The Marxist group in Nicaragua's civil war was known as the ______________________.

4. The group opposed to the Marxists in Nicaragua's civil war was called the ______________________.

5. The ______________________ held power in Mexico for many years.

6. ______________________ was Luis Muñoz Marín's plan to improve the Puerto Rican economy through outside investment and industrialization.

7. Argentineans who were arrested and never seen again are known as ______________________.

8. The Maoist terrorist group in Peru was called the ______________________.

9. The ______________________ signed in 1983 promoted negotiation to settle regional conflicts and a reduction in foreign military presence.

10. In Latin American nations, ______________________, ______________________, and the Catholic Church have a growing voice in government.

UNDERSTANDING IDEAS *(3 points each)* For each of the following, write the letter of the best choice in the space provided.

______ **1.** Which is NOT a solution used by Latin American leaders for economic problems?
a. develop national industries
b. obtain loans
c. form a regional trade group
d. bring in foreign corporations

______ **2.** Relying on one or two crops or minerals for export is known as
a. nationalization.
b. pastoralism.
c. substitution.
d. monoculture.

_____ **3.** Latin American debt ultimately led to
a. inflation.
b. import substitution.
c. monoculture.
d. reduced taxes.

_____ **4.** Population growth in Latin America has been caused by
a. movement from cities to rural areas.
b. movement from rural areas to cities.
c. low death rates and high birth rates.
d. high death rates and high birth rates.

_____ **5.** One issue that led to tense relations between Mexico and the United States was
a. PRI domination.
b. illegal immigration.
c. student protests.
d. peasant uprisings.

_____ **6.** Panama's Manuel Noriega was convicted of
a. embezzlement.
b. war crimes.
c. taking bribes.
d. drug trafficking.

_____ **7.** Who landed in Cuba in the Bay of Pigs invasion?
a. the CIA
b. Cuban exiles
c. United States special forces
d. Guatemalan forces

_____ **8.** "The Brazilian Miracle" resulted in
a. economic prosperity.
b. increased civil rights.
c. the reduction of national debt.
d. domination of world markets.

_____ **9.** Which nation is Latin America's leading producer of coca, the plant from which cocaine is made?
a. Colombia
b. Chile
c. Peru
d. Argentina

_____ **10.** Augusto Pinochet's regime in Chile was noted for
a. freedom of speech.
b. political repression.
c. full employment.
d. support of all citizens.

TRUE/FALSE *(2 points each)* Mark each statement *T* if it is true or *F* if it is false.

_____ **1.** The Mothers of the Plaza de Mayo is a group of Latin American women who oppose the abuse of power by the government and the military.

_____ **2.** The end of the civil war in Nicaragua allowed the country to solve its economic problems.

_____ **3.** Fidel Castro's government was openly communist from the time it came to power.

_____ **4.** Puerto Rico is a United States commonwealth.

______ **5.** Eva Perón was the first woman elected to lead a country in the Western Hemisphere.

PRACTICING SKILLS *(5 points each)* The map below shows the average percentage of calories required for well-being consumed per day by the people of the Western Hemisphere. Study the map and answer the questions that follow.

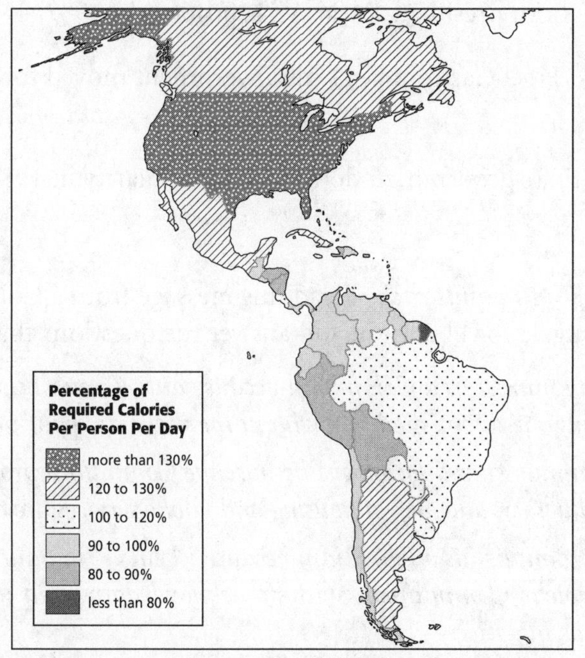

From *The Great World Atlas,* updated edition published by CLF, a division of Quadrillion Publishing Ltd., Surrey, UK, 1999.

1. In what region of the hemisphere do people receive less than 100 percent of the calories they need for well-being?

____

2. How does the United States compare to other nations with respect to calories consumed for well-being?

____

COMPOSING AN ESSAY *(20 points)* On a separate sheet of paper, write a brief essay in response to one of the following.

1. Which Cuban citizens supported Fidel Castro when he first came to power, and why did they support him?

2. Why and how have Colombia's fortunes changed since World War II?

Name ______________________ Class ______________ Date ____________

Chapter Test Form B

Modern Chapter **25**

Latin America Since 1945

SHORT ANSWER *(10 points each)* Provide brief answers for each of the following.

1. What has been the effect of the growth of cities in Latin America?

2. What has been the condition of Mexico's economy since World War II?

3. What did Costa Rican president Oscar Arias propose in 1987?

4. What actions did Fidel Castro take as his government moved toward communism in late 1959?

5. What did Argentina's government do to regain popularity in 1982, and with what result?

PRIMARY SOURCES *(10 points each)* Read this message from a Colombian priest who joined the armed struggle for liberation and answer the questions that follow.

> *I am not anti-Communist as a Colombian because anti-Communism in my country is bent on persecuting the dissatisfied, . . . who in the main are poor people.*
>
> *I am not anti-Communist as a sociologist because the Communist proposals to combat poverty, hunger, illiteracy, and lack of housing and public services are effective and scientific.*
>
> *I am not anti-Communist as a Christian, because I believe that anti-Communism condemns the whole of Communism, without acknowledging that there is some justice in its cause, as well as injustice. . . .*
>
> *I am not anti-Communist as a priest because, whether the Communists realize it or not, there are within their ranks some authentic Christians. . . .*
>
> *The Communists must be fully aware of the fact that I will not join their ranks, that I am not nor will I ever be a Communist. . . .*
>
> *Yet I am disposed to fight with them for common objectives: against the oligarchy and the domination of the United States, and for the takeover of power by the popular class.*
>
> From *Latin American Civilization: The National Era, Vol II, Third Edition,* edited by Benjamin Keen. Copyright © 1974 by Houghton Mifflin Company. Reprinted by permission of **Benjamin Keen.**

1. Why is this priest willing to fight alongside the Communists?

2. What is he fighting for?

COMPOSING AN ESSAY *(30 points)* Write an essay on one of the following subjects. Remember to give examples to support your essay.

1. Discuss the role played by the United States in the nations of Latin America and the success of the United States in achieving its aims.

2. Discuss the types of economic reforms attempted in Latin American countries and which seemed to be most effective.

Name ______________________ Class ______________ Date ____________

Chapter Test Form A

Modern Chapter **26**

The Superpowers in the Modern Era

MATCHING *(3 points each)* In the space provided, write the letter of the name or term that matches each description. Some answers will not be used.

_____ **1.** Conservative prime minister of Great Britain who ordered troops to defend the Falkland Islands

_____ **2.** German leader from 1982 to 1998 who presided over the reunification of Germany

_____ **3.** king of Spain after the death of Francisco Franco

_____ **4.** United States president forced to resign because of the Watergate scandal

_____ **5.** United States president who pardoned the president who resigned after Watergate

_____ **6.** United States president whose administration was marked by the Iran-contra affair

_____ **7.** United States president who was impeached for lying to a grand jury

_____ **8.** Soviet prime minister who suppressed Czechoslovakia's Prague Spring reforms in 1968

_____ **9.** Soviet prime minister who oversaw the perestroika and glasnost reforms in the 1980s

_____ **10.** Russian prime minister who oversaw Russia's transition to democracy in the 1990s

a. Bill Clinton
b. Boris Yeltsin
c. Gerald Ford
d. Helmut Kohl
e. John Major
f. Juan Carlos
g. Leonid Brezhnev
h. Margaret Thatcher
i. Mikhail Gorbachev
j. Richard Nixon
k. Ronald Reagan
l. Yuri Andropov

UNDERSTANDING IDEAS *(3 points each)* For each of the following, write the letter of the best choice in the space provided.

_____ **1.** The Watergate scandal was about
a. accusations of sexual misconduct.
b. selling weapons to free hostages.
c. a politically motivated break-in and cover-up.
d. the killing of antiwar protesters.

_____ **2.** The result of President Reagan's economic stimulus activities in the 1980s was
a. increased United States government debt.
b. decreased United States government debt.
c. the nationalization of United States industries.
d. the breakup of United States business monopolies.

_____ **3.** In the 1990s, the main energy source for the United States was
a. coal.
b. oil.
c. nuclear power.
d. solar power.

_____ **4.** One factor in the economic improvement in Britain during the 1980s was
a. heavy industry.
b. North Sea oil fields.
c. colonial resources.
d. increased welfare benefits.

_____ **5.** Which was NOT a concern of France in the 1990s?
a. unemployment
b. recession
c. immigration
d. separatist movements

_____ **6.** The result of the meeting of 35 nations in 1975 to discuss European security and cooperation was the
a. European Union.
b. European Economic Community.
c. Helsinki Accords.
d. Maastricht Treaty.

_____ **7.** In 1997 NATO expanded to include
a. Turkey, Poland, and Portugal.
b. Spain, Greece, and the Czech Republic.
c. Serbia, Hungary, and Austria.
d. Poland, Hungary, and the Czech Republic.

_____ **8.** What was the MAIN cause of the breakup of the Soviet Union?
a. economic problems
b. demands for independence
c. foreign intervention
d. military spending

_____ **9.** The campaign of terror and murder aimed at driving the Muslims out of Bosnia was
a. ethnic cleansing.
b. the Final Solution.
c. glasnost.
d. détente.

_____ **10.** Transition to democracy was especially smooth in
a. Czechoslovakia.
b. Romania.
c. Yugoslavia.
d. Albania.

TRUE/FALSE *(2 points each)* Mark each statement *T* if it is true or *F* if it is false.

_____ **1.** The United States economy remained stable throughout the last quarter of the 20th century.

_____ **2.** The reunification of Germany resulted in new prosperity for the German economy.

_____ **3.** The easing of relations between the Soviet Union and the United States during the 1970s was known as détente.

______ **4.** After the terrorist attacks of September 11, 2001, President Bush appointed Donald Rumsfeld to head the office of Homeland Security.

______ **5.** The Commonwealth of Independent States was established to coordinate defense and economic policies among the 15 independent republics of the former Soviet Union.

PRACTICING SKILLS *(5 points each)* The following chart shows the number of refugees from ten countries and where they took asylum. Study the chart and answer the questions that follow.

Origin of Ten Largest Refugee Populations in 1999

Country of Origin	Main Countries of Asylum	Number of Refugees
Afghanistan	Pakistan, Iran	3,580,400
Burundi	Tanzania	568,000
Iraq	Iran	512,800
Sudan	Uganda, D.R., Congo, Ethiopia, Kenya, C.A.R., Chad	490,400
Bosnia-Herzegovina	Yugoslavia, Croatia, USA, Sweden, Netherlands, Denmark	478,300
Somalia	Kenya, Ethiopia, Yemen, Djibouti	447,800
Angola	Zambia, D.R., Congo, Namibia	432,700
Sierra Leone	Guinea, Liberia	400,800
Eritrea	Sudan	376,400
Vietnam	China, USA	370,300

From "Refugees by Numbers 2001 Edition" from *UNHCR: The UN Refugee Agency* website, accessed January 30, 2002, at www.unhcr.ch/cgi-bin/texis/vtx. Copyright © 2002 by the **UN Refugee Agency.** Reprinted by permission of the publisher.

1. How many refugees are there from Vietnam, and where did they go?

____

2. How many people escaped the violence in Bosnia-Herzegovina, and where did they go?

____

COMPOSING AN ESSAY *(20 points)* On a separate sheet of paper, write a brief essay in response to one of the following.

1. Describe the relations between Canada and the United States during the late 1900s.

2. Discuss the challenges faced by Boris Yeltsin during the 1990s.

Name ________________ Class ________________ Date ________________

Chapter Test Form B

Modern Chapter 26 The Superpowers in the Modern Era

SHORT ANSWER *(10 points each)* Provide brief answers for each of the following.

1. What effect did the Vietnam War have on the United States?

2. What was the result of the Maastricht Treaty?

3. What was Margaret Thatcher's approach to economic and foreign policy?

4. What reforms were made under perestroika and glasnost?

5. Explain how the Bush administration sought to fight terrorism using economic, diplomatic, and military means.

PRIMARY SOURCES *(10 points each)* Read this passage from the *Time* magazine description of the opening of the Berlin Wall, and answer the questions that follow.

When the great breach finally came, it started undramatically. . . . Word spread rapidly through both parts of the divided city . . . . At Checkpoint Charlie, in West Berlin's American sector, a crowd gathered well before midnight. . . .

On the stroke of midnight, East Berliners began coming through, some waving their blue ID cards in the air. West Berliners embraced them, offered them champagne and even handed them [money] to finance a celebration. . . .

West Germany, the country most immediately and strongly affected, was both overjoyed and stunned. In Bonn members of the [West German parliament], some with tears in their eyes, spontaneously rose and sang the national anthem. . . .

Running through the joy in West Germany, however, was a not-so-subtle undertone of anxiety. Suppose the crumbling of the Wall increases rather than reduces the flood of permanent refugees? . . . . West Germans fear they simply could not handle so enormous a population shift. . . .

The West German government has done little or no planning to absorb the refugees: it has left the task of resettlement to states, cities and private charity.

1. Why were West Germans happy about the opening of the Wall?

2. Why was the West German government anxious about the opening of the Wall?

COMPOSING AN ESSAY *(30 points)* Write an essay on one of the following subjects. Remember to give examples to support your answer.

1. Discuss the role of nationalist movements in the Western democracies during the late 20th and early 21st centuries.

2. Discuss the role of nationalist movements in Eastern Europe during the late 20th and early 21st centuries.

Name ______________________ Class ______________ Date ____________

Chapter Test Form A

Modern Chapter **27**

The Modern World

FILL IN THE BLANK *(3 points each)* For each of the following statements, fill in the blank with the appropriate name, term, or phrase.

1. ______________________ was a leading American abstract expressionist artist.

2. ______________________ was a Russian exile who founded and directed the New York City Ballet.

3. The Italian director who produced films that criticized social and political injustice was ______________________.

4. The books and poetry of ______________________ explored the African American experience in the South.

5. The plays of East German playwright ______________________ brought attention to their own artificiality.

6. A Soviet cosmonaut named ______________________ was the first person to orbit Earth.

7. The International Space Station that was occupied in November 2000 is called ______________________.

8. ______________________ wrote *Silent Spring* to warn about the effects of pesticides on the environment.

9. ______________________ was the first American to travel in space.

10. ______________________ kill or limit bacterial growth.

UNDERSTANDING IDEAS *(3 points each)* For each of the following, write the letter of the best choice in the space provided.

______ **1.** Andy Warhol's work is an example of
- **a.** abstract expressionism.
- **b.** conceptual art.
- **c.** pop art.
- **d.** the "theater of the absurd."

______ **2.** Samuel Beckett's *Waiting for Godot* is an example of
- **a.** abstract expressionism.
- **b.** conceptual art.
- **c.** pop art.
- **d.** the "theater of the absurd."

______ **3.** Ballet was MOST strongly influenced by artists from
a. the United States.
b. the Soviet Union.
c. France.
d. Germany.

______ **4.** According to the New Wave film directors, the director should
a. avoid making personal statements in a film.
b. use ideas from a commercial studio.
c. act as the auteur of a film.
d. tell an engaging story.

______ **5.** Lasers are NOT used in
a. architecture.
b. medicine.
c. communications.
d. manufacturing.

______ **6.** The genetic code is expected to
a. make it possible for people to live in space.
b. reverse the effects of pollution on the environment.
c. better match people with products.
d. help cure cancer, heart disease, drug addition, and mental illness.

______ **7.** One effect of the explosion at the Chernobyl nuclear power plant was
a. an increase in birth defects.
b. that the use of nuclear power was oulawed.
c. that laws controlling the use of nuclear power were passed.
d. a greater use of coal to generate power.

______ **8.** Urbanization has led to
a. worldwide population decline.
b. overcrowding and pollution.
c. discovery of the genetic code.
d. reduction in poverty and disease.

______ **9.** The interests of the individual are less valued than the interests of the community in some
a. Western democracies.
b. island nations.
c. non-Western countries.
d. the entire world.

______ **10.** Communist rule continues in
a. the Soviet Union.
b. Cuba.
c. Syria.
d. Indonesia.

TRUE/FALSE *(2 points each)* Mark each statement *T* if it is true or *F* if it is false.

______ **1.** Modern architecture is characterized by a single, easy-to-recognize style.

______ **2.** The treatment of Islam in works by Salman Rushdie and Naguib Mahfouz offended some Muslims and led to violence.

______ **3.** Support for the arts in the United States is related to education, increased leisure time, and an expanding cultural awareness.

Name _______________ Class _______________ Date _______________

_______ **4.** The former Soviet Union and the United States are the only countries that have participated in space exploration.

_______ **5.** The international community agrees that the United Nations should enforce the Universal Declaration of Human Rights.

PRACTICING SKILLS *(5 points each)* The following table shows life expectancy and infant mortality rates. Study the chart and answer the questions that follow.

Life Expectancy and Infant Mortality Rates

Life expectancy is the estimated number of years a baby is expected to live.
Infant mortality rates are the estimated number of deaths of children less than one year old per 1,000 children in a year.

Nation	Life Expectancy at Birth		Infant Mortality Rate	
	Male	Female	Male	Female
Bangladesh	60.6	60.8	14.2	15.7
Canada	76.2	81.8	1.6	1.4
Egypt	66.7	69.9	2.8	3.0
Japan	77.8	85.0	0.4	0.3
Russian Federation	60.0	72.5	1.2	0.9
Tajikistan	65.2	70.8	9.0	8.5
United States of America	74.6	80.4	0.4	0.3

1. Which of the countries listed appears to have the poorest medical system? Why?

____

2. Which of the countries listed appears to have the best medical system? Why?

____

COMPOSING AN ESSAY *(20 points)* On a separate sheet of paper, write a brief essay in response to one of the following.

1. Discuss the role of experimentation in modern culture.

2. Discuss the status of democracy in the world at the start of the 21st century.

Name ______________________ Class ______________ Date ______________

Chapter Test Form B

Modern Chapter **27**

The Modern World

SHORT ANSWER *(10 points each)* Provide brief answers for each of the following.

1. What is the relationship between social criticism and modern plays?

2. What is the relationship between social criticism and modern literature?

3. In what ways have miniaturization and computerization changed modern life?

4. What is the cause of reduced biodiversity, and what effect could it have?

5. What are often the roots of human rights violations?

PRIMARY SOURCES *(10 points each)* Read this passage from *Future Shock* by Alvin Toffler and answer the questions that follow.

> *We cannot and must not turn off the switch of technological progress. Only romantic fools babble about returning to a "state of nature." A state of nature is one in which infants shrivel and die for lack of elementary medical care, in which malnutrition stultifies the brain, in which, as Hobbes reminded us, the typical life is "poor, nasty, brutish, and short." To turn our back on technology would be not only stupid but immoral.*
>
> *At the same time, it is undeniably true that we frequently apply new technology stupidly and selfishly. In our haste to milk technology for immediate economic advantage, we have turned our environment into a physical and social tinderbox.*

1. Why, according to the author, is technological progress important?

2. What does the author see as a problem of technological progress?

COMPOSING AN ESSAY *(30 points)* Write an essay on one of the following subjects. Remember to give examples to support your essay.

1. Have science and technology changed the lives of people around the world for the better or for the worse? Explain.

2. Does the future look promising or threatening for people around the world? Explain.

Name ______________________ Class ______________ Date ____________

Unit Test Form A

Modern Unit **6**

The World Since 1945

UNDERSTANDING IDEAS *(3 points each)* For each of the following, write the letter of the best choice in the space provided.

______ **1.** At the end of World War II, the United States and the Soviet Union
- **a.** agreed about war reparations and postwar boundaries.
- **b.** agreed about reparations, but not about boundaries.
- **c.** agreed about boundaries, but not about reparations.
- **d.** disagreed about both reparations and boundaries.

______ **2.** After World War II, the Philippines and Indonesia were
- **a.** newly independent.
- **b.** dictatorships.
- **c.** Communist.
- **d.** socialist.

______ **3.** Conflict among the people of India after the war resulted mainly from differences in
- **a.** religion.
- **b.** education.
- **c.** political ideology.
- **d.** feelings about self-rule.

______ **4.** Which was NOT a problem faced by new African nations?
- **a.** ethnic violence
- **b.** military dictatorships
- **c.** lack of their own cultures
- **d.** limited economies

______ **5.** The contras in Nicaragua
- **a.** were funded by the Soviet Union.
- **b.** were funded by the United States.
- **c.** were helped by Cuba.
- **d.** were helped by China.

______ **6.** Under Castro, Cuba's economy
- **a.** boomed because of the sugar crop.
- **b.** became fully industrialized.
- **c.** was harmed by the U.S. boycott.
- **d.** was harmed by the Soviet boycott.

______ **7.** After World War II, West Germany's economy was
- **a.** unable to grow because Germany was split in two.
- **b.** unable to grow because the Soviet Union removed all materials.
- **c.** able to grow, but more slowly than other Western nations.
- **d.** able to grow more quickly than some other nations.

______ **8.** Starting in the 1970s U.S.
- **a.** heavy industry declined.
- **b.** heavy industry increased.
- **c.** service jobs declined.
- **d.** advanced technology declined.

______ **9.** In the Soviet Union, glasnost
a. freed satellite nations.
b. added satellite nations.
c. allowed dissent.
d. prohibited dissent.

______ **10.** The computer was a result of
a. quantum theory.
b. miniaturization.
c. mechanization.
d. biodiversity.

MATCHING *(3 points each)* In the space provided, write the letter of the name or term that matches each description. Some answers will not be used.

______ **1.** program of economic assistance to European nations after World War II

______ **2.** association of nations formed after World War II to maintain international peace and security

______ **3.** association of Western nations formed after World War II for mutual self-defense

______ **4.** treaty signed in 1954 between France and Vietnam, ending France's war in Vietnam

______ **5.** idea that if one Southeast Asian nation became communist, all the nations would

______ **6.** framework for a peace settlement between Egypt and Israel in 1978

______ **7.** government policy of segregation and economic exploitation in South Africa

______ **8.** economic alliance between Mexico, Canada, and the United States

______ **9.** general improvement in Soviet-American relations in the 1970s

______ **10.** organization of European nations working toward common economic practices

a. apartheid
b. Camp David Accords
c. Contadora Principles
d. détente
e. domino theory
f. European Union
g. Geneva Accords
h. Marshall Plan
i. NAFTA
j. NATO
k. nonalignment
l. United Nations

TRUE/FALSE *(2 points each)* Mark each statement *T* if it is true or *F* if it is false.

______ **1.** Although the Cold War was mostly a war of ideas, local wars occasionally broke out.

______ **2.** Population growth has had little effect on the economies of Asian and African nations.

______ **3.** North and South Vietnam remained separate nations with separate capitals through the end of the 20th century.

______ **4.** The September 11 terrorist attacks on the United States hit only the World Trade Center's Twin Towers.

______ **5.** Eva Perón was a political liability to her husband, and her expenditures led to his overthrow.

PRACTICING SKILLS *(5 points each)* Study the following map of Europe after World War II and answer the questions that follow.

1. Into how many occupation zones was Germany divided after World War II?

____

2. What three countries on the Baltic Sea were entirely taken over by the Soviet Union?

____

COMPOSING AN ESSAY *(20 points)* On a separate sheet of paper, write a brief essay in response to one of the following.

1. What problems did Europe face after World War II?

2. What factors led to the recovery of the Japanese economy after World War II?

Name ______________________ Class ______________ Date ______________

Unit Test Form B

Modern Unit **6**

The World Since 1945

SHORT ANSWER *(10 points each)* Provide brief answers for each of the following.

1. Describe the economies of the Soviet Union and its Eastern European satellite countries after World War II.

2. Describe the economic goal of the Communist Chinese government in the 1950s.

3. Explain the reasons for war between Israel and the Arab nations.

4. Describe two of the economic impacts experienced by the United States following the September 11 terrorist attacks.

5. Describe Margaret Thatcher's economic policies in Britain in the 1980s.

PRIMARY SOURCE *(10 points each)* Read this passage from a report by a Polish journalist who visited Moscow in 1996 and answer the questions that follow.

> *The capitalism that came to Russia at the start of the 1990s looked different from the one constructed in Europe several centuries ago. . . .*
>
> *[T]he advance guard of capitalism that arrived in Moscow was armies of speculators, barons of the black market, gangs of drug dealers, armed aggressive racketeers, brutal, ruthless, powerful mafias. People were terrified. . . .*
>
> *[In 1996] a tremendous social revolution is taking place in Russia; a still weak and contradictory yet nevertheless "normal" society is coming into being here, a society of people with "normal" expectations and aspirations; this country is ruled by a new élite (or a new class), composed of varying groups with varying interests yet with a common desire to maintain stability. . . .*
>
> *Conversations revolved around making money, buying a new car, a better apartment. This gold-rush atmosphere, the sudden potential for everything, this interpretation of freedom to mean simply the chance to acquire goods, is a source of great divisiveness. For the table at which Russian capitalism is banqueting is still small; there aren't many places around it, but everyone wants to pull up a chair.*

From "A Normal Life" by Ryszard Kapuscinski from *Time,* May 27, 1966. Copyright © 1996 by Time, Inc. Reprinted by permission of **Liepman Agency.**

1. How did Russian people feel about capitalism in the early 1990s?

2. How did they feel about capitalism in 1996?

COMPOSING AN ESSAY *(30 points)* Write an essay on one of the following subjects. Remember to give examples to support your answer.

1. Discuss whether the lives of the world's people are better or worse today than in 1945, and explain how and why peoples' lives are better or worse.

2. Compare and contrast the problems, solutions, successes, and failures of the nations that were formerly colonies in Africa, Asia, and Latin America.

Name ______________________ Class ______________ Date ______________

EPILOGUE Chapter Test Form A

The Modern World

MATCHING *(3 points each)* In the space provided, write the letter of the name or term that matches each description. Some answers will not be used.

______ **1.** philosophical movement based on the belief that reason and the scientific method could explain human nature

______ **2.** political philosophy that places the needs of the state above those of the individual

______ **3.** program to help European nations rebuild after World War II

______ **4.** policy of total racial segregation

______ **5.** policy of openness

______ **6.** system in which labor controls production and profits

______ **7.** system in which the central government controls many important powers, while the states and the people keep other powers

______ **8.** the ambition of a powerful nation to dominate another nation

______ **9.** economic system in which the government owns the means of production and operates them for the people

______ **10.** economic system in which individuals control the factors of production

a. apartheid
b. capitalism
c. communism
d. Enlightenment
e. fascism
f. federal system of government
g. glasnost
h. imperialism
i. Marshall Plan
j. nationalism
k. New Deal
l. socialism

UNDERSTANDING IDEAS *(3 points each)* For each of the following, write the letter of the best choice in the space provided.

______ **1.** Which nation did NOT experience a revolution or civil war between 1600 and 1900?
a. England
b. the United States
c. Russia
d. France

______ **2.** The Industrial Revolution involved
a. organizing businesses.
b. freeing colonized nations.
c. creating monarchies.
d. computerization.

______ **3.** The spark that set off World War I was the
a. assassination of the czar of Russia by communist revolutionaries.
b. assassination of the Austria-Hungarian heir by a Serbian nationalist.
c. invasion of Poland by Germany.
d. invasion of Serbia by Austria-Hungary.

______ **4.** The purpose of the League of Nations was to
a. maintain world peace.
b. divide colonies among world powers.
c. draw new borders for occupied nations.
d. collect reparations.

______ **5.** The Great Depression affected
a. only the United States.
b. only North America.
c. only the democracies.
d. the world.

______ **6.** The trade agreement between Canada, Mexico, and the United States is
a. NATO.
b. NAFTA.
c. the New Deal.
d. OPEC.

______ **7.** After World War II, Japan's economy
a. became socialistic.
b. became colonial.
c. recovered quickly.
d. recovered slowly.

______ **8.** In China, Deng Xiaoping
a. began the Cultural Revolution.
b. introduced democratic government.
c. reunited China and Taiwan.
d. introduced economic reforms.

______ **9.** In Eastern Europe, the fall of communism led to
a. stable democratic governments.
b. economic problems.
c. widespread prosperity.
d. the Warsaw Pact.

______ **10.** Which did miniaturization make possible?
a. development of the desktop computer
b. development of the telephone
c. elimination of smallpox
d. space satellites

TRUE/FALSE *(2 points each)* Mark each statement *T* if it is true or *F* if it is false.

______ **1.** During the 19th century, nationalist movements led to the breakup of large, powerful nations.

______ **2.** When Czar Nicholas II abdicated his throne in Russia, the Bolsheviks took over the government.

______ **3.** The British Empire was stronger before World War I than after it.

Name ______________________ Class ______________ Date ____________

______ **4.** The Philippines, Vietnam, Indonesia, and Thailand established communist governments in the 1950s.

______ **5.** After the terrorist attacks of September 11, 2001, President Bush appointed Donald Rumsfeld to head the office of Homeland Security.

PRACTICING SKILLS *(5 points each)* Study the following map of troop strength during World War I and answer the questions that follow.

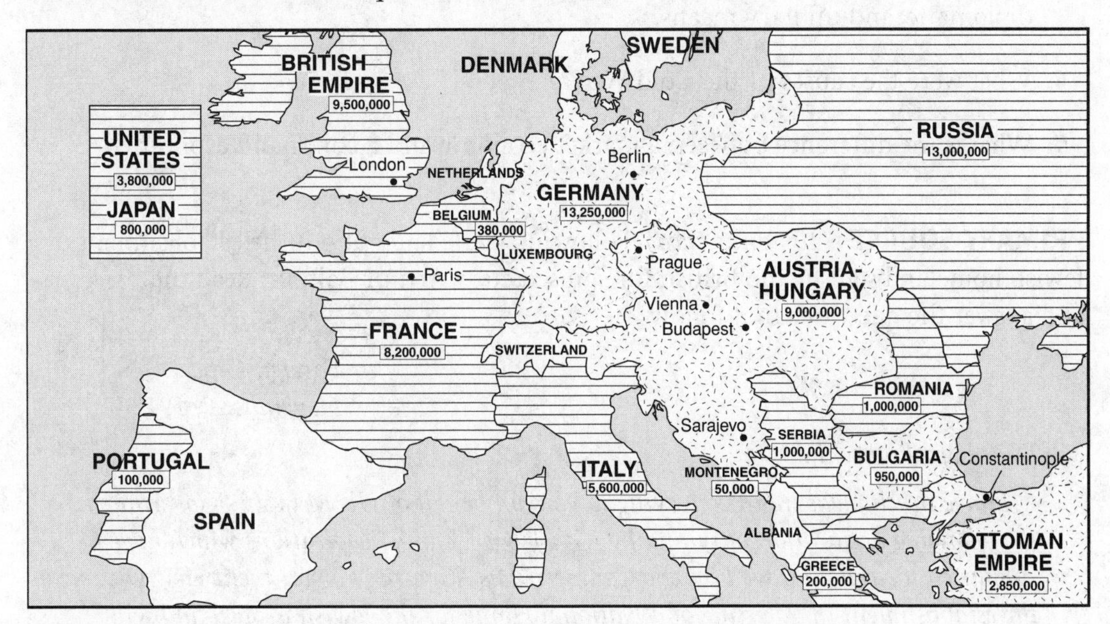

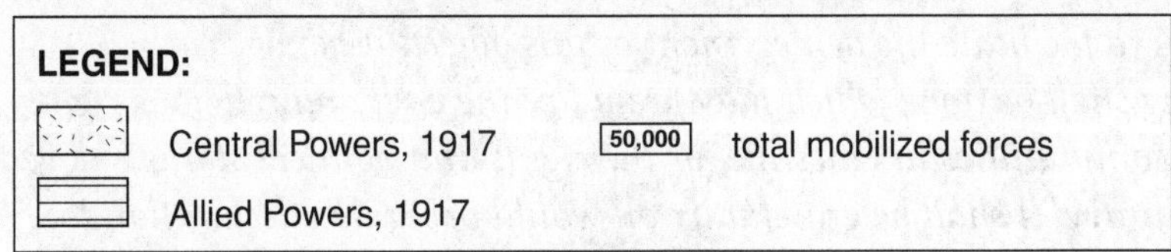

1. What countries belonged to the Allied Powers, and what countries to the Central Powers?

____

2. What countries supplied at least one million soldiers to the war effort?

____

COMPOSING AN ESSAY *(20 points)* On a separate sheet of paper, write a brief essay in response to one of the following.

1. Compare and contrast the British, French, and American civil wars/revolutions.

2. Discuss the changes in China between the late 1800s and today.

Name ______________________ Class ____________ Date ____________

EPILOGUE — Chapter Test Form B

The Modern World

SHORT ANSWER *(10 points each)* Provide brief answers for each of the following.

1. What effect did nationalism have on Europe and Latin America?

2. What is the relationship between nationalism and imperialism?

3. Explain how the Bush administration sought to fight terrorism using economic, diplomatic, and military means.

4. What were the causes of the Cold War?

5. What is the difference between a market economy and a command economy?

PRIMARY SOURCE *(10 points each)* Following is the letter about the establishment of a Jewish homeland sent by the British foreign secretary Arthur Balfour. Read the passage and answer the questions that follow.

Foreign Office
November 2, 1917

Dear Lord Rothschild,

I have much pleasure in conveying to you, on behalf of His Majesty's Government, the following declaration of sympathy with Jewish Zionist aspirations which have been submitted to, and approved by, the Cabinet: "His Majesty's Government view with favor the establishment in Palestine of a National Home for the Jewish people, and will use their best endeavors to facilitate the achievement of this object, it being clearly understood that nothing shall be done which may prejudice the civil and religious rights of existing non-Jewish communities in Palestine, or the rights and political status enjoyed by Jews in any other country." I shall be grateful if you would bring this declaration to the knowledge of the Zionist Federation.

Yours sincerely,
(Signed) ARTHUR JAMES BALFOUR

1. Does this letter promise a homeland for the Jewish people?

2. How might Jews and Arabs have interpreted it?

COMPOSING AN ESSAY *(30 points)* Write an essay on one of the following subjects. Remember to give examples to support your essay.

1. Analyze the roles played by nationalism and imperialism in the modern world.

2. Discuss whether the forces of nationalism and imperialism that created the modern world are likely to have an equal effect in the 21st century and beyond.

Name ______________________ Class ______________ Date ____________

PROLOGUE

Chapter Test Form A

The Ancient World

MATCHING *(3 points each)* In the space provided, write the letter of the name or term that matches each description. Some answers will not be used.

_____ **1.** American people who built earthen mounds in which they buried their dead

_____ **2.** established the first ruling dynasty in China

_____ **3.** first emperor of the Roman Empire

_____ **4.** founder of Buddhism

_____ **5.** poet who wrote the Greek epic poems the *Iliad* and the *Odyssey*

_____ **6.** formed city-states and developed one of the first civilizations in the Fertile Crescent

_____ **7.** philosopher who established a method of learning through questioning

_____ **8.** East African language that has Persian and Arabic influences

_____ **9.** pyramid-building advanced people of the Americas

_____ **10.** ruler who compiled a collection of laws that governed business, work, and property rights

a. Augustus Caesar
b. Hammurabi
c. Homer
d. Hopewell
e. Julius Caesar
f. Mansa Mūsā
g. Maya
h. Shang
i. Siddhartha Gautama
j. Socrates
k. Sumeria
l. Swahili

UNDERSTANDING IDEAS *(3 points each)* For each of the following, write the letter of the best choice in the space provided.

_____ **1.** The first civilizations in India, China, Egypt, and Mesopotamia all
a. were organized into city-states.
b. developed along rivers.
c. were ruled by pharaohs.
d. disappeared for some unknown reason.

_____ **2.** The Greeks' conquests under Alexander the Great mixed Asian and Mediterranean cultures to create a way of life that became known as
a. the golden age.
b. Hellenic culture.
c. Hellenistic culture.
d. the Homeric Age.

_____ **3.** One of the characteristics that makes a culture also a civilization is
a. taking up agriculture.
b. having religious beliefs.
c. domestication of animals.
d. a division of labor.

_____ **4.** The two most powerful and important Greek city-states were
a. Thebes and Parthenon.
b. Parthenon and Sparta.
c. Sparta and Athens.
d. Athens and Thebes.

_____ **5.** Which two peoples depended on a highly developed road network in their empires?
a. Inca and Roman
b. Roman and Hellenistic
c. Hellenistic and Aztec
d. Aztec and Inca

_____ **6.** The Chinese philosophy that emphasizes the importance of family, respect for elders, and respect for the past is
a. Buddhism.
b. Confucianism.
c. Daoism.
d. Legalism.

_____ **7.** Which was NOT a cause of the Roman Empire's decline?
a. government weakness
b. invasions by Germans
c. economic problems
d. the rise of the Byzantine Empire.

_____ **8.** The kingdoms that developed in sub-Saharan Africa were based mainly on
a. trade.
b. agriculture.
c. religion.
d. hunting.

_____ **9.** The rulers responsible for a "golden age" in early India were the
a. Indo-Aryans.
b. Assyrians.
c. Gupta.
d. Harappans.

_____ **10.** Early Chinese civilization reached its height under
a. Zhou and Han rulers.
b. Han and Maurya rulers.
c. Maurya and Qin rulers.
d. Qin and Ming rulers.

TRUE/FALSE *(2 points each)* Mark each statement *T* if it is true or *F* if it is false.

_____ **1.** A series of texts known as the Five Classics were used to educate scholars in ancient Egypt.

_____ **2.** The most important contribution of the ancient Hebrews to Western civilization was ethical monotheism.

_____ **3.** Christianity gained popularity in the Roman Empire because it offered hope to people in a time of instability.

_____ **4.** The Hittites and the Chaldeans lived in two of the more advanced kingdoms of sub-Saharan Africa.

______ **5.** The Aztecs that invaded central Mexico developed a calendar, used mathematics, and practiced human sacrifice.

PRACTICING SKILLS *(5 points each)* The chart below diagrams the development of the major ethnic and racial groups in the world today. Study the chart and answer the questions that follow.

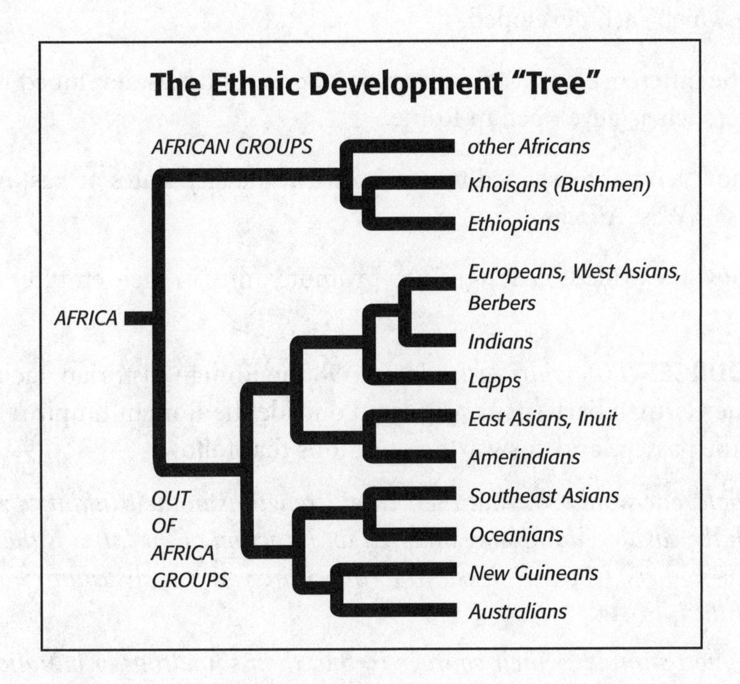

1. According to the chart, what is the geographic origin of all of the races and ethnic groups that exist in the world today?

____

2. Are the original peoples of East Asia (China, Japan, etc.) more closely related to the peoples of Southeast Asia (Vietnam, Thailand, etc.) or to the peoples of Europe? Explain how you know.

____

COMPOSING AN ESSAY *(20 points)* On a separate sheet of paper, write a brief essay in response to one of the following.

1. Identify beliefs that early Hindus and Buddhists shared as well as beliefs that were unique to each religion.

2. Describe the growth of democracy in ancient Greece.

Name ________________________ Class ______________ Date ____________

PROLOGUE Chapter Test Form B

The Ancient World

SHORT ANSWER *(10 points each)* Provide brief answers for each of the following.

1. Explain why early peoples who created towns and cities would also be likely to have developed some form of government.
2. Explain why the first civilizations developed in river valleys and name the four river valleys in which each developed.
3. Explain the difference between a direct democracy, such as developed in Athens, and a republic, such as developed in Rome.
4. Explain how geography shaped the economy of the city-states of East Africa and the kingdoms of West Africa.
5. Explain how Inca rule was designed to promote unity in their empire.

PRIMARY SOURCES *(10 points each)* In A.D. 98 the Roman historian Tacitus described the army of the German barbarians who lived outside the Roman Empire's northern border. Read the passage and answer the questions that follow.

> *On the whole, one would say that their chief strength is in their infantry, which fights along with the cavalry; admirably adapted to the action of the latter is the swiftness of certain foot-soldiers, who are picked from the entire youth of the country and stationed in front of the line. . . .*
>
> *And what most stimulates their courage is, that their squadrons or battalions, instead of being formed by chance . . . are composed of families and clans. Close by them, too, are those dearest to them, so that they hear the shrieks of women, the cries of infants. They are to every man the most sacred witnesses of his bravery—they are his most generous applauders. The soldier brings his wounds to mother and wife, who shrink not from counting or even demanding them and who administer both food and encouragement to the combatants. . .*

1. What factors does Tacitus identify in the organization of the Germans' army that he believes account for its success?
2. In what ways does Tacitus believe German women contribute to the bravery of German soldiers in battle?

COMPOSING AN ESSAY *(30 points)* Write an essay on one of the following subjects. Remember to use examples to support your essay.

1. Identify the achievements of the early Egyptians, Indians, Chinese, Maya, and Aztec in mathematics, medicine, science, and technology.
2. Explain how the growth of agriculture led to the development of civilization.

Chapter 1

TEST FORM A

Fill in the Blank

1. culture
2. Neolithic agricultural revolution
3. hominids
4. irrigation
5. domestication
6. civilization
7. artifact
8. division of labor
9. nomads
10. gathering

Understanding Ideas

1. c
2. a
3. a
4. c
5. a
6. d
7. c
8. b
9. d
10. b

True/False

1. F
2. T
3. F
4. F
5. T

Practicing Skills

1. Africa
2. to Europeans, because East Asians and Europeans come from the same main "branch" of the "tree," while Southeast Asians developed along a different main "branch"

Composing an Essay

1. Developing a form of language helped people to communicate, which allowed them to work better together in groups. Written language made it easier to pass on information and ideas among peoples and over time.
2. As the number of people living in a place grew larger, society would become more complicated. Leaders would be needed, and it would be more important to have rules for living together. These things comprise government.

TEST FORM B

Short Answer

1. A culture consists of the beliefs, knowledge, and living patterns a group of people develop. A civilization is a culture whose living patterns include towns and forms of government, the ability to produce extra food, a division of labor, and often a calendar and writing system.
2. better tools and weapons, such as spear-throwers; cave art; migrated, lived in, adapted to, and succeeded in a variety of environments
3. Floods and other water from these rivers helped to grow enough food to increase population and turn small villages into towns and cities.
4. The invention of the plow turned farming into a man's job. Women's loss of control over food production made them less powerful in ancient society.
5. They helped groups exchange extra food and goods for other products and also passed along ideas from one group to another.

Primary Sources

1. the arrow symbols and emphasis on game animals in these paintings
2. that these paintings may have had religious significance or showed an appreciation for art

Composing an Essay

1. Agriculture enabled groups to produce their own food, which allowed them to give up nomadic hunting and gathering and settle in one place. As farming methods improved, it took fewer farmers to feed larger populations. Over time, this led to a division of labor. Some people developed special skills such as making tools, engaging in trade, and creating calendars to help farmers and writing systems to help traders. These developments, along with the population growth that eventually turned their villages into towns and cities, advanced the cultures of such groups to civilizations.

2. Paleolithic peoples were hunter-gatherers who lived in small groups. Their diet consisted of wild plants and game animals they were able to kill. They had stone tools. As their technology improved, they became better hunters and moved over great distances in search of food. Neolithic peoples also had stone tools. But they had better technology and their tools were more specialized. This enabled some of them to scrape the ground and plant seeds in the first attempts at growing their own food. Such people gave up their nomadic ways, settled in villages, and domesticated animals as another source of food.

Chapter 2

TEST FORM A

Matching

1. k
2. g
3. f
4. h
5. a
6. l
7. i
8. d
9. c
10. j

Understanding Ideas

1. c
2. d
3. b
4. a
5. c
6. a
7. d
8. b
9. a
10. c

True/False

1. F
2. F
3. T
4. T
5. F

Practicing Skills

1. B
2. the location of Babylon

Composing an Essay

1. Both worshipped many gods, and the gods of each were associated with nature and heavenly bodies. Religion and religious beliefs were central to each society. Each believed in an afterlife and buried objects with the dead. But, unlike the Egyptians, the Sumerians did not mummify their dead and did not believe in judgment after death.
2. The Nile River, with its predictable annual floods, provided the water and rich soil that allowed the food surpluses, population growth, and division of labor that led to, and were characteristic of, an advanced civilization. At the same time, deserts to the east and west isolated and protected the Egyptians, which also promoted their civilization's growth.

TEST FORM B

Short Answer

1. In a money economy, a buyer pays for goods or services with coins or similar units of value. In a barter economy, the buyer "pays" for goods or services by providing other goods or services in return.
2. Government of both peoples was guided by a written set of laws. Religions differed in that Babylonians worshipped many gods, while Hebrews practiced monotheism.
3. Their land was not very suitable for agriculture, and mountains discouraged their expansion to the east. Their lumber resources and coastal location made trade a good alternative.
4. Both passed religious teachings to their peoples—Zoroaster to the Persians and Moses to the Hebrews—that were based on ideas of good, evil, and proper behavior.
5. The region's agricultural resources attracted many outside peoples through the centuries. Over time, each invader gradually weakened, and new invasions occurred.

Primary Sources

1. It is a prayer to the god Osiris, the judge of the dead, appealing for a favorable judgment and afterlife.
2. It was important, as shown by the prayer's citation of proper behaviors toward land and livestock, as a reason for admission to a happy afterlife.

Composing an Essay

1. Both the Sumerians and the Egyptians developed advanced agricultural societies

in the fertile valleys of the Tigris-Euphrates and Nile rivers, respectively. Both societies practiced irrigation, developed a division of labor, produced metal and other objects, and traded their goods and food with distant peoples. Both developed impressive architecture—for example, the Egyptians built pyramids of stone blocks, and the Sumerians built brick ziggurats. Each made important scientific and technological contributions—for example, the Egyptians' knowledge of the human body, the Sumerians' use of the arch and wheel, and each groups' numbering system. Both peoples also had a writing system and an educational system. They both were polytheistic, and religion was very important in each culture.

2. Trade allowed the mixing of goods, ways of life, beliefs, technology, and other ideas among the cultures of the region. For example, the Phoenicians became skilled metal workers using techniques they learned through their trade with the Egyptians. The lumber they produced and traded with other peoples promoted building throughout the ancient world. Through trade, they also spread alphabetical writing—an improvement on the earlier picture-based systems—throughout the Mediterranean region, along with elements of Egyptian and Babylonian culture. Later, Lydian traders spread the concept and use of coins. This helped replace the traditional, but economically restrictive, barter system with a more sophisticated method of exchange.

Chapter 3

TEST FORM A

Matching

1. e
2. c
3. l
4. d
5. i
6. j
7. b
8. a
9. k
10. g

Understanding Ideas

1. b
2. c
3. d
4. b
5. c
6. a
7. c
8. d
9. a
10. c

True/False

1. F
2. T
3. T
4. T
5. F

Practicing Skills

1. the Koreans because it spread to Japan from Korea
2. no, because it did not have to spread as far to reach Ceylon

Composing an Essay

1. Both believed in the eternal nature of the soul and in people's continued rebirth, or reincarnation, and new lives during which they gain the knowledge and experience they need to reach a state of enlightenment, salvation, and peace called nirvana. However, the Buddha did not accept the Hindu gods, the sacredness of the Vedas, the elevated position of the Brahmins, or the caste system in general.
2. The collapse of both empires resulted from a combination of internal division and external threats—the Mauryan Empire ended as Aśoka's sons fought over the throne and northern and eastern invaders attacked the empire, while decentralization and central Asian invaders combined to end the Gupta Empire. One contrast is that the last Maurya ruler was assassinated by an internal rival, while the last Gupta ruler depleted the treasury fighting external invaders.

TEST FORM B

Short Answer

1. The Indus River valley provided the fertile soil and water that led to the growth of agriculture, population and urban growth, and a division of labor that produced crafts and trade.

2. They migrated to India from north of the Black and Caspian seas after about 1750 B.C. Unlike the darker, settled Harappans, they were light-skinned and nomadic herders.
3. The Vedas are the religious works of the Indo-Aryans, and the Upanishads are later, written explanations of the Vedic religion. Together these works formed the basis for the development of Hinduism.
4. Power was held by local rulers called rajas until the Magadha kingdom tried to unify rule in the 500s B.C. The Persian Empire also ruled part of India for a time. Then, Magadha regained control and held power until the Maurya Empire was established.
5. Women had some protections but did not have equal rights with men. They could not own property or study sacred writings. They had to obey their fathers or husbands or, if widowed, their sons. Polygyny and suttee were common.

Primary Sources

1. Hindu, because of the reference to Brahman (Brahma) the Hindu god, which Buddhism does not accept
2. The passage indicates that Brahman is indistinguishable from the world around him, which he created. This is the essence of monism.

Composing an Essay

1. The Harappans of northwestern India developed a thriving urban, farming, and craft culture until they were supplanted by nomadic Indo-Aryan invaders who brought their own gods, eventually settled in villages, and took up farming, too. Protected by geography against invasion from the north or unification, southern peoples developed diverse lifestyles related to their locations and resources. Some were hunter-gatherers, while others farmed, and still others, who lived in coastal areas, depended on trade.
2. The Mauryans standardized weights and measures, established standards for physicians, and dug mines and centers for spinning and weaving. The Gupta Empire was a "golden age" in Indian culture. Drama flourished and architects designed great Hindu temples. The Buddhist university Nalanda became a center of learning. Achievements in mathematics included understanding the concepts of negative numbers, zero, and infinity; the use of algebra; and the invention of Arabic numerals. Astronomers identified several planets, understood the rotation of the earth, and accurately predicted eclipses of the sun and moon. Medical advances included bone setting, plastic surgery, and the development of inoculation and vaccines.

Chapter 4

TEST FORM A

Fill in the Blank

1. Qin
2. Confucius
3. loess
4. acupuncture
5. Mandate of Heaven
6. civil service system
7. dikes
8. yin, yang

Understanding Ideas

1. b
2. d
3. a
4. c
5. d
6. b
7. d
8. c
9. a
10. c

True/False

1. T
2. F
3. T
4. T
5. T
6. F
7. F
8. F

Practicing Skills

1. Qin
2. Chu

Composing an Essay

1. China's size, the mountains to the west, northwest, and southwest, and deserts such as the Gobi isolated early peoples from most outsiders. This allowed a distinctive Chinese culture to develop

relatively free of outside influences and gave the Chinese a strong sense of identity. The lack of contact also gave Chinese the belief that they were culturally superior to foreign peoples, whom they called barbarians.

2. The Shang came to power by invading China. The Shang and Zhou dynasties both fell because of the prolonged pressures of warlike neighboring states. In fact, the Zhou were responsible for overthrowing the Shang. Invasions eventually weakened the Zhou, however, and powerful neighbors called the Warring States fought for power. The Qin were victorious in this struggle and founded a new dynasty. Unlike the Shang and Zhou, the Qin dynasty fell from within when a ruler's policies angered the people, causing them to revolt and overthrow the empire.

TEST FORM B

Short Answer

1. As people built dikes against flooding, the river rose due to silt build-up until it was higher than the surrounding land. Then when it flooded, the water could not return to the river and remained covering the fields.
2. Great distances and geographic features, like mountains and deserts, caused early Chinese civilization to develop in relative isolation. They had little contact with, or knowledge of, outsiders. This gave them a strong sense of identity and feelings of superiority.
3. It was a largely agricultural civilization, so the Shang worshipped gods of natural forces and held religious festivals related to agriculture. Their ancestor worship was related to their use of oracle bones.
4. Women had few legal rights and powers compared to men, and could not own property. When a woman married, she became like a servant in the household of her husband's family, where the father ruled. But once the wife had children, especially sons, she gained respect and power in the family and household.
5. Chinese astronomers built instruments to track the planets, as well as inventing sundials and water clocks to track time. They improved the accuracy of calendars, developed medicines based on herbs and minerals, and introduced acupuncture. Their invention of paper and printing changed the world.

Primary Sources

1. by individuals bringing order first to their minds, and then to successively larger units around them, like their personal lives and their families
2. Confucianism, which taught that order and good government could be achieved through people performing their roles in society, including virtuous behavior, self-improvement, and focus on the family

Composing an Essay

1. The Han dynasty illustrates Confucianism because Han emperors stressed government by well-educated officials and an interest in the happiness and welfare of the people. For example, Lin Ch'e expanded civil service and established a university to educate would-be officials in an attempt to improve the quality of government. His creation of the leveling program showed his concern for the welfare of his people. The rule of the Qin, on the other hand, was harsh. Qin rulers such as Cheng enforced harsh laws, like those which required forced labor for public works. The Qin executed scholars who opposed the government, and they showed little concern for the people's happiness. This is characteristic of Legalism, which taught that people were selfish and untrustworthy and had to be controlled.
2. Opinions will vary, and students' responses should show reasoned judgment and good use of evidence. Under the Shang, Chinese arts such as pottery developed, silk production occurred, and a writing system and calendars were created. The Qin advanced China's security by completing the Great Wall. The Han encouraged advances in Chinese government and trade—some of which, like civil

service, began under the Qin—by expanding and improving civil service and improving the calendar and spreading the use of a new invention—paper. The Han also increased trade, most notably along the Silk Road that connected China and the Mediterranean region.

Unit 1

TEST FORM A

Understanding Ideas

1. d
2. c
3. a
4. b
5. b
6. b
7. d
8. c
9. d
10. a

Matching

1. h
2. l
3. j
4. c
5. d
6. f
7. b
8. a
9. k
10. e

True/False

1. T
2. F
3. F
4. T
5. F

Practicing Skills

1. Europe
2. north and northwest out of Africa into Europe and east into Asia

Composing an Essay

1. The Neolithic agricultural revolution, which was the long process of shifting from food gathering to food producing, had a great impact on the development of the elements of civilization. Early peoples, who were nomads, gradually learned that they could plant seeds from the plants they gathered for food and grow it themselves. A dependable food supply meant that they no longer had to roam in search of food and could settle in villages to farm. As farming increased their food supply, they could feed larger numbers of people, and villages grew into towns and cities.

   Large groups led to the need for government, to regulate their living together. A larger food supply through farming also meant that everyone did not have to be involved with finding or providing food all the time. This allowed people to perform other kinds of jobs, and a division of labor developed. As communities became larger and more complex, people needed a way other than speech to pass on information. This resulted in the development of written language. In addition, calendars developed because farmers needed to know when the seasons would change.

2. The Egyptians developed a calendar based on their observations of the stars and the moon. They also developed a number system based on 10, similar to today's decimal system, as well as fractions, and used geometry to build their pyramids. They also used herbs and medicines to treat disease and developed the mummification process for preserving the dead.

   Early Indian medicine included plastic surgery, and physicians developed the technique of inoculation. They also understood infection long before Western medicine. Like the Egyptians, Indian astronomers also studied the stars. They knew that the Earth rotated and accurately predicted eclipses. Indian mathematicians understood the concepts of negative numbers, zero, and infinity. They also introduced Arabic numerals and used algebra.

   The early Chinese made similar accomplishments, doing mathematical calculations to produce an accurate calendar. They built instruments to track the movements of the planets and invented the sundial and water clock. Like the Egyptians, they developed medicines based on herbs and they also introduced the technique of acupuncture. The Chinese invention of paper replaced Egyptian papyrus as the main writing material. The Chinese also invented the printing process.

TEST FORM B

Short Answer

1. They dig up and study the artifacts that a people left behind. They combine their study of the artifacts with their knowledge of geography and climate of the region to make educated guesses about how the people lived.
2. A culture is the set of beliefs, knowledge, and living patterns a people develop. A civilization is a culture characterized by permanent settlement, ability to produce surplus food, and a division of labor. Therefore, a culture may or may not be a civilization. But, by definition, no civilization can exist without a culture.
3. They developed a society that was based on trade. Through this trade they spread the influences of Egyptian and Mesopotamian civilization throughout the Mediterranean region. They also spread their alphabet, which was adopted by the Greeks.
4. Answers may include writing systems, calendars, and/or related advances in astronomy and mathematics. Reasons should center around the need to collect, use, disseminate, and preserve information in order to foster agricultural and commercial development.
5. Both peoples were fierce warriors who invaded to establish their empires. Both were the first to effectively govern a large empire in their region. In each, a ruler headed a well-organized bureaucracy of government officials. Significant cultural advances occurred under each rule.

Primary Sources

1. People should love, serve, and revere their parents and elders. Those who do this will be loyal and obedient citizens.
2. represents Confucianism; from the emphasis on reverence for parents and ancestors, loyal and obedient government service, and the importance of the family as a social unit

Composing an Essay

1. (Accept any of the following.) Judaism holds the belief that there is only one God. The major tenets of the religion, which include the Ten Commandments, are outlined in the Torah. The Jewish religion places a high value on proper conduct and is sometimes known as ethical monotheism.

   Hindus are monistic, believing that God—in all incarnations—and creation are one. A central belief in Hinduism is that people must recognize that the world they see is illusion in order to be saved, and that souls are reincarnated many times in their efforts to reach this perfection. The caste system plays an important role, as do dharma, one's moral duty in life, and karma, the good or bad force created by people's actions.

   Buddhism also accepts reincarnation, but not the Hindu gods. It also rejects the caste system, believing that virtue cannot be inherited. Founded by the Buddha, Buddhism holds that all human life involves suffering, that desire is the root of suffering, and that letting go of desire leads to salvation. Theravada Buddhists follow the Buddha's teachings. Mahayana Buddhists view the Buddha as a god and savior.
2. The Egyptian civilization that developed along the Nile was separated from the east and west by vast expanses of desert. This provided the isolation that allowed the civilization to develop relatively free from invasion and conquest by other peoples, and the outside influences such events bring. As a result, Egyptian civilization was unique and reached a state of advancement that was unparalleled at the time. The pyramids are the most visible and best-known example of this.

   The desert was also a geographic factor in China's development. The Gobi, along with the mountains and the vast size of the region, kept the outside influences in China at a minimum. The civilization that developed viewed China as the only civilized land and considered other peoples to be culturally inferior "barbarians." As with Egypt, Chinese art and other cultural characteristics—such as the roles of family and ancestors in Chinese society—were culturally unique and did not show the influences of outside ideas and values to the degree that characterized development in Mesopotamia and India.

Chapter 5

TEST FORM A

Fill in the Blank

1. Persia
2. Solon
3. aristocracies
4. Persia
5. helots
6. epics
7. trade
8. Athens
9. Pericles
10. Homer

Understanding Ideas

1. c
2. b
3. a
4. c
5. d
6. b
7. a
8. c
9. d
10. b

True/False

1. T
2. F
3. T
4. F
5. T

Practicing Skills

1. the Assembly
2. representative democracy, because they are elected by the citizens (Assembly) to govern for them

Composing an Essay

1. Hoplites were an infantry of commoners that was formed to help the aristocrats fight. The hoplites became more powerful fighters than the aristocrats, and as their importance to defending the city-state grew, they demanded more say in its government. Tyrants were leaders who illegally took power and had the people's support because they ruled in the people's best interests. The tyrants weakened the nobles' power. When some tyrants became unjust, they were overthrown. In some city-states, the former supporters of these former tyrants decided to try ruling themselves.
2. The Peloponnesian War began when Pericles tried to unite the Greek city-states under Athenian rule. Tensions grew between Athens and rival Sparta until war broke out in 431 B.C. The war lasted 27 years and other city-states were drawn in—as was Persia, which helped Sparta. After a weakened Athens finally surrendered, a struggle broke out between the other city-states for control of Greece. This resulted in a long period of instability in Greece.

TEST FORM B

Short Answer

1. Trade was encouraged by the long coastline and the seas that connected Greece with Italy and Asia Minor. Trade inside Greece was discouraged by mountains and the shortness of rivers.
2. The mountains separated the Greeks and, along with the short rivers, discouraged interaction. Politically, the polis or city-state, was an organization that promoted independence and regional, rather than national, loyalty and identity.
3. It was a group of city-states allied against the threat of Persian invasion. This created unity but became a divisive factor when members resisted Athenian attempts to control the league, resulting in a long war and a long period of disunity after.
4. In a representative democracy, people elect their leaders to make decisions and govern for them. In a direct democracy, the people make the decisions of government themselves.
5. Both had three classes: citizens, called "equals" in Sparta, at the top, with most of the power; slaves, called "helots" in Sparta, on the bottom; and a middle group, called "half citizens" in Sparta and "metics" in Athens, that was free but politically powerless.

Primary Sources

1. to instill discipline, obedience, and bravery
2. in Sparta; because of its references to discipline, obedience, bravery, and training for later dangers and battle, which are all characteristic of the great importance Sparta attached to military service by young males

Composing an Essay

1. At first the city-states were ruled by kings who were dependent on wealthy landowners to form armies and defend them. These landowners became nobles who eventually overthrew the kings and took power themselves. As city-states became prosperous, commoners could afford to arm themselves and help the nobles with defense. Eventually these hoplites became stronger than the nobles, and they began to demand a say in government. In many city-states, tyrants, who had the support of the commoners, seized power and ruled on behalf of the people. As some tyrants' rule became unjust, they were overthrown by their supporters, who began to think that the people could and should rule themselves. At first, this process was not very democratic, as only some residents chose the leaders, and even fewer were allowed to hold office. However, democracy grew over time, especially in Athens, where eligibility for office-holding expanded, as did the number of people who had a direct voice in governing and in choosing these officeholders.
2. Answers will vary. Those who view it as democratic may suggest that drawings for office eliminate the possibility of voters being swayed by a candidate's wealth or status. Those who do not view the process as democratic may argue that it puts leaders who may have absolutely no support among the people into office by the "luck of the draw."

Chapter 6

TEST FORM A

Matching

1. d
2. k
3. f
4. h
5. a
6. g
7. i
8. b
9. j
10. c

Understanding Ideas

1. b
2. c
3. b
4. d
5. a
6. b
7. c
8. a
9. b
10. d

True/False

1. F
2. T
3. F
4. T
5. T

Practicing Skills

1. wine and slaves
2. Major trade routes from India, Arabia, and east and north Africa ended there.

Composing an Essay

1. He tried to fuse the two by spreading Greek culture to the places he conquered in the old Persian Empire and by encouraging his soldiers to marry Persian women. Both policies were aimed at hastening the fusion of the two cultures because the perpetuation of cultural differences would weaken the unity of the empire.
2. Answers will vary but should cite and explain the significance of three of the following: Democritus's development of atomic theory; the Pythagorean Theorem; Euclid's contributions to geometry; Archimedes's calculation of pi; Hipparchus's use of trigonometry to predict eclipses; and Archimedes's application of mathematics to the development of machines like levers, pulleys, and screws.

TEST FORM B

Short Answer

1. (Accept any two of the following.) Artists glorified human beings by creating statues of people who exhibited strength, beauty, and other valued qualities. They created temples and other public buildings to honor the gods and bring attention and glory to their polis. They expressed the Greek belief that beauty should be useful by creating functional art, such as vases, that had a purpose.
2. Unlike most teachers, whose students learned by memorization, Socrates held that students should learn by thinking for themselves. He achieved this by asking questions that forced students to test their values and ideas. Some of these questions made public officials and other powerful people look foolish, and they accused Socrates of corrupting young minds.
3. (Accept any two of the following.) He tried to involve conquered peoples in helping him govern them. He spread Greek culture. He encouraged cultural diffusion by asking his soldiers to marry Persian women and marrying two himself. The reason for these tactics was to minimize differences and division between the conquerors and the conquered.
4. (Accept any three of the following.) They provided a means for social criticism and commentary. Traditional values could be defended. War could be opposed. Religious questions could be examined. Old beliefs and ideas could be questioned. New ideas and their proponents could be mocked.
5. The Cynics taught that the goal in life should be to live simply, without regard for pleasure, wealth, or status. The Epicureans taught that the goal in life should be to seek pleasure and avoid pain.

Primary Sources

1. Alexander, because he did what Plato only wrote about doing
2. No, because he views them as uncivilized, and Hellenistic values were more favorable toward peoples of different cultures

Composing an Essay

1. As trade expanded across the Hellenistic world, opportunities for wealth increased. This made more people prosperous, and the middle ranks grew. With this prosperity and growth, education became more widespread, new values took hold, and women gained new rights and status in society. New ideas arrived from Asia, Egypt, and other places. The concept of "Greek" culture was altered to include the influences of regions now within the empire. Alexandria and other centers of Hellenistic trade also became centers of science and learning that combined the Greeks' knowledge with the contributions of those formerly great civilizations. As traditional Greek culture faded and the importance of the local polis declined, some people turned to religions and to philosophies like Skepticism, Stoicism, and Cynicism in a search for identity and meaning amidst all this change.
2. Answers will vary but should show reasoned judgment and an understanding of the influence of Greek history and politics. For example, the city-states had successfully opposed invasions before, such as by the Persians. The Spartans, in particular, with their long military tradition, might have felt they could defeat Philip. In addition, Demosthenes was an Athenian. The city-states were fiercely independent, and many would have resisted any suggestion that they organize a common defense, especially under Athenian leadership. That had been tried before, in the Delian League, and had resulted in tensions, rivalries, and eventually war among the city-states. On the other hand, those who favored the unification of Greece might have welcomed Philip's invasion instead of opposing him.

Chapter 7

TEST FORM A

Fill in the Blank

1. Punic Wars
2. aqueducts
3. Greek
4. Julius Caesar
5. Conflict of the Orders
6. Vandals
7. dictator
8. Pax Romana
9. Constantine
10. gladiators

Understanding Ideas

1. b
2. c
3. a
4. d
5. a
6. c
7. b
8. c
9. d
10. c

True/False

1. F
2. F
3. T
4. F
5. F

Practicing Skills

1. They were cremated.
2. that the Romans adopted the burial practices of these cultures

Composing an Essay

1. The Senate was the most powerful governing body. It controlled public funds and set foreign policy. Popular assemblies of citizens voted on laws, served in courts, and elected three types of magistrates: consuls, who ran the government and commanded the army in peacetime; praetors, who oversaw the legal system in peacetime and commanded the army in time of war; and censors, who registered citizens according to wealth, appointed senators, and oversaw the public morals. Tribunes elected by the assemblies oversaw the actions of the Senate and other public officials.
2. At first, the Romans granted full or partial citizenship to nearby people, depending on their distance from Rome. This gave them some or all of the rights that were enjoyed by Romans. More distant peoples were made allies of Rome and kept their independence. As the empire grew and conquered peoples became more distant and "un-Roman," these policies changed. Newly-added peoples were not offered citizenship or independence. Instead they were governed by Roman officials as subjects of Rome. This change caused such peoples to be less loyal to Rome, which weakened the unity of the empire.

TEST FORM B

Short Answer

1. The Twelve Tables were the first set of written laws in Rome, which were displayed in the public square. By putting the laws on record and making them accessible, the patricians were giving up power because, until then, only they knew what the laws were. Gaining knowledge of the laws they were living under empowered the plebeians.
2. At first, the Romans granted full or partial citizenship to nearby people, depending on their distance from Rome. More distant peoples were made allies and kept their independence. As the empire continued to grow, Rome stopped these practices and began to treat newly-conquered peoples as subjects.
3. He believed that the empire had grown too large for one ruler and that if it were divided and a co-emperor named, each half could be managed more effectively.
4. As Rome's economy weakened, and invaders threatened, rule became more harsh as emperors tried to restore the empire's stability. The resulting growth of poverty and the loss of rights, freedoms, and security made life more difficult. Christianity offered hope and comfort to people affected by these changes by expressing the idea that the poor and troubled were blessed and promising a better future in the afterlife.
5. The Romans built a network of bridges and paved roads throughout their empire. This promoted communication and trade and facilitated control because it allowed troops to be moved to trouble spots quickly.

Primary Sources

1. The observation that, after facing the animals, they are being turned over to the "spectators" to be burned, lashed, and killed suggests that executions are taking place.
2. His report that he experienced the reverse of the fun and relaxation he expected, coupled with his report of the spectators' blood lust, indicates his disapproval.

Composing an Essay

1. The functions of government were divided among three main groups: the magistrates, the assemblies of citizens, and the Senate. A complex system of checks and balances was interwoven among and within these groups. The magistrates ran the day-to-day government. But their power was checked by the assemblies, which elected them, passed the laws they administered, and served as courts of law. In addition, the assemblies elected tribunes, who could veto certain actions of the magistrates. Among the magistrates, two consuls served as chief executives, but each had veto power over the other. Although the consuls commanded the army in peacetime, in time of war this power belonged to other magistrates, called praetors, who in peacetime headed the courts and interpreted the laws passed by the assemblies. Besides depending on election by the assemblies, the praetors' military power was balanced by the power of the assemblies to make war and peace. The Senate served as a check on this entire system through its control over the republic's finances. It also balanced the military power of the magistrates and war power of the assemblies by setting the republic's foreign policy. However, the Senate's power was balanced by a third type of magistrate—the censors—who appointed its members. But censors, like the other magistrates, depended on election by the assemblies, thus bringing this complex system of checks and balances full circle.
2. Answers will vary. Students should note that Pax Romana means "Roman Peace." Supporters of the "appropriate" position might argue that, while fighting continued along the edges of the empire as it expanded, the situation within the empire itself—and especially with regard to political conditions in Rome—was one of relative peace and stability. The internal divisions, civil wars, and other military and political crises that had marked the decline of the republic and the rule of the First and Second Triumvirates were quieted by the accession of Augustus in 27 B.C. His rule—and those of the three Flavian Emperors and the Five Good Emperors who came later—brought stability to the empire for most of the next 200 years. Some invasions did occur late in the period, and there were instances of "bad" rule—such as in the 50 years after Augustus's death—but these were minor events compared to the instability that came before, and the internal unrest and invasions that would follow. Students who deem the label "inappropriate" may focus on the exceptions noted, as well as on the military expansion of the empire as not indicative of a period of peace.

Chapter 8

TEST FORM A

Matching

1. g	**6.** h
2. j	**7.** b
3. d	**8.** c
4. k	**9.** a
5. l	**10.** f

Understanding Ideas

1. a	**6.** d
2. c	**7.** b
3. b	**8.** d
4. a	**9.** c
5. b	**10.** a

True/False

1. T
2. F
3. T
4. T
5. F

Practicing Skills

1. at Meroë
2. from North Africa in a generally southern direction into the interior

Composing an Essay

1. The East African societies developed on the Indian Ocean. In this location they came into contact with Arab and Asian merchants who sailed the ocean conducting business. The merchants were attracted by the Africans' gold, ivory, and other goods. Many of them settled on the coast, and trade became a major economic activity in this part of Africa. At the same time, Islam became important in East Africa, as these traders spread their faith to their African trading partners.
2. In West Africa, peoples who lived along the routes that brought salt from the Sahara into the Sahel developed economies that were based on trade. The northern traders wanted gold that was mined further south in West Africa. The West Africans willingly made this exchange because they needed salt to preserve their food. In places where the gold-for-salt exchange took place, cities like Timbuktu developed and became major centers of commerce and trade. At the same time, the West Africans adopted the Islamic faith that the salt merchants brought with them from North Africa.

TEST FORM B

Short Answer

1. In matrilineal societies, families are organized around the mother's relatives. This means that a person would trace his or her ancestry through the mother's side, and property would pass to children from mothers instead of fathers.
2. Penetration of the interior on major rivers was blocked by rapids. The harsh Sahara made it difficult for northern traders to reach the interior. Jungle made travel in or through some interior regions difficult.
3. Christianity began to spread after King ʻĒzānā of Aksum converted and made it the kingdom's official religion around A.D. 350. Islam was spread in East and West Africa by Arab, Persian, and other Muslim traders.
4. Great Zimbabwe was a major African fort and trading center on the Indian Ocean in East Africa in the 1300s and 1400s. Timbuktu was a major commercial city and cultural center in West Africa during the same period of time, and was also a leading center of Islamic learning.
5. He made a pilgrimage from his kingdom of Mali to Mecca, the Islamic holy city in Arabia. The size and dress of his group, and the gold they carried, showed others that a great and wealthy civilization existed in West Africa. His development of Timbuktu into a major learning center also made this point.

Primary Sources

1. The agents are trading with the natives for their gold.
2. that they do not speak the same language

Composing an Essay

1. Gold was important in East and West Africa, as well as in the early African kingdoms along the Red Sea, chiefly as a natural resource that was mined and traded for other items that they needed or desired to improve their quality of life. For example, Aksum traded gold along with other regional resources, such as ivory and rhinoceros horns, to Mediterranean countries for products like glass, pottery, and olive oil. Later, East African city-states along the Indian Ocean—like Great Zimbabwe, Mogadishu, and Kilwa—found that they could trade their gold and other natural resources to Arab and Asian merchants who sailed in the region, to obtain tools

and cloth, as well as salt to preserve their food. In West Africa, people of the Sahel, who lived in kingdoms such as Ghana, Mali, and Songhai, prospered by trading gold mined by others further south, with Islamic traders who brought salt mined in north across the Sahara. Gold had some limited intrinsic cultural and ornamental value in these civilizations, but its main use in each region was as a medium of exchange.

2. Since the societies in each region were built on trade, the loss of control over trade would have been an important factor in their decline. For example, Kush declined after Aksum gained control of its trade routes, and Aksum declined when it lost control of its trade routes to the Arabs from across the Red Sea. In West Africa, a similar situation occurred with Ghana, when neighboring peoples took over the salt trade. In some cases, another reason for decline may have been the society's depletion of its natural resources. Kush's decline may have occurred when the fertility of its land was exhausted. Great Zimbabwe's collapse may have been due to its population exhausting its food and water supply. But by far the most common factor behind the fall of these civilizations was conquest by a rival or neighbor. Kush ceased to exist when Aksum conquered it. Ghana fell to the people who created Mali; Mali fell to the people who created Songhai; and Songhai was ended by an invasion of Moroccans.

Chapter 9

TEST FORM A

Matching

1. h
2. f
3. i
4. k
5. c
6. l
7. e
8. d
9. a
10. j

Understanding Ideas

1. c
2. b
3. a
4. c
5. d
6. b
7. a
8. c
9. a
10. d

True/False

1. F
2. T
3. T
4. T
5. T

Practicing Skills

1. basalt
2. from a site in present-day Guatemala

Composing an Essay

1. The people of the Southwest were farmers who lived in permanent towns. Some of these villages, like those of the Pueblo, were constructed of adobe—sun-dried bricks. The people of the Northwest relied on fishing. They were weavers and woodworkers who are known for their totem poles. The Great Plains peoples hunted buffalo. They lived in tepees of buffalo hides. Some plains people farmed and lived in rectangular houses. The Eastern Woodlands peoples lived in towns, farmed, and built earthen mounds for burial or religious purposes. They also carried on trade with peoples in other regions.
2. Many of the large animals hunted by the first peoples in North America became extinct as the Ice Age gradually ended. This forced prehistoric peoples to rely more on plants for food, which led to the development of farming. Later, in the A.D. 1300s and 1400s, changes in climate in the Southwest caused one farming people who lived there, the Hohokam, to abandon their communities. At about the same time, a series of droughts on the Great Plains forced some peoples there to also give up farming and move in order to survive.

TEST FORM B

Short Answer

1. The coming of the Ice Age lowered sea levels, causing a land bridge to develop across the Bering Strait. This climate change forced animals and the Asian peoples who hunted them across the bridge and then south in search of warmer climates in the Americas.
2. Many large animals became extinct as the Ice Age ended and climate again warmed. This forced hunter-gatherers to rely more on plants for food, which led to the development of farming.
3. The Maya were an agricultural people. This is why the rain god was one of their most important gods. The Maya's use of astronomy to develop a calendar was also related to their farming economy.
4. The development of agriculture caused people to stop wandering in search of food and to remain in one place so they could farm. This reliable source of food allowed populations to grow, which resulted in the development of villages and towns.
5. Both cultures offered human sacrifices as gifts to their gods. The Aztec sacrificed people to their sun god, while the Maya sacrificed people to their rain god.

Primary Sources

1. They worshipped it because it represented the Inca sun god.
2. Since the Inca believed the sun gave the idol/sun god its power, they would likely have feared that its power would be lost during an eclipse.

Composing an Essay

1. Both the Aztec of Mexico and the Inca of Peru built and ruled empires that contained other Native American peoples. The success and unity of each empire depended on keeping these subject peoples loyal and under control. The Aztec tried to accomplish this through military power and intimidation. They used force to dominate other peoples, requiring them to pay tribute and making human sacrifices of those captured in war. In contrast, the Inca approach was more sophisticated. They built forts, so, like the Aztec, military power was part of the equation. But they relied less on brute force and intimidation. Instead, they tried to keep control by eliminating regional differences within the empire. To do this, they relocated people and established schools through which they spread their language and culture to the peoples they ruled. They also built roads to tie the empire together. All these techniques were designed to weaken resistance to Inca rule. Thus, the "force" they applied was more cultural, while the Aztec relied more on military force. The fact that the Inca empire was stronger and more stable than the Aztec empire suggests that the Inca approach was the better one.
2. The most common characteristic of the peoples of the Pacific Coast, Southwest, Great Plains, and Eastern Woodlands was that the lifestyles they developed all relied on their surrounding natural resources. For most, this meant living in villages or towns. Farming was their main activity and source of food. The Northwest fits this pattern least, because peoples along the Pacific Coast relied heavily on the fish that were readily available. Great Plains peoples also developed cultures that relied less on farming because of the ready availability of buffalo as a source of food, as well as hides for clothing and the tepees in which they lived. But Plains peoples also farmed, as did the peoples of the Southwest and Eastern Woodlands. The geography of the Southwest required farmers to use irrigation to water their crops. Some, like the Pueblo, built their houses of adobe—earthen bricks that they dried in the hot southwestern sun. Like the peoples of the Southwest, the Eastern Woodlands peoples also depended more heavily on farming. Unlike all the others, however, they built large mounds of earth which they used for burial or religious purposes.

Unit 2

TEST FORM A

Understanding Ideas

1. a
2. d
3. c
4. a
5. c
6. b
7. c
8. a
9. a
10. d

Matching

1. e
2. i
3. j
4. f
5. c
6. h
7. b
8. d
9. a
10. l

True/False

1. T
2. T
3. T
4. T
5. F

Practicing Skills

1. inside: Gaul; outside: Germania
2. olive oil; it was available through trade with several places in the empire (Spain, Greece, Asia Minor, North Africa) Spices had to come from outside the empire—all the way from the Arabian Peninsula.

Composing an Essay

1. Both Greece and Rome practiced direct and representative democracy. Direct democracy existed in the assemblies of citizens that met in each city. These are similar to the town meetings that are held in some parts of America today, and in the meetings of other groups of people, such as neighborhood associations. Representative democracy existed in the election of certain leaders such as the archons of Athens and the consuls, praetors, and censors of Rome. In the United States, this system is found in the election of almost all our leaders, such as legislatures, mayors, governors, and presidents. Checks and balances existed in Roman government, which is a major principle of U.S. government, as is the veto power of executive officials like governors and the president. This copies the veto power of the Roman consul. Another important principle is that in both societies, only citizens could take part in government (though not all citizens could do so). This is also true in the United States, where only citizens can vote in elections.
2. Answers will vary but should show reasoned judgment and an accurate understanding of the different geographic and cultural environments on each continent. Among the general observations that students may make is the more ready presence of outside influences—such as ironworking technology, Islam, and the cultural heritage of ancient civilizations—that influenced development in East and West Africa. After the Ice Age ended, the Americas were cut off from the rest of the world and developed in isolation from these influences. For example, this deprived the Americas of the horse, the plow, and the wheel, which greatly impacted development. Although trade existed in North America, it was not nearly the factor that it was in Africa, and this too accounts for developmental differences.

TEST FORM B

Short Answer

1. Accept any two: peninsula, coastline, sea, mountains, rivers, or islands; surrounded by water and with its long coastline, Greece was easily involved in overseas trade and influenced by ideas from other cultures, such as from Egypt and the Fertile Crescent, as well as spreading Greek culture elsewhere. The mountainous terrain, short rivers, and many islands made communication more difficult and contributed to cultural and political disunity.
2. Accept any three: sculpture became more lifelike; human beings glorified, especially their strength, intelligence, pride, grace, and courage; gods and goddesses potrayed; ideals of beauty, harmony, order, moderation (simplicity), and utility (art was to be functional as well as aesthetically pleasing); pride in the city-

state—evidenced by architecture (which also demonstrated the ideals of functionality and honoring the gods)

3. Accept any three: writing—we use numbers and letters taken from Rome; language—Latin is the basis of the Romance languages, and many English words have Latin roots; government—Rome practiced direct and representative democracy, republican government, dictatorship, and the principles of checks and balances and the power of veto, which are present in U.S. as well as many other governments today; religion—through the Roman Empire, Christianity became a major world religion
4. In East Africa, coastal locations on the Indian Ocean and monsoon winds brought contact between Arab and Asian traders and African cultures, developing trade for African gold and other natural resources in return for products from throughout the Mediterranean and Asia. In West Africa, peoples of the Sahel benefited from their position between the gold mines further south and the salt-producing regions of the Sahara, or needed salt that came across the Sahara from the north. Powerful kingdoms developed along and controlled the trade routes by which the gold came north to be exchanged for the needed salt that came south—and trading centers like Timbuktu grew to facilitate this exchange.
5. The Aztecs controlled through military power and fear, while the Incas controlled by military power and by promoting unity and cultural blending. The Aztec forced subject peoples to pay them tribute and made religious sacrifices of prisoners they captured in war. The Inca established a network of forts and roads within their empire over which moved not only their armies but also peoples and ideas. The Inca spread their language, culture, and religion to subject peoples, thereby blending cultures and promoting unity.

Primary Sources

1. They coordinate cavalry and infantry well. Elite foot-soldiers are placed in front to lead the attack. The soldiers who fight together are related to one another as family or clan members.
2. Women encourage bravery by witnessing and honoring it. In addition, their fearful shrieks during battles motivate the soldiers to fight harder, as do the expectations—and even the demands—of women that their husbands and sons will be wounded in the fighting.

Composing an Essay

1. Answers will vary, but, at a minimum, students should demonstrate recognition of the following points: the Greek polis, or city-state, was geographically small and had a small population—fewer than 10,000 people in most cases, and most of these were slaves and other noncitizens. This enabled Greek government to be participatory and personal. Decisions could be and were made and enforced at the local level. Communications and commercial and other interactions were easy. Road networks were limited and only small armies were needed in most city-states, except when the Greeks faced an outside threat, such as the Persians. Then they would unite militarily, but never politically. Except for the Delian League, which itself was a cause of unrest in Greece, the city-states were markedly independent.

   The Roman Empire, on the other hand, became a huge governmental unit. At its height, it covered much of western Europe, Asia Minor, and North Africa and contained a large number of people. Early Rome had a participatory government that was much like the Greek polis—and in many ways, one that was more democratic that that of the early Greeks. However, as the territory that Rome governed expanded, this form became less and less appropriate to the task. Government had to be both centralized and decentralized in order to effectively govern the large area to be ruled, in the sense that decisions came from strong rulers in Rome and had to be carried out in the provinces. Communication was slower and more difficult than in the Greek polis and government was more bureaucratic and complicated.

2. Answers should include the following basic points: the Greeks were polytheists who attributed human qualities and personal characteristics to their gods and goddesses and communicated with them through a priesthood at places called oracles. They looked to the gods to explain natural phenomena and human behavior, and for good luck. But they did not expect their religion to save them from sin, nor for the gods to reward or punish them in the afterlife. The Greeks held special athletic competitions—the Olympics—to please and honor their gods.

The early Romans belived that spirits inhabited everything. Home spirits, including those of ancestors, were especially important. By the time of the empire, Roman religion became heavily influenced by Greek culture, and a state religion evolved that was based on a combination of family religion and the Greek gods, with temples, ceremonies, and a priesthood. Its purpose became loyalty and patriotism to the state, and the emperor became Rome's religious leader as well as its temporal one.

As Roman power expanded into the Middle East, Judaism and, later, Christianity became influential. Monotheistic religions like Judaism and Christianity taught love for God and self, the blessedness of the poor and oppressed, the importance of God over human law, and salvation and forgiveness of sin. Both religions proved disruptive. Although the Romans did not require the Jews to honor the Roman gods, Judaism became associated with the Jews' desire to be free of Roman political control. Christianity was disruptive because it appealed to large numbers of poor and oppressed Roman subjects and undermined the state religion, as well as the emperor's religious and temporal authority. However, its popularity prevented the Romans from stamping it out, and it rapidly spread, eventually converting even emperors and becoming the official religion of the empire.

Chapter 10 (Modern Chapter 1)

TEST FORM A

Fill in the Blank

1. boyars
2. czar
3. Justinian
4. Polovtsy
5. Rus
6. Ivan the Terrible
7. Kievan Russia
8. Vladimir I
9. Moscow
10. *Pravda Russkia*

Understanding Ideas

1. d
2. a
3. b
4. d
5. c
6. a
7. d
8. a
9. c
10. b

True/False

1. T
2. F
3. F
4. T
5. T

Practicing Skills

1. southeast
2. about two miles (3.3 kilometers)

Composing an Essay

1. The Byzantine Empire's capital, Constantinople overlooked the Bosporus Strait, which connected the Black and Mediterranean Seas. This location gave the Byzantines control over the trade between peoples who lived around the Black Sea and all the peoples along the Mediterranean shores of Africa and Europe. Because the narrow Bosporus Strait was also the place where major land routes crossed between Europe and Asia, the Byzantines benefited from their influence over overland trade as well. However, this location later worked against the empire. The Bosporus was much too narrow a barrier to protect the Byzantine capital from being attacked and conquered by the Ottoman Turks when they rose to power across the strait in Asia Minor.

2. Kievan wealth and power began to decline after 1054, when powerful rulers began dividing their holdings to be ruled by their sons. These princes and their descendants fought among themselves and against Kiev, the region's most powerful principality. This helped the Turkish Polovtsy, who gained control of the region south of Kiev, to disrupt Kievan trade. Further weakened by these developments, the principalities were not able to withstand an invasion out of Asia by the Mongols in the 1200s. By 1240 nearly every Kievan city had been conquered or destroyed, and the Mongols were in control of the region.

TEST FORM B

Short Answer

1. Religious leaders split over the role of icons in Christianity. Icons were venerated by the Byzantines. The pope in Rome approved this practice, but Byzantine church leaders opposed it. This friction helped to create the split.

2. A network of rivers crossed the region and connected to the Black Sea. In addition, the fertile soil of the steppe and the plentiful rainfall of the taiga were ideal for agriculture. The trade that resulted from these two factors helped Kievan Russia to become wealthy and strong.

3. (1) Kievan rulers began dividing their holdings to be ruled by their sons. (2) The debilitating struggles that resulted allowed the Turkish Polovtsy to gain control of the region south of Kiev and disrupt Kievan trade. (3) This further weakened Kievan Russia and allowed it to be conquered by the Mongols in the 1200s.

4. Ivan the Great was so known for his role in asserting Moscow's independence from the Mongols and increasing the city's power by conquering more territory. Ivan the Terrible got his name because he arrested boyars who resisted him and even murdered his oldest son.

5. Constantinople became known as the "second Rome" because the glory of the Roman Empire lived on there after Rome fell to the invasion of Germanic tribes. After Constantinople fell to the non-Christian Ottoman Turks, Moscow became the "third Rome" because leadership of the Orthodox Church became centered there.

Primary Sources

1. to not flee at this time; that having been an emperor, he will not like the lifestyle of a fugitive and that later he will wish he had remained to fight

2. She says that she would rather stay and risk death than give up being royalty. ("May I never be separated from this purple.")

Composing an Essay

1. Judgments will vary but should be supported with arguments and evidence that show an accurate understanding of Byzantine history. Some students may point to the value of the empire's strong central rule and code of laws, while others may attribute its longevity to Byzantine military power, especially its navy. Still others may call attention to the clever way in which Byzantine rulers used marriage to forge alliances with foreign powers, or point to the western help that "bought" a few hundred more years by saving Constantinople from the Seljuq Turks. A few may focus on Byzantine culture and be able to adequately argue that it was the most important factor in the Empire's longevity.

2. Answers will vary, but students should recognize that the Mongols strengthened Russia by providing a controlling hand at a time when Russia had splintered into numerous fractious principalities that had resisted Kievan domination and struggled among themselves. With Kiev's decline, the Mongols provided a unifying force, even if it was not a Russian one. In addition, the Mongols let Russians alone as long as they caused no trouble and paid their taxes. This combination of stable state and self government was one that Russians had rarely experienced. The obstructive dimension of Mongol rule came when Moscows leaders decided that they wanted to be free of Mongol control. The Mongols were successful in resisting this until Ivan III successfully created a Russian state under Moscow's leadership.

Chapter 11 (Modern Chapter 2)

TEST FORM A

Matching

1. l
2. i
3. e
4. a
5. j
6. d
7. k
8. g
9. c
10. f

Understanding Ideas

1. b
2. d
3. c
4. b
5. d
6. a
7. d
8. a
9. a
10. b

True/False

1. F
2. T
3. F
4. T
5. T

Practicing Skills

1. Mindanao
2. from Java/Bali and Moluccas

Composing an Essay

1. The bedouins lived in the desert, where they were not able to grow crops. Instead, they moved around in search of grazing areas for their flocks. At the same time, caravan traders moved across the Arabian Peninsula from towns such as Mecca and Yathrib (Medina), that were located near the coast. There, Muhammad, himself a trader, had converted some of the townspeople to the new religion of Islam. As traders who accepted Islam came into contact with the bedouins of the interior, they spread their religion to these beduoins, who, in turn, spread the religion to others they met in their nomadic existence.

2. Over time, beautiful mosques were built across the Islamic world. Because they served as community centers as well as places of worship, many of them became very large and elaborate and demonstrated an increasingly sophisticated architectural style. Religious art was restricted by the Islamic ban on depicting God in human form, and by the Muslims' reluctance to show any human figures in their art. Instead, Muslim artists created beautiful geometric and floral designs. In nonreligious art, however, they sometimes showed scenes of people in battle or in daily life.

TEST FORM B

Short Answer

1. Muhammad experienced a vision in which God spoke to him through the angel Jibreel (Gabriel), commanding him to teach God's word to the Arabs. Muhammad began teaching Islam in the trading cities of Mecca and Yathrib (Medina), where he attracted followers. He then spread the religion to the desert tribes

2. The bedouins were nomadic herders who, once they had been converted to Islam, spread the religion among their tribal groups and to other peoples they met in their wanderings.

3. Muslim factions disagreed about from which clan caliphs should come. More fundamentally, the Shi'ah believed that religious leaders called imams should decide worldly and religious matters, while the Sunni believed that religious matters should be settled by agreement of the Muslim people.

4. Both caliphs and secular rulers who were Muslims spread Islam by sending armies to conquer neighboring regions as far as Spain in the west and India in the east. Muslims traders also spread the faith in their commercial dealings with peoples in Africa, Asia, and throughout the Middle East.
5. Wherever they went, Muslims spread their art and architecture, as well as education, literature and advanced learning in science, mathematics, and medicine.

Primary Sources

1. Be brave, merciful, and honest with enemies, and do not kill old men, women, or children.
2. that Muslims should treat others as they themselves would like to be treated

Composing an Essay

1. Answers will vary but should show recognition of the following points. Before the rise of the Turks, caliphs often held both political and religious power in Arab Muslim societies. As the Turks conquered the Arabs and established the Turkish (Ottoman) empire across the Middle East and elsewhere, governing power transferred to the Turkish sultans, which relegated the caliphs to a more narrow religious role. Thus the military spread of Islam became less a "religious war" and more a case of a secular Muslim ruler extending his empire—and only secondarily his faith—to the regions he conquered. This change in priorities is best demonstrated by the conquest of the Arabs, who were already Muslims when they became part of the Turkish empire.
2. Opinions will vary but should be supported with reasoned arguments and appropriate examples. Students who argue the importance of Islamic culture as an influence will likely note the spread of Islamic science and other higher learning to Africa and Europe as Muslims conquered and settled or traded in these regions. They may note, for example, the medical advances of Muslim physicians, such as Abū al-Qāsim in Spain and al-Rāzī in Baghdad, whose writings formed the basis of European medicine for centuries. Students who argue the other position will note that most of the math, science, and medical knowledge that Muslims spread did not originate in the Middle East, but was knowledge and technology that Muslims acquired and spread from other parts of the Islamic empire. For example, Islamic physicians drew upon the work of the early Greeks in medicine, spread mathematical achievements that came from India, and papermaking methods from China.

Chapter 12 (Modern Chapter 3)

TEST FORM A

Fill in the Blank

1. Zen
2. Sui
3. Genghis Khan
4. Vietnam
5. samurai
6. Tang
7. Kublai Khan
8. Shinto
9. Batu
10. Sung

Understanding Ideas

1. b
2. d
3. c
4. d
5. c
6. b
7. a
8. d
9. b
10. a

True/False

1. F
2. T
3. T
4. F
5. F

Practicing Skills

1. Karakorum
2. Yuan

Composing an Essay

1. Production increased as farming methods improved—such as water-control projects that allowed farmers to irrigate more fields and thus grow more rice. Also, a new type of quick-ripening rice was introduced that let farmers harvest two

rice crops per year instead of the usual one. However, life also became harder for peasants because of new taxes imposed by the government. Those who could not pay these taxes had to sell their farms and became tenant farmers, paying high rent to landlords.

2. In both societies the emperor was the titular head of the government, and in both the position was hereditary. However, through history China's emperors have been of several dynasties, or families of rulers, while Japan's emperors are believed to all have come from the same family. Another notable difference is that China's emperors generally held real power, while for much of Japan's history the real power of government was in the hands of the shoguns or daimyo.

TEST FORM B

Short Answer

1. Their superior generals, quickly moving cavalry, massed firepower, and powerful weapons overwhelmed many peoples.
2. Chinese cultural influences included written language, Confucianism, Buddhism (and Zen Buddhism), model of government, and civil service system. Differences include elements of traditional Korean beliefs in Korean Buddhism, the development of a powerful nobility in Korea, and more sharp divisions in Korea between noble and peasant classes because, unlike China, Korea never developed a large middle class of merchants, government officials, and scholars.
3. (Accept any of the following.) Trade and trade routes with India and Persia were improved. Communication within the empire was improved, and unity and order increased. Contacts with the outside world, and especially with Europe, grew. The central government grew stronger as local governments became more accountable to Beijing. Population, which had dropped due to a century of war, began to rise again. However, heavy taxes created hardships for farmers and merchants. Chinese people could not hold important government positions, and Mongols did not allow intermarriage between different groups of people.
4. Politically, China controlled northern Vietnam through much of its history. Culturally, Mahayana Buddhism, Daoism, and Confucianism influenced Vietnamese culture. Vietnam also used the writing system and political organization of the Chinese.
5. Both are linked to Zen Buddhism, which arrived in Japan from China. Like Bushido, the samurai code, Zen taught values, like self-discipline and acceptance of death and pain, that were helpful in battle. For this reason, Zen was popular with the samurai. The Noh plays that developed in Japan were a Zen art form, thereby making them the indirect result of an aspect of Chinese culture.

Primary Sources

1. because it has a bitter taste and the Japanese do not like bitter things
2. It has qualities that strengthen the heart, which is important to dispelling illness and achieving long life.

Composing an Essay

1. Opinions will vary but should weigh the following factors: In agriculture, production increased during both dynasties as farming methods improved. Water-control projects allowed farmers to irrigate more fields and thus grow more rice. Also, a new type of quick-ripening rice was introduced that let farmers harvest two rice crops per year instead of the usual one. Achievements in the arts included the growth of literature under the Tang, such as the poetry of Li Bo and Du Fu. Under the Sung, Chinese artists perfected porcelain making and produced beautiful vases which became a valuable export item. Foreign trade greatly expanded under the Sung, and they improved China's service system to make it more honest and efficient. The Sung found a practical use for gunpowder—in warfare—and printing technology improved during both

dynasties. On the other hand, although each dynasty experienced external threats, those threats were much greater during Sung rule.

2. Throughout the entire feudal period, the emperor was the titular head of Japan. At first, he was under the control of powerful families, such as the Fujiwara clan, that came to control the central government. In 1185, when the Minamoto clan gained power over the emperor, he appointed one of them as his chief general, or shogun. The shoguns gained control of the military, finances, and laws, so the emperor became more of a figurehead. Away from the capital, in the countryside, local lords called daimyo were in control. Their power depended on the loyalty of warriors called samurai. At the bottom of society were the peasants, who also served in the army of their local daimyo. This power structure shifted during the 250-year Ashikaga shogunate, which began around 1330, as the daimyo and their samurai gradually became the most powerful people in Japan.

Chapter 13 (Modern Chapter 4)

TEST FORM A

Matching

1. g
2. l
3. j
4. f
5. c
6. k
7. d
8. h
9. b
10. i

Understanding Ideas

1. b
2. a
3. d
4. c
5. b
6. c
7. d
8. a
9. d
10. a

True/False

1. T
2. T
3. T
4. F
5. F

Practicing Skills

1. Norway and Denmark
2. Swedish Vikings, who reached the Black and Caspian Seas

Composing an Essay

1. William I increased the power of the king by making all feudal nobles swear loyalty directly to him. In addition, he scattered their fiefs across England to prevent them from uniting against him. He also created a central tax system. William's son, Henry I, built on this by creating a department to handle the king's finances and thereby make the government more efficient. He also set up royal courts that took power from the courts of the feudal lords. His son, Henry II, allowed nobles to pay a fee in lieu of the military service required under feudalism. This allowed the king to hire an army independent of the nobles and more loyal to him. Henry II also increased the royal courts' appeal by establishing trial by jury to replace the harsh methods used by feudal lords' courts to determine guilt or innocence.
2. The Capetian kings increased their power in several ways. One was to increase the territory they controlled through marriage, by taking the lands of noble families that had died out, and by taking lands held by England's Norman kings. They also strengthened their governments by appointing well-trained officials to run things and by extending the jurisdiction of royal courts. To gain control over the church's power in France, they began to tax the clergy. Philip IV made himself stronger by increasing his popularity among the French people. He did this by

convening the Estates General, a representative body of commoners, nobles, and church officials and making it a part of his government.

TEST FORM B

Short Answer

1. He brought unity to western Europe for the first time since the fall of Rome. In doing so, he also spread effective government, education, and Christianity in Europe during this "barbarian" period.
2. It arose with the collapse of Charlemagne's empire. With no central authority in place, powerful nobles granted land to lesser nobles in return for their loyalty and military assistance. Grantees established estates on their land that were farmed by peasants, who also provided loyalty (serfs were bound to the land forever) and labor in return for protection.
3. The pope was at the top and was advised by cardinals. Under the cardinals were the archbishops, who controlled several geographical dioceses, each headed by a bishop. The bishop of each diocese was in charge of its local priests. The church controlled almost every aspect of everyday life, from birth to death—including education and salvation and such integral components of spiritual life as baptism, holy communion, and marriage.
4. The basic conflict was over who was the ultimate power and authority in a kingdom. The pope, as head of God's church, thought that he was above temporal rulers and that his authority had no political boundaries. Kings, on the other hand, wished to be sovereign within their realms.
5. This was the land ruled by the Germanic kings, starting with Charlemagne, whom the pope had designated "emperor of Rome." Its borders varied with the emperors' power, but it generally included parts of what is now Germany and Italy.

Primary Sources

1. to provide on demand a specific number of knights, at the noble's expense, to the king for 40 days and 40 nights; only for the defense of the kingdom, and the king pays their expenses
2. only during their 40 days of compulsory service

Composing an Essay

1. Answers will vary but should demonstrate reasoned judgment and an understanding of the power dynamics of the era. Most students will likely accept the stated view. These should note that the feudal system made kings weak, while at the same time, the church was fundamentally involved in the everyday lives of people in every country and at every level of society. This degree of involvement gave the pope, as head of the church, tremendous power and influence. In addition, it made the papal practices of excommunication and interdiction especially potent weapons in struggles with kings over issues of authority within their realms. The powers of popes were demonstrated by the capitulation of Henry II in England and Holy Roman Emperor Henry IV in conflicts over church versus state power.

   Students who reject the stated view may note that popes often had to rely on the armies of kings to protect them, as was the case with Pope John XII and Otto I of Germany. In times of poorer relations, German emperors were able to threaten the popes' rule of the Papal States. They may also note the common practice of lay investiture and that French king Philip IV was even able to influence the selection of a pope, as well as having another pope arrested. Finally, these students may note that, in the end, kings were able to establish states where royal power was sovereign.

2. In both countries, land was important to power. The early French kings tried to increase their holdings through marriage, conquest, and seizure. By contrast, William I in England increased his power by making all vassals swear loyalty directly to him, and by scattering his vassals' fiefs to hinder their uniting against him.

In both countries, kings attempted to increase their power by creating efficient governments, by giving themselves an independent source of income, and by gaining control over the system. In England, William I established a system for taxing people's holdings, whereas in France, Philip IV taxed the clergy. This also gave the king some control over the church, which was powerful in both countries. In England, however, Henry II's attempts to control the church by taking power from its courts met with failure. But the English kings set up royal courts that traveled the countryside, trying cases that otherwise would have been heard in the lords' feudal courts. These courts also established trial by jury. This gave royal courts some appeal over the lords' courts, which determined guilt or innocence by ordeal or combat. The kings of France also increased their power by expanding the authority of royal courts.

Democracy began in the two countries in very different ways. In France it was the result of Philip IV's attempt to increase his popularity by calling the Estates General, a representative body of clergy, nobles, and commoners, and giving it a role in his government. In England, however, democracy was born of conflict rather than cooperation. King John's efforts to expand his power caused the nobles to force him to sign Magna Carta, which gave some basic rights to the people. Also, the first Parliament was the effort of nobles and the middle class to resist the king, not to cooperate with him as in France.

Chapter 14 (Modern Chapter 5)

TEST FORM A

Fill in the Blank

1. Pope Urban II
2. domestic system
3. scholasticism
4. Joan of Arc
5. John Wycliffe
6. vernacular languages
7. craft guilds
8. market
9. Thomas Aquinas
10. Dante

Understanding Ideas

1. b
2. d
3. c
4. a
5. c
6. b
7. a
8. d
9. a
10. c

True/False

1. T
2. F
3. T
4. T
5. F

Practicing Skills

1. church service
2. 4.5 hours in each season

Composing an Essay

1. The war resulted from the attempt of England's King Edward III, whose land-holdings in France made him a vassal of the French king, to gain the throne of that country. It was a long struggle—interspersing periods of war and peace over 116 years—during which France finally gained control over all the English-held lands on its soil except Calais. However, it brought heavy loss of life and property in France, where most of the war was fought. The fighting also cost many English lives. Public unhappiness over this situation in both countries allowed the English Parliament and the French Estates General to gain power over their kings. The war and the resulting weakening of the king stimulated civil war in both England and France—the English conflict was the War of the Roses, which began after the Hundred Years War ended—for control of the throne in each country. Ultimately, however, restoration of peace returned strong kings to each throne.

2. The growth of trade was accompanied by the growth of towns. Trade attracted people to towns because of the economic opportunities that they offered. Some lords tried to benefit from these changes by encouraging trade fairs on their lands and raised money by taxing these fairs. But, over time, as the manor villages where these events took place grew, merchants and workers began to unite. With the rise of craft guilds and the expansion of the middle class, the manor system weakened.

TEST FORM B

Short Answer

1. The First Crusade was the most successful because it brought much of the Holy Land under crusader control and was the only Crusade to capture Jerusalem. The biggest failure was the Children's Crusade, which was poorly organized, ill-equipped, and ended in slavery or death for many of the young crusaders.
2. freedom: anyone, including escaped serfs, who lived in a town for more than a year and a day became free; exemption: townspeople could not be required to perform work on a lord's manor; justice: towns had their own courts which heard cases that involved townspeople; commercial privileges: townspeople could sell goods freely in the town market and charge outsiders who wanted to sell goods there
3. It became more available because authors began to write in vernacular languages instead of in Latin. This allowed more people to read it or, more commonly, to listen to it being performed by troubadours. The classics of the period include the French epic *The Song of Roland,* Italian writer Dante's *The Divine Comedy,* and English writer Chaucer's *The Canterbury Tales.*
4. The war resulted from the attempt of England's King Edward III, whose landholdings in France made him a vassal of the French king, to gain the throne of that country. During the long, sporadic struggle, which brought heavy losses of life and property on both sides, public unhappiness allowed the English Parliament and the French Estates General to gain power over each king.
5. Around 1300, Philip IV of France influenced the selection of a new pope, who moved the church's capital from Rome to France. It remained there for about 70 years in what is called the Babylonian Captivity. When a later pope returned the capital to Rome, the Great Schism occurred. A second pope was chosen, who continued to live in France. These events weakened the church in other countries because it seemed that the pope was being controlled by French kings.

Primary Sources

1. He says that a lender can rightly expect and ask for some other "consideration," by which he means interest, as a "reward" for making a loan.
2. People who lend money are taking a risk that it might not be repaid. Furthermore, people are bound by honor to reward someone who does them a favor, such as extending them a loan. Since this behavior is not unnatural, it is not unlawful to require some kind of compensation to a lender as part of the loan contract.

Composing an Essay

1. Answers will vary but should include the following basic points: People joined the Crusades for many reasons. Some saw opportunity. Knights were lured by land and plunder, while merchants saw a chance to make money. Others were inspired by their faith. They hoped to free the Holy Land from the Turks. Some believed that being a crusader would provide salvation and a place in heaven.

The Crusades affected Europe in many ways. Europeans leaned new military techniques, such as the use of the crossbow and possibly gunpowder. The power of kings was increased as they led armies from their entire countries, and as many feudal lords who became crusaders died, bringing a decline in feudalism. The church also became more powerful because it was the spiritual force behind the Crusades. The middle class and towns grew as the Crusades stimulated trade between Europe and the Middle East. New products such as rice and sugar were introduced to Europe through the Middle East, as well as new ideas and knowledge gained from the crusaders' interactions with the Byzantine and Muslim peoples they met.

2. Students' opinions will vary but should be supported by accurate evidence and sound reasoning. Responses should show recognition of the following points: Trade began to revive as Europeans became more interested in goods from Asia, many of which they discovered as Crusaders returned home. The revival of trade encouraged the growth of towns, markets and fairs, a manufacturing system, a banking system, the practice of investing capital, and the development of guilds. Many of these consequences, such as town growth, fairs, banking, and investment were themselves important factors behind the growth of trade as well.

Unit 3 (Modern Unit 1)

TEST FORM A

Understanding Ideas

1. c
2. b
3. d
4. a
5. d
6. c
7. d
8. b
9. a
10. a

Matching

1. h
2. c
3. i
4. d
5. b
6. e
7. k
8. g
9. j
10. f

True/False

1. T
2. F
3. T
4. F
5. F

Practicing Skills

1. from the northeast, out of western or central Asia
2. before the Crusades, because Asia Minor is shown as still in Byzantine hands

Composing an Essay

1. Muslims believed in the jihad, or the struggle to defend their faith. To spread the faith, they conquered non-Muslim lands in the Middle East, as well as in Europe, Africa, and Asia. War and conquest brought Islam into Spain, via the Berber invasions, and into eastern Europe, when the Ottoman Turks conquered the Byzantine Empire. Muslims also defended their lands and faith against non-Muslim invaders, such as in the Crusades. Religion was also a motivation for war and conquest in Europe—for example, the pope's call on Christians to participate in the Crusades. Four major Crusades were launched between about 1100 and 1300, plus numerous other, smaller Crusades, all to "free" the Christian "Holy Land" (which happened to be holy to Muslims and Jews, as well) from the Turks.
2. All three peoples were conquerors who created empires that temporarily unified parts of Europe, the Middle East, and Asia, spreading culture as well as bringing stabilizing political control. The Franks under Merovingian and Carolingian rules—most notably Charlemagne—unified Western Europe in the A.D. 400s to 800s, bringing order and political stability, and helping to establish Christianity and

spread education throughout the region. The collapse of the Frankish kingdom, following Charlemagne's death, launched the feudal period in Europe.

In Asia, the Mongols, led by Genghis Khan and his grandsons, swept out of central Asia to conquer China, southwest into Persia, and west across Asia into eastern Europe in the 1100s and 1200s. One of Genghis Khan's grandsons, Kublai Khan, established a harsh but productive rule in China, bringing one of the few periods of true unity in that nation's long history. Mongol rule was a factor in the creation and rise of Russia in eastern Europe.

In the Middle East, the Ottoman Turks invaded and politically unified much of the Islamic empire in the 900s and after, and also spread Islam as they expanded their empire west into Europe and east as far as India. The Turks' expansion eastward was halted by the Mongols invasion of Persia in the 1200s, but their western expansion continued, and they conquered the Byzantine Empire, bringing Islam to the Balkans in Europe, in the 1300s and 1400s.

TEST FORM B

Short Answer

1. Accept any five: powerful emperor; strong central government; skilled and efficient government officials; clever diplomacy, such as alliances through marriage with foreign powers; military strength and strong navy; economic strength through trade; strategic location of Constantinople; military help from western European armies
2. Accept either of the following: Muslim culture flourished in Spain after the Berbers invaded and conquered it in the A.D. 700s. Over the next 700 years, Islamic knowledge and technology spread from Moorish Spain throughout Europe. Muslims and Europeans came into contact in the Holy Land when Europeans invaded it during the Crusades in the 1100s and 1200s. There the crusaders learned of Muslim technology, ideas, and trade goods that advanced European culture.
3. Extensive water-control projects were built to increase the number of irrigated rice fields, thereby increasing rice production. Also, a quick-ripening rice was introduced that allowed two crops to be harvested each year, which also increased production. These changes gave peasants surplus food to sell at market, which promoted population growth and the growth of towns and cities.
4. He unified the kingdom of the Franks, set up an efficient form of government for the empire, strengthened the role of the Christian church in western Europe, and encouraged the establishment of schools.
5. Serfs could become free of the manor by escaping to a town and living there for a year and a day. Also they could sell their produce in town and thereby pay for the use of their land with money rather than with labor. As towns became centers of such commerce, other people began to produce manufactured items for sale there. At first this manufacturing centered in the homes of the employees, but later shops appeared and apprentice and guild systems developed for learning and regulating skilled crafts and trades.

Primary Sources

1. a generally favorable one; the writer admits that William was an extremely hard and unforgiving ruler, but seems to admire him for bringing order to the country through his harsh methods
2. Answers will vary but should note that the passage demonstrates the feudal system William created, in which he held supreme authority by making each lord the king's direct vassal and requiring personal loyalty to the monarch.

Composing an Essay

1. Answers will vary but should demonstrate reasoned judgment and be supported by appropriate evidence. Depending on the position they take, students should make some of the following observations: Those

who accept that religion was the greater force may note that much of the military conflict in Europe, the Middle East, and parts of Asia during this period was religiously motivated. For example, Muslims believed in jihad, or the struggle to defend the faith, a practice that often had military dimensions. They conquered lands in Europe, Africa, and Asia to spread their faith and used force to defend it against non-Muslim invaders, such as in the Crusades. Christians also used religion to justify military conflict—for example, the pope's call to Christians to participate in the Crusades. In addition, religion was a key factor in some of the non-military conflicts in Europe. Kings and popes often struggled over political issues that centered around church-state power, such as the conflict over lay investiture. Excommunication, interdiction, and the clergy's control over the sacraments all demonstrate how religion was a powerful, non-military weapon in secular conflicts and events in Europe.

Students who take the position that war was the greater force may observe that the Mongols' wars of conquest in Asia and Europe were motivated by a temporal desire for empire, as was the Ottoman Turks' creation of an empire in the Middle East and North Africa. Many of the peoples the Turks conquered were already Muslims, so the spread of Islam was not a factor. The Turkish sultan, who headed the empire, was a secular leader, not a religious one, and the Turk's spread of Islam into places such as the Byzantine Empire was motivated by the desire for a temporal empire, not a religious one. The Chinese brought Buddhism into Korea and Vietnam. But here, too, the primary motivation was a temporal desire for empire and not a quest to spread the faith. In addition, important feudal conflicts in Europe and Japan, which tremendously shaped the history of both regions, were not religious in nature. Major wars in Europe during this period, such as the Hundred Years' War, also had no religious motivation.

2. Answers will vary but should note the following factors: Feudalism in both societies had a tightly organized social structure, with kings or emperors at the top and peasants or serfs at the bottom. Both developed as a way of protecting the society, with European vassals and Japanese daimyos—served by European knights and Japanese samurai respectively—helping their lord to protect their domain. Soldiers in both cultures were bound by codes of honor, knights by chivalry and samurai by Bushido.

A fundamental difference in the two systems is that feudal Japan had two conflicting power structures—a central government under a figurehead emperor and a shogun, who held the real power, and local military rule under the daimyo and samurai. For much of Japan's feudal period, the local rulers were more powerful than the central government. Local lords were also the locus of power in the European system. But no central governments existed in feudal Europe until the system began to break down and kings began to assert their power, gradually unifying their rule and creating nations. In Japan, the nation and central government existed from the beginning of feudalism, and its power declined as the power of the daimyo increased. In Europe, the situation was exactly the reverse.

Chapter 15 (Modern Chapter 6)

TEST FORM A

Matching

1. g
2. d
3. j
4. f
5. l
6. b
7. i
8. n
9. k
10. a
11. m
12. c

Understanding Ideas

1.	d	**5.**	c
2.	c	**6.**	d
3.	b	**7.**	b
4.	a	**8.**	a

True/False

1. T
2. F
3. T
4. T
5. F

Practicing Skills

1. 1470–1480
2. slowed down; the graph shows that 63 new printing centers developed between 1480 and 1490, but only 46 between 1490 and 1500

Composing an Essay

1. The humanists believed that it was important to understand how things worked. For this reason they attached a great value to education. Although most were committed Christians, they viewed life as not just preparation for the afterlife, but as a joy in itself. They valued human dignity and individual achievement. This led them to believe that leading a meaningful life was very important. To the humanists, this meant active involvement in practical affairs, such as scientific investigation, writing, or supporting the arts.
2. One of the greatest differences between Luther's beliefs and those of the Church concerned salvation. He rejected the Church's teachings that the sacraments could atone for sin and claimed that neither priests nor indulgences had any special role in helping people to salvation. He claimed instead that people gained salvation through an inner faith in God rather than though actions. The key, to Luther, was not good deeds, but God's grace. Coinciding with this view was Luther's belief that the Bible was the sole religious authority and that popes and bishops should not be telling people what to believe.

TEST FORM B

Short Answer

1. Answers will vary but should accurately name, locate, and attribute a writer and an artist of each movement.
2. The printing press helped to spread Renaissance ideas, as did the return home of northern European students who had studied in Italy. Also, merchants and wealthy northern Europeans brought Renaissance art and other goods, as well as ideas, to northern Europe.
3. He was declared a heretic and excommunicated by the pope. When he still refused to renounce his views, he was declared an outlaw in the Holy Roman Empire (within which he lived) and the printing and sale of his works was banned.
4. France's Catholic monarchs persecuted Protestant converts, called Huguenots, and civil wars resulted. England's King Henry VIII withdrew his country from the Catholic Church when the pope refused to grant him a divorce. Henry then created a Protestant church, called the Anglican Church, as the official church of England in order to receive his divorce.
5. Accept any two: frustration and resentment of privileged people, such as kings or bishops, who ruled them; fear or resentment of neighbors who upset their traditions or sense of proper behavior; anger over high taxes, food shortages, and other economic hardships

Primary Sourcess

1. reasons: because other people are treacherous and will not keep their promises to the ruler and because the rulers who accomplish the most do so by cunning rather than by honesty; circumstances: when keeping his word would damage him or when the reasons he gave his word no longer apply
2. Niccolò Machiavelli. He, of all the people discussed in this chapter, is most likely to espouse this view of ethics.

Composing an Essay

1. Many reformers believed that the church had lost sight of its spiritual mission and that it was more concerned with ceremony, leadership and control, and making money than it was with saving souls. Related to these concerns, for some reformers, was discontent over basic church teaching and practices. Martin Luther, for example, rejected the church doctrine that the way to salvation was through good works and forgiveness of sin. Salvation, he said, came through God's grace and a person's inner faith. It could not be achieved through the sacraments offered by church officials. John Calvin believed in predestination and in clear instruction on what the faithful should believe and how they should act.

   One result of these conflicts was religious war, as Holy Roman Emperor Charles V tried to stop the spread of Protestantism. These efforts failed and many new churches arose. Another result was an increased interest in education. Many Protestant reformers supported education because of their belief in the people's need to read the Bible. Catholics also renewed their educational efforts. Groups like the Jesuits founded colleges, in part to strengthen students' commitment to the Church. Another result was an increase in the power of national governments and a decrease in the power of the pope. In both England and Switzerland, for example, a "state" religion was organized, under the leadership of Protestant religious or secular officials.
2. Answers will vary but should include many of the following points: The humanists of the 1300s and villagers of the 1500s shared a common desire to understand the world around them. For the humanists this meant study and investigation. For the villagers it often meant a search for supernatural explanations. As scholars, the humanists were well-educated in Christian doctrine. The villagers were Christians too, but they had little education. They remained rooted in the superstitions of the past. For example, a humanist would want to investigate the cause of a lightning strike, and perhaps conduct scientific experiments. Villagers would merely dismiss lightning as the work of spirits. The humanists attached great importance to classical learning and its value in helping them to better know their world. Villagers also looked to others for knowledge of their world, but this was usually some village member who was thought wise because he or she knew about the spirit world, and was perhaps thought to be a witch. Not until villagers started moving to cities in greater numbers did this traditional culture and lack of sophistication begin to change and the common villagers adopted a world view more like that of the humanists.

Chapter 16 (Modern Chapter 7)

TEST FORM A

Fill in the Blank

1. Johannes Kepler
2. Hernán Cortés
3. mercantilism
4. Descartes
5. Portuguese
6. balance of trade
7. Ferdinand Magellan
8. Middle Passage
9. Vasco da Gama
10. Philip II

Understanding Ideas

1. b
2. a
3. d
4. c
5. b
6. d
7. a
8. c
9. d
10. a

True/False

1. F
2. T
3. F
4. T
5. T

Practicing Skills

1. Americas: coffee, sugar; Asia: calico, silk
2. coffee, because it is found in both Asia (East Indies) and America (West Indies), suggesting that its cultivation spread from one hemisphere to the other

Composing an Essay

1. Technological improvements that made exploration possible came in the areas of mapmaking, navigation and shipbuilding. Renaissance Europeans' interest in ancient geographers inspired a rebirth of mapmaking. Renaissance geographers updated earlier maps to make them more accurate. This encouraged sea captains to find new trade routes to Asia. Improvements to navigational instruments, and new ones such as the compass, enabled captains to venture far from coastlines without getting lost in the open sea. Shipbuilders made improvements in the size and shape of ships and their sails, and relocated ships' rudders. These changes allowed ships to be steered more easily, to sail against the wind, to move at greater speeds, and to be more reliable in different types of weather conditions.
2. Answers will vary but should show recognition of the following points: The Dutch primarily colonized for the purpose of trade, while the Spanish and Portuguese settled in and exploited their colonies, and the native peoples therein, to a much greater degree. The Spanish in particular took huge amounts of gold and silver from their colonies, partly by plundering native peoples and partly by conscripting them to work in the Spaniards' mines. Both the Spanish and the Portuguese made heavy use of enslaved Africans in their colonies, while the Dutch did not. On the other hand, both the Dutch and the Portuguese were heavily involved in the buying and selling of slaves (the slave trade), while the Spanish were less so. Missionary work—converting the natives to Christianity (Catholicism)—was a major part of Spanish and Portuguese policy. However, the Dutch did not force their subject peoples to change their religions.

TEST FORM B

Short Answer

1. Early scientists had believed that one could learn about the physical world by observing things and understanding them through logic and reasoning. Later scientists believed those observations had to be verifiable through mathematical proof or demonstrated by repeatable experiments that produced the same results.
2. The compass encouraged captains to venture beyond the sight of land and into the open sea. Improvements in the size and shape of ships and their sails, and in the location of their rudders allowed them to be steered more easily, sail against the wind, move at greater speeds, and be more reliable in bad weather.
3. Joint-stock companies were businesses financed by individual investors through their purchase of stock in the company. The money thus raised paid the huge cost of an exploratory expedition or a new colony. The joint-stock approach meant that no single investor had to advance a large sum and risk a large loss if the venture failed. This made the money for such projects easier to raise.
4. At first the Spanish and Portuguese enslaved Native Americans to provide the workers for their mines and farms. However, it proved difficult to enslave a people in their own land. In addition, huge numbers died due to their lack of immunity to European diseases. So enslaved Africans were transported to the Americas to do this work.
5. Because of their location on the North Sea, the Dutch were already a seafaring people. After they threw off Spanish rule and became independent in the late 1500s this tradition quickly made them leaders of European overseas commerce. They established their own trade-based empire in the East and West Indies and North and South America, as well as trade with Japan.

Primary Sources

1. that he is in Asia, as suggested by his references to "reaching the Indies" and to his continuing search for the mainland of China ("Cathay")
2. He asks for their continued support and promises them in return all the gold, cotton, spices and slaves they wish.

Composing an Essay

1. Answers will vary but should be supported by reasoned judgment and appropriate factual evidence. Most students will eliminate the Dutch because their empire was based on trade more than on colonization, thereby making them less exploitative of native peoples than were the Spanish and Portuguese. Nor did the Dutch try to convert subject peoples to Christianity. However, the Spanish and Portuguese settled in and plundered the resources of the areas they controlled, as well as attempting to enslave the native peoples. In addition, when disease and other factors reduced the native populations, the Spanish and Portuguese imported and exploited African slaves in their colonies. However, although their colonial polices and practices were similar, the Spanish Empire was more extensive than the Portuguese Empire. On this basis, some students may conclude that the Spanish inflicted more damage on non-Europeans than the Portuguese did. On the other hand, the Portuguese were much more active in the enslavement of peoples in Africa and in the related slave trade, which may cause some students to choose them.
2. Mercantilism was a theory that held that a country's government should do all it could to increase the country's wealth, which was measured by the amount of gold and silver it possessed. One way to do this was to mine gold and silver at home or in colonies that the country developed. Another way was to sell more to other countries than it purchased from them. This surplus of sales over purchases would create a favorable balance of trade, causing a nation to receive more gold and silver from other countries than it paid out to them. A nation could obtain a favorable trade balance in several ways. One was to impose tariffs on imported goods, making them more expensive and thereby discouraging citizens from buying other countries' products. Another was to increase the value of the nation's exports to other countries. Since finished products were more valuable than raw materials, the growth of manufacturing was encouraged. The government would grant subsidies to certain companies to help them get started. Yet another way was for the nation to become self-sufficient by producing all it needed plus a surplus for export.

   Colonies played several roles in mercantilism. One of the most important was to produce gold and silver. Another was to produce raw materials needed by the home country. If it could get these from its colonies, it would not have to buy them from rival countries. Colonies also provided ready markets for the home country's exports. According to mercantilism, control of colonial markets and raw materials was the key to a nation's success.

Chapter 17 (Modern Chapter 8)

TEST FORM A

Matching

1. c
2. j
3. f
4. h
5. l
6. i
7. b
8. a
9. k
10. d

Understanding Ideas

1. a
2. d
3. c
4. b
5. c
6. a
7. c
8. d
9. a
10. d

True/False

1. T
2. T
3. T
4. F
5. F

Practicing Skills

1. 1830–1840 (also accept 1832–1842)
2. It had little if any effect; about the same amount of peasant unrest occurred in the 1830s, before Perry's opening of Japan, as in the decade following it (1860–1870). The data thus suggests that Japan's opening was not a significant factor in the unrest that existed in Japanese society.

Composing an Essay

1. External forces played a large part in the fall of both rules, but China was also internally weaker than Japan. Like the Tokugawa shoguns in Japan, the Qing emperors of China enjoyed more than 250 years of power. However, the Qing Dynasty went into a long period of decline following the White Lotus Rebellion in 1796 and was further damaged by the long and destructive Taiping Rebellion in the 1850s and 1860s. These factors, coupled with the increasing pressures from foreign powers, seriously weakened the Qing dynasty and eventually led to its collapse in 1912. In contrast, the Tokugawa became stronger during their rule, gaining power over the daimyo and samurai. Probably at least partly for this reason, they were better at resisting foreign pressures than were the Qing. Nevertheless, internal conflict resulting from Perry's opening of Japan in the 1850s led to the shogunate's fall in the 1860s.
2. China's rulers were not able to resist the internal pressures for overseas trade, nor the pressures from the British and others to expand trade opportunities for foreigners. The Opium War illustrates the lengths to which the British were willing to go to expand their trade in China. As an island nation, Japan's geography was more amenable to isolation and Japanese leaders were generally more successful at it than were China's Qing emperors. However, in the end, foreign pressures, this time from the United States, also were too powerful for Japan to ignore or overcome.

TEST FORM B

Short Answer

1. The Opium War broke out in 1839 after the Chinese government tried to forcibly stop the British sale of opium in China. The Chinese were easily defeated by the British and in 1842, in the Treaty of Nanjing, agreed to cede Hong Kong to Britain, open more ports to British trade, and accept the principle of extraterritoriality for British subjects in China.
2. Accept any two: increased government corruption; declining government efficiency; tax increases; continuing interference by foreign powers in domestic affairs; rebellions such as the White Lotus Rebellion and the Taiping Rebellion
3. They required the daimyo to spend every other year in the capital, thereby keeping the daimyo under closer control and increasing the daimyo's expenses. They required that daimyo families remain in the capital when the daimyo returned to their estates to live, thereby holding them hostage for good behavior. They also may have prohibited daimyo alliances.
4. The Qing recognized that Chinese converted to Catholicism by the Jesuits had to promise faith and allegiance to the pope. They worried that this would undermine the people's loyalty to the emperor. The shoguns harbored a similar concern that Japanese Christians' allegiance to the Church would weaken their authority, as well as become a divisive force in their tradition-based society.
5. President Fillmore's desire to open Japan to American trade was presented in a visit by U.S. warships commanded by Matthew Perry in 1853. After considerable debate within Japan's government, the shogun agreed to this in the Treaty of Kanagawa in 1854. This opened the door to similar treaties between Japan and other foreign powers, which intensified Japanese criticism of the government and its perceived weakness toward foreigners, culminating in civil war and the overthrow of the shogunate in 1867.

Primary Sources

1. A determined person is able to lead many others persuasively.
2. He should be able to rise above them and have standards for himself that surpass the level of the average person.

Composing an Essay

1. Answers will vary but should focus on the idea that by pursing similar policies as the Japanese, China might have been better able to resist Western demands, such as the "unequal" treaties, and thereby have maintained a greater degree of independence. Students should note, however, the difficulty the Qing would have had in following such a course because of the different internal situation in China. Commerce was much more important in Chinese society, and these internal pressures made isolation much more difficult. In addition, the Tokugawa had a strong hold on Japan. Qing control was weak, causing foreign powers to have little respect for China's sovereignty or government.
2. Answers will vary, but students should recognize that the Qing were Manchu and not Chinese, and that they were numerically overwhelmed by the Chinese people. Policies requiring the study of Manchu culture and language, regarding marriage, emigration, and segregation, and others such as requiring Chinese men to wear queues and the establishment of a Manchu homeland were all designed to protect the Manchu's cultural identity and to keep it from being swallowed up in the majority Chinese culture.

Chapter 18 (Modern Chapter 9)

TEST FORM A

Fill in the Blank

1. Rajputs
2. Janissaries
3. India
4. Akbar
5. Iran
6. Süleyman
7. Bābur
8. Esmā'īl
9. Turkey
10. Mughal

Understanding Ideas

1. b
2. a
3. d
4. c
5. b
6. b
7. d
8. c
9. c
10. a

True/False

1. T
2. T
3. F
4. T
5. F

Practicing Skills

1. the imperial council or divan
2. sultan, court and divan

Composing an Essay

1. Answers will vary, but students should note that government policy in regard to religion was a central part of each dynasty's program to keep its empire stable and that, in one way or another, they all maintained control over this aspect of life in their empires. The Ottomans allowed religious freedom but only in separate religious communities, called millets, of Muslims, Christians, Jews, and other religions. Each millet had its own laws, courts, customs, and education system. On the other hand, the Safavids required their peoples to convert to Shi'ah Islam. The Mughals allowed religious freedom for a time, and even encouraged it when Akbar lifted religious taxes imposed on non-Muslims. But later, Aurangzeb persecuted all but Sunni Muslims. In terms of stability, the "hardline" policy appears to have been best. Religious tension existed in the Ottoman Empire and great unrest accompanied the rise of the Sikhs in Mughal India. Only the Safavids, who had no religious tolerance, seem to have been free from religious conflict undermining their empire.
2. The decline of the Ottoman Empire began with the death of Süleyman in 1566. It was aggravated by military defeats in Europe as the Ottomans tried to expand their empire, and later by Russian and French seizure of its territory, as well

as by power struggles that led to unrest within the empire. Its collapse finally occurred in 1923. The decline of the Mughal Empire also began following the death of a great ruler, Shah Jahān, in 1658, and, like in the Ottoman Empire, it was exacerbated by internal unrest and revolts. Similarly, the death of the great shah 'Abbās in 1629 sent the Safavid Empire into decline. Its collapse occurred much more quickly, in 1736, following a series of inept rulers. Internal unrest was also a factor, as evidenced by the fact that the empire split into a number of small states.

TEST FORM B

Short Answer

1. The sultan was at the top, followed by a secondary level called grand viziers. The people were organized into self-governing millets, according to the religion they followed. Each millet had its own laws, courts, taxes, and education system.
2. The decline began with the death of Süleyman in 1566. It was aggravated by defeats in Europe as the Ottomans tried to expand their empire, and by Russian and French seizure of its territory. Power struggles, government corruption, and rebellions among the Janissaries were also factors.
3. 'Abbās the Great reformed the Safavid military, using the Ottoman army as a model, and then recaptured all the lands that his predecessors had lost to the Ottomans and Uzbeks. He also founded a new capital on the Plateau of Iran.
4. He appointed the Indian warrior princes, the Rajputs, to government positions; married a Rajput princess; used military force; introduced humane tax reforms; and allowed religious freedom.
5. Safavid: Persian rugs; Mughal: Taj Mahal

Primary Sources

1. He relied upon the Qur'an and prayer before taking any action in government.
2. God, by governing the actions of 'Abbās through the Qur'an

Composing an Essay

1. Answers will vary, but students' choices and explanations should demonstrate a clear and accurate understanding of the comparative economic, cultural, and sociopolitical conditions in these empires as well as a conclusion that is based on the evaluation criteria each student sets forth. In general, the factors that students' essays might consider and weigh, according to their relative importance to each student, are these:
   (1) religious policies and practices (most open in Akbar's India and in the Ottoman Empire and most repressive in the Safavid, and later the Mughal, Empires); (2) comparative social organization and social mobility (for example, the segregation of the Ottoman millets and the opportunities there for social advancement); (3) cultural and economic variables, including commercial activities and standard of living (each had a highly developed culture, with a variety of skilled crafts and a flourishing trade).
2. Answers will vary, but students should note that all three thrived on rule by strong leaders and were to a great extent based on and maintained by military power. To varying degrees, each empire recognized the cultural traditions of its peoples. But tight controls also existed, particularly in the area of religion. The Ottomans illustrate both concepts. Their empire was organized into segregated millets, where each people could follow their own religion and have their own laws, courts, and educational system. The Safavids, on the other hand, exercised religious control by requiring peoples to convert to Shi'ah Islam. The Mughals allowed religious freedom for a time, but later imposed heavy taxes on Hindus and persecuted all but Sunni Muslims.

ANSWER KEY

Unit 4 (Modern Unit 2)

TEST FORM A

Understanding Ideas

1. d
2. b
3. c
4. a
5. c
6. d
7. b
8. a
9. a
10. c

Matching

1. i
2. l
3. a
4. n
5. c
6. h
7. m
8. f
9. k
10. g

True/False

1. F
2. F
3. T
4. T
5. F

Practicing Skills

1. Asia (also accept China, Indies, or East Indies)
2. Answers will vary but should suggest that it would have spread more quickly over sea routes, where travel was more direct, than it would have over land.

Composing an Essay

1. Both experienced a long period of decline. Internal unrest, as well as external factors, played a large part in the fall of both rules. The Qing dynasty began to decline following the White Lotus Rebellion in 1796 and was further damaged by the Taiping Rebellion in the 1850s and 1860s. Increased government corruption and declining government efficiency were also factors. The decline of the Ottoman Empire began with the death of Süleyman in 1566. Ottoman government also became corrupt over time, and revolts by the Janissaries weakened the sultans as well.

   The weakness of later rulers in both empires encouraged foreign interference in their sovereignty. The Russians and French seized Ottoman territory, while following the Opium War with Great Britain, the Qing rulers were forced into signing "unequal treaties" that gave foreigners unprecedented rights and powers in China. All these factors weakened both powers and eventually led to their collapse—the Qing dynasty in 1912 and the Ottoman Empire in 1923.
2. Before the Scientific Revolution, scientists relied on the work of classical scholars for their understanding of the world. These early scientists had believed that one could learn about the physical world by understanding things through logic and reasoning. Although the ancients made observations of the phenomena they studied, the conclusions they drew from those observations were based on deductive assumptions and were not tested. Later scientists believed that observations had to be verifiable in order to be considered valid and useful. The scientific method developed during the Scientific Revolution stressed verification through mathematical proofs or by experiments that could be repeated over and over to make sure they produced the same results. For example, Galileo Galilei and Johannes Kepler both proved the heliocentric theory of the solar system developed earlier by Copernicus was correct—Kepler doing this through mathematical proofs. Through repeated experiments, Isaac Newton also proved a series of observations and conclusions about gravity and motion.

TEST FORM B

Short Answer

1. Answers will vary, but students should correctly identify Renaissance writers and artists and accurately describe the contribution of each.
2. Before the Scientific Revolution, scientists relied on the work of classical scholars for their understanding of the world. This information, though based on observations by the ancients, was also based on deductive assumptions and conclusions that had not been tested for veracity. The scientific method developed during the Scientific Revolution called for conclusions to be verifiable through mathematics or by repeatable experiments before they were accepted.
3. The basic reason for both exploration and colonization was mercantilism, which itself was related to the even more fundamental reason of trade. Mercantile theory held that a favorable balance of trade—exports over imports—was critical to a nation's strength and to the related acquisition of gold. The initial voyages of exploration were to find routes to develop this trade. The European colonies that were established in the Americas and Asia were also trade-related—serving as sources of needed products for the home country and as markets for the home country's products.
4. Both were beset by internal unrest, such as the Janissaries' rebellions in the Ottoman Empire and the White Lotus and Taiping Rebellions in China. Both were also weakened by European military and other interventions—the French and Russians taking territory from the Ottomans and the British and European powers destroying Qing sovereignty through the Opium War and the "unequal treaties."
5. The Ottomans allowed religious freedom but only in separate, segregated religious communities of Christians, Jews, and other non-Muslims. In contrast, the Safavids required their peoples to convert to Shi'ah Islam. The Mughals allowed religious freedom, and even encouraged it for a time; but later all but Sunni Muslims were taxed and persecuted.

Primary Sources

1. gold; he makes mention of it twice, implies that it is what attracts him about the larger island which the natives have reported to him, and holds it out as a lure or incentive for further help from his sponsors
2. that they are not Christians; he promises to enslave and ship as many of "these idolators" as his sponsors desire.

Composing an Essay

1. Answers will vary, but students should recognize that both exploration and the Reformation were outgrowths of the awakening of interest in learning and knowledge that characterized the Renaissance. Renaissance humanists like Erasmus were among the first to criticize the Catholic Church and question its teachings and practices. They urged like-minded persons to join them. From these criticisms and this call, the Reformation gradually took shape.

   The spirit of curiosity, investigation, and discovery that characterized the Renaissance was also responsible for stirring Europeans' interest in what lay beyond the world with which they were familiar. Improvements in mapmaking, navigation, and general knowledge of the physical world that resulted from the Scientific Revolution—another outgrowth of the Renaissance spirit—made such voyages of exploration more possible.

   Later, the sociopolitical unrest that the Reformation stirred throughout Europe, as well as missionary zeal of the Counter-Reformation, helped to fuel European settlement in many of the lands the explorers encountered. The Huguenots, Calvinists, and Puritans who settled in North America were the direct or indirect result of Reformation-related conditions and events in Europe.

2. Answers will vary, but students should realize that both movements were influenced by revolutionary thinkers, that both involved new ways of thinking, and that both questioned existing beliefs and practices, as well as the authority on which they were based. The Reformation came about because of new ways of thinking about church authority. The reformers wanted people to become more spiritual and less concerned with the ceremonies and rituals of their traditional religion. They stressed new ways of thinking about God, salvation, and faith. The leaders of the Scientific Revolution also stressed new ways of thinking and rejected many traditional—in this case classical or historical—authorities and their views. They, too, questioned beliefs that were long held, and accepted largely for that reason. Instead, they advocated investigation over reliance on traditional assumptions.

   A basic difference in the two movements is that the Reformation focused on the spiritual world while the Scientific Revolution centered on the natural or physical one. In addition, the methods each advocated—prayer and study of the Bible and other historical texts versus observation and experimentation—were fundamentally different. In sum, the Reformation taught people to have faith while the Scientific Revolution taught people to doubt.

Chapter 19 (Modern Chapter 10)

TEST FORM A

Fill in the Blank

1. Frederick William (the Great Elector)
2. Frederick I
3. Frederick William I
4. Frederick II (Frederick the Great)
5. Louis XIV
6. the (Spanish) Armada
7. Catholic
8. Poland
9. Turks (Ottomans)
10. Scotland

Understanding Ideas

1. b
2. c
3. d
4. a
5. c
6. b
7. a
8. b
9. d
10. d

True/False

1. F
2. T
3. F
4. T
5. T

Practicing Skills

1. King Philip II of Spain and Queen Mary I of England; her maternal grandparents and his maternal great-great grandparents were the same, making his wife also his great aunt.
2. James I was the son of Mary Queen of Scots and King Francis II of France

Composing an Essay

1. Russia was separated from Europe both culturally and geographically. The Mongols' nearly 200-year domination before 1480 had given Russia a strong Asian orientation and influence. When Western civilization did come to Russia, it came through Constantinople and the Byzantine Empire rather than through western Europe itself. For example, Russian Christians followed the Eastern Orthodox church, not the church in Rome. In addition, Russia used the Cyrillic alphabet, which made communication with the rest of Europe difficult. Geographically, the nation was virtually landlocked. Sweden and Poland blocked access to the Baltic and the Ottoman Turks controlled the coast of the Black Sea. Nor did Russia's major rivers flow into seas that encouraged commerce or communication.
2. The issue that set off some 100 years of religious unrest was the dispute between Henry VIII and the Catholic Church over Henry's wish for a divorce. This led to the establishment of the Anglican Church. Henry's Catholic daughter

Mary came to the throne upon his death and tried to make England a Catholic nation again. This resulted in persecution of Protestants and rebellions against the crown. Upon Mary's death, her Anglican half-sister Elizabeth became queen. Catholics hoped to replace her with her Catholic relative, Mary Queen of Scots, but Elizabeth had Mary beheaded. This failure to restore Catholic rule caused Philip II, the Catholic king of Spain, to send his Armada to conquer England. Its failure solidified Elizabeth's rule and strengthened the Protestants. However, a split developed among them over reforming the Anglican Church, producing the Puritans, whose increasing power in Parliament created conflict with Elizabeth's successor, James I, who was also king of Scotland and a strong supporter of the Anglican Church.

TEST FORM B

Short Answer

1. They centralized authority by weakening the nobility's power, appointing regional officials to represent the king, and by first destroying the Protestant Huguenots' military power and later driving them from the country by ending religious freedom in Catholic France.
2. The war was fought on three continents. Besides fighting in Europe, the British and French fought in India and in North America, where the conflict actually began, and where it was known as the French and Indian War.
3. The king's lavish rule, capped by the construction of his huge palace at Versailles strained the French treasury, as did the four wars he fought during his reign. On the other hand, his adviser Colbert strengthened the economy through tax reform and by promoting development with subsidies to new industries and high tariffs on imports.
4. Frederick William (the Great Elector) strengthened the small German state of Brandenburg-Prussia by unifying its armies, and improving agriculture, industry, and the tax and transportation systems. Frederick I united all the Hohenzollern lands under his rule as the first true King of Prussia. Frederick William I made Prussia's government and army more efficient and better equipped. He trained the army, and doubled its size to make it one of Europe's most powerful forces.
5. James was both an absolutist and king of Scotland before becoming king of England, making some doubt his commitment to England's system of government. James intensified these fears by trying to involve himself in the affairs of the House of Commons. He was also a strong Anglican at a time when the Puritans were powerful in Parliament. His financial polices and attempts to negotiate an alliance with Catholic Spain were additional irritants.

Primary Sources

1. that some may dismiss her because she is a woman, but although she has less physical strength than a king, she has the same inner strength and courage
2. that she respects her subjects, that the source of her ruling power comes from their loyalty and support, and that she is willing to die to defend their continued freedom

Composing an Essay

1. Answers will vary but should include the following major points. Peter wanted to expand Russia's borders, but mainly tried to westernize the nation. Catherine continued Peter's reforms, but mainly tried to expand Russia's borders. Domestically, both consolidated their power within Russia by eliminating competition from the nobility. Peter created a highly centralized government that controlled the nobles, church, and local government. He controlled the nobles by isolating them and restricting their freedom of movement, as well as by rewarding loyal nobles with grants of land and serfs and through

his "service nobility" system in which their rank depended on performance in his government. Catherine bought nobles' support through her support of the arts and sciences. In foreign affairs, both waged war around the Black Sea, but Catherine had greater success, gaining its north shore and the Crimea from the Turks. Peter gained access to the Baltic in a war against Sweden. Catherine also expanded the nation west by dividing up Poland with Austria and Prussia.

2. The Thirty Years' War benefited France by making it stronger at the expense of its European rivals. France, as well as Denmark and Sweden wanted to weaken the Holy Roman Empire and its ruling family, the Habsburgs. France accomplished its goals largely by staying out of the war but encouraging continued fighting by the others. As a result, Germany, where most of the fighting took place, was weakened, as was the Holy Roman Empire and its political center, Austria. Austria's Habsburg rulers lost control of most of the German states, whose princes became increasingly independent of Habsburg rule after their defeat in the war. At the same time, the German weakness that resulted from the war allowed Prussia to consolidate its power in the region. Blocked by the increased power of France on the west, and of Prussia to its north, Austria was weakened. This encouraged Prussia to seize the Austrian territory of Silesia, which it did easily, precipitating the War of the Austrian Succession, which Austria lost in 1748. This loss caused Austria's major ally, Britain, to become Prussia's ally instead. To keep Prussia from becoming too powerful, France joined with Austria and Russia. This entire chain of events was set in motion by the Thirty Years' War and its consequences.

Chapter 20 (Modern Chapter 11)

TEST FORM A

Matching

1. l
2. f
3. h
4. a
5. c
6. k
7. d
8. i
9. g
10. b

Understanding Ideas

1. a
2. c
3. b
4. a
5. c
6. b
7. d
8. a
9. c
10. b

True/False

1. T
2. F
3. T
4. F
5. T

Practicing Skills

1. It raised expenses to levels that exceeded income (deficit spending).

2. to make up for the deficits, or pay off the debts it incurred between about 1757 and the end of the war

Composing an Essay

1. Locke believed that people had a social contract with their rulers in which they gave up many of their individual rights but kept their natural rights, which were the right to life, liberty, and the enjoyment of their property. He believed that if a ruler violated these rights, the people had the right to overthrow and replace the ruler with another who pledged to observe and protect those rights. Neither Charles I or James II, as absolutist monarchs, were willing to recognize these rights or the House of Commons as representative of the people. Neither were receptive to Parliament's attempts to assert the people's rights. Thus Locke's ideas provided the justification for removing both from the throne.

2. Answers will vary, but students should note that mercantilism was a prime motivator for establishing colonies established in both regions. However, British activities in India at first were more directed toward trade and less toward exploration, land acquisition, and permanent settlement than in North America. Another factor was that an empire, albeit one in decline, existed in India. No such situation existed in America (although the British did have to deal with regional Native American groups). Another similarity was the competing French interests that developed in both regions, which the British won out in both colonies.

TEST FORM B

Short Answer

1. Parliament forced Charles I to sign the Petition of Right, which limited his power to tax without Parliament's consent. Charles, however, ignored the Petition, dismissed Parliament and ruled for the next 11 years. When a rebellion broke out in Scotland, he called it back into session to approve new taxes. When another rebellion began in Ireland, Parliament insisted on control over the army. When Charles refused, civil war began.
2. Catholic James II, who became king when his brother, King Charles II, died childless, had a Protestant daughter, Mary, by his first wife and a Catholic son by his second wife. By law, the son would be king when James died. Instead, Parliament forced James to step down and invited Mary and her husband, William of Orange, to be joint rulers.
3. In India, mercantilism was responsible for the emphasis on trade and trading posts that dominated early relations with the Mughals and that gave the East India Company so much power. In America it was responsible for shaping the colonies' economic development through such things as restrictions on manufacturing and trade, a tax on non-British sugar, and smuggling to avoid these laws.
4. Having to defend the colonies from the French in the French and Indian War caused the British government to run up a huge debt. Britain decided that the colonies should repay these costs of their defense. So the British began to raise money in the colonies by taxing them in various ways.
5. Government under the Articles was weak and ineffective. The Articles denied Congress important power, such as to tax and regulate trade. The legislative process was cumbersome, requiring approval of 9 of the 13 states. There was no chief executive or national courts. Americans soon realized that a more effective national government would be needed to build a strong nation.

Primary Sources

1. for performing his duty to rule on behalf of the people—thereby freeing them of the need to rule themselves, so that they can enjoy their lives—and for refusing to give in to the "arbitrary" demands of Parliament to change laws in ways that are not in the people's bests interests
2. He claims that rulers and their people are "clean different things," and that the people do not need to "share in government" in order to obtain the laws necessary for them to enjoy liberty and freedom. Providing such laws, he says, is the king's job and "nothing pertaining to them."

Composing an Essay

1. Answers will vary but, at a minimum, should note the following points: Hobbes believed that people gave their rulers absolute power and retained only the right to protect their own lives. The Declaration declares that this absolute power to rule lies with the people as their own rulers, and that only by their consent can they delegate it to others. The Declaration is closer in line with Locke, whose ideas about natural rights correspond to the three rights enumerated in the Declaration. Like Locke, Jefferson

believed that a ruler's key function was to safeguard these rights of the people. Jefferson also accepted Locke's argument that leaders who violated the social contract to protect these rights could be justifiably overthrown by the people and replaced by another government. This argument is what provided the justification for the Revolution's armed resistance of British authority and the declaration of separation from Great Britain.

2. Britain was a "monarchy" in that the nation had a king or queen. It was a "limited" monarchy in that the prime minister became the real head of government. The prime minister selected the other members of the cabinet and, together, they planned and executed government policy. In addition, the monarch had to consult Parliament in order to exercise any power. The government was "constitutional" in that government power, and the power of the monarch in particular, was limited by a series of documents that, together, comprise Britain's "constitution." These documents include the Magna Carta, the Petition of Rights, the English Bill of Rights, the Habeas Corpus Act, the Act of Settlement, and other acts of Parliament.

Students' lists of political developments will vary, but should include and discuss three of the following: Each of the documents mentioned above, as well as the Toleration Act, reduced the monarch's power to rule absolutely. The powers of Parliament were gradually increased, including the power to declare war. As Parliament gained strength, the monarch's veto power disappeared. The office of prime minister and cabinet developed and, instead of meeting with their traditional advisors, monarchs met with ministers to discuss problems. Under the leadership of Robert Walpole, from the 1720s to the 1740s, the authority of the prime minister grew to exceed that of the monarch.

Chapter 21 (Modern Chapter 12)

TEST FORM A

Fill in the Blank

1. nobles (the nobility)
2. Marie-Antoinette
3. radicals
4. Legislative Assembly
5. Catholic clergy
6. Directory
7. Concordat
8. National Convention
9. Consulate
10. peasants

Understanding Ideas

1. a
2. c
3. c
4. b
5. b
6. d
7. c
8. b
9. d
10. a

True/False

1. T
2. T
3. T
4. F
5. F

Practicing Skills

1. It gave him a base from which to invade Russia.
2. France

Composing an Essay

1. During the reign of Terror, which lasted from September 1793 to July 1794, the National Convention, led by the Jacobin radicals Danton and Robespierre, attempted to suppress all opposition to the revolution. Through the Convention's Revolutionary Tribunal, they executed people of all classes who were even suspected of disloyalty. Among the first were their political opponents in the National Convention. Eventually, twice as many people from the bourgeoisie were victims as nobles, and more than twice as many workers and peasants as bourgeoisie. Even Danton became a victim. His loyalty became suspect when he suggested that the Reign of Terror had met its goal and should be stopped. However, not until other members of the National Convention intervened and executed Robespierre did the Reign of Terror come to an end.

2. Napoléon reorganized and centralized the government of France. Among his reforms were the organization of all French law into a system called the Napoléonic Code, and the establishment of a central Bank of France, as well as a public education system that included high schools, universities, and technical schools. He also ended a conflict that had developed between the French government and the Roman Catholic Church. Napoléon's conquests spread his ideas about centralized government across Europe. He merged small states in Germany and Italy into two kingdoms under his control. Everywhere his armies went they introduced the Napoléonic Code, putting an end to the last vestiges of feudalism and serfdom. Ironically, French ideas about human rights that Napoléon's forces spread across Europe awakened feelings of nationalism among the peoples he conquered.

TEST FORM B

Short Answer

1. It wrote a new constitution to create a constitutional monarchy in which the king had severely limited powers; ended the vestiges of feudalism, tithing, and the privileges of the First and Second Estates; issued the Declaration of the Rights of Man and of the Citizen; and made major reforms in the Catholic Church. It took these actions in hopes of heading off more radical changes in France.
2. the National Convention, because it executed Louis XVI and conducted the Reign of Terror
3. He abolished the Holy Roman Empire and organized the small states of Germany and northern Italy into a confederation and kingdom, respectively, under his control. He also directly ruled the Netherlands and Spain, and forced most of the rest of Europe to sign treaties of alliance with France.
4. The Russians used Russia's climate and size by retreating in front of Napoléon's army as it advanced deep into Russia. As the Russian army retreated, they practiced a scorched-earth policy, destroying anything Napoléon's army could use. When winter came, Napoléon's army had to retreat back across this expanse of land in bitter cold without proper clothing or supplies. By the time Napoléon's army left Russia, two-thirds of the army had been destroyed. The Russians then invaded Napoléon's empire. The Russian disaster caused Napoléon's allies to desert him and join the Russians against him.
5. Territorial settlements made at the Congress of Vienna caused tensions between nations. Internally, nations faced rising nationalism and other unrest inspired by Napoléon's spread of French revolutionary ideas. In response, the nations of Europe formed an alliance system called the Concert of Europe to help one another maintain a balance of power.

Primary Sources

1. at first surprise, followed by admiration, followed by fear
2. She rejects that she was uneasy because of his power, because at the time he had none. Instead, she attributes her uneasiness to his personality, which blocked any insights into his true character.

Composing an Essay

1. Summaries will vary, but students may suggest that French society became less structured and more people had freedoms. In addition, the French people, and Europeans in general, became aware that oppressive political systems could be changed. Human rights emerged as a widespread concept, and nationalism also grew. On the other hand, countless thousands of French and other people lost their lives in the internal unrest and foreign wars that accompanied the

revolution. Student judgments of its success will vary but should be supported by sound and valid arguments.

2. Answers will vary. Some students may focus on the immediate political events that precipitated the uprising, such as the meeting and actions of the Estates General or Louis XVI's actions, which inflamed a tense political situation into a crisis. Students who argue social factors might cite growing family size or the class structure of the Old Regime—for example, the disparity between class size, wealth, and political power. Power and privilege were concentrated in the First and Second Estates, which comprised less than three percent of the population. The large and wealthy bourgeoisie had much less power, were burdened by government regulations, and paid more taxes. Peasants and workers, the largest part of French society, had no voice and the heaviest burden of all.

Other students may cite purely economic factors. Declining economic conditions fell hardest on peasants and urban workers, who struggled to feed their families while facing rising prices, rents, and taxes. On the other hand, the nobility and clergy were determined to use their power and status to minimize the effects of economic problems on themselves, and they shifted the economic burden to the Third Estate.

Unit 5 (Modern Unit 3)

TEST FORM A

Understanding Ideas

1. c
2. d
3. b
4. b
5. a
6. d
7. c
8. a
9. c
10. b
11. a
12. d

Matching

1. f
2. l
3. b
4. j
5. d
6. g
7. a
8. c

True/False

1. F
2. T
3. T
4. T
5. F

Practicing Skills

1. the U.S. system; they elect the chief executive and both houses of the legislature, whereas in the British system they elect only the House of Commons

2. In the British system the lower house (House of Commons) selects the chief executive (prime minister) and cooperates in the selection of his or her cabinet. In the U.S. system the upper house (Senate) cooperates in the selection of the cabinet and neither house has any role in the selection of the chief executive (president).

Composing an Essay

1. Answers will vary but should show recognition of the following basic points. The English civil war and the French Revolution were both initially internal power struggles between the legislature and the king, while the American Revolution was a struggle of colonies for independence from both the legislature and the king. In England the power struggle itself was the cause of the conflict, while in France the cause was rooted in basic political and economic inequities of French society. The causes of the American Revolution were a blend of both. The colonists wanted to take governing power from Parliament and the king, but economic inequities and grievances with Britain were a factor as well. One issue that all three conflicts shared, in one form or another, was that of taxation.

2. Answers should touch on the following points. By the early 1600s, the struggle between Catholics and Protestants over which faith would be the state religion had quieted to a degree in both nations. The defeat of the Spanish Armada had solidified the Anglican hold on England, and in France the Edict of Nantes granted a measure of toleration to the Huguenots in what remained an officially Catholic nation. So, in both countries, religious conflict began to center around the exercise of political power. In France the Huguenots exercised religious freedom until the monarch thought they weakened his power and their religious freedom was revoked by Louis XIV. By contrast, in England the basic issue was the religion of the monarch. The Protestant-controlled Parliament went to great lengths to manipulate the answer to this question, although often not successfully. They finally reached their intended goal, however, in 1688, when the Catholic James II was deposed and replaced with Protestants Mary and William of Orange. This "Glorious Revolution" ended Catholic rule in England. The Act of Settlement in 1701, which banned Catholics from the throne, made the Protestant victory complete.

TEST FORM B

Short Answer

1. Both created highly centralized governments. Richelieu did this by establishing regional governments controlled by intendants who were directly responsible to the king. Peter did this by making the nobles his agents in a system of service nobility, under which their rank depended on the performance of service to his government. Peter also required the most powerful nobles to live in the capital and spend time at court, so he could keep watch over their actions.
2. Frederick William, prince of Brandenburg-Prussia, unified his armies into one force and strengthened his small state by improving its government and economy. His successor, Frederick I, consolidated all Hohenzollern lands into the kingdom of Prussia and became its first king. His son, Frederick William I, streamlined the government and doubled the size of the army. Frederick William I's son, Frederick II (the Great) spent half of his 46-year rule at war to expand Prussia's territory and power, and the remaining 23 years strengthening Prussia internally by improving its government, economic development, and education system.
3. Locke taught that people form governments to protect their "natural rights" to life, liberty, and property, and that if the government they form does not do this, they have a right to replace it with another. This argument provided the justification for revolution expressed by Jefferson in the Declaration of Independence. The later Enlightenment thinker Baron de Montesquieu believed that the best form of rule was one in which power was distributed among branches of government, with a system of checks and balances in place between them. This approach was reflected in the three-branch system created in the Constitution.
4. Accept any two of the following internal reforms: organized French law into the Napoléonic Code; established the Bank of France as a central financial institution; created a system of public high schools, universities, and technical schools; reached an agreement with the pope to allow religious freedom. Accept any two of the following European reforms: organized the German principalities into the Confederation of the Rhine; organized small northern Italian states into the Kingdom of Italy; brought Spain under his direct rule; abolished the Holy Roman Empire.
5. Accept any two of the following: the Congress of Vienna shuffled borders to restore the balance of power in Europe and keep any nation from becoming too powerful; former ruling families were restored to their thrones; an alliance system, including the Quadruple Alliance and the Holy Alliance, allowed countries to discuss and coordinate their common interests; the Concert of Europe produced a spirit of cooperation that maintained the balance of power until 1848.

Primary Sources

1. that they pay taxes and the local nobles do not, and that they pay many taxes for which they are unaware of any legal basis; their demand is that all taxes not approved by the nation's legislature be eliminated
2. France, because the peasants there were heavily taxed and the nobles paid few if any taxes, which was a cause of the French Revolution and which is the situation described in the petition

Composing an Essay

1. Answers will vary, but students' essays should show recognition of the following points: In terms of their nature, the English civil war and the French Revolution were both internal power struggles, while the American Revolution was an effort for independence from an external rule. The Americans were resisting both Parliament and king, while in England the conflict was between legislature and king, and the French Revolution also began that way. All three were caused by what was perceived to be the repressive rule of those in power—the king in England and France, and the king and Parliament in America. In all three, the underlying causes were both political and economic—the perception of an unfair and oppressive tax burden and the inability of those being oppressed to have a voice in their government, as well as other forms of perceived political and economic oppression. Another underlying issue was taxation without consent—in England and France, it being the king's taxation of the people without the consent of Parliament or the Estates General, the people's representatives, both of which had not been summoned for a long time. In America the "no taxation without representation" issue was important because the colonists had no representatives in Parliament.

   All three were military conflicts involving armies on each side and formal battles, although less so in France, where the Revolution was somewhat more in the nature of an insurrection. In all three, a republic was established by the revolutionaries. In England and France, the republic went through several phases before ending in dictatorship—the Consulate of Napoléon and the Protectorate of Cromwell. In France, the dictator eventually became emperor, while in England Cromwell was eventually replaced by a restored monarchy (albeit with severely reduced powers). The American republic also went through phases in the aftermath of revolution, with government under the Articles of Confederation being replaced by the Constitution. The French also wrote several new constitutions during their various phases of government.

   All three conflicts lasted years, although the military aspect of the French Revolution was over rather quickly as the republican forces seized control. However, the French Revolution had a radical phase, the Reign of Terror, that the other two did not.
2. Answers will vary, but students should realize that Britain was least interested in expanding its borders and most interested in building an empire, while the reverse was true for Russia. France fell between these extremes, acting both to expand its national territory and to secure an empire, primarily in the Americas. Britain also pursued an American empire by founding colonies there, while establishing a presence in India to exploit trade. In both India and America, British and French imperial interests competed, resulting in war in both of the empires and in Europe and victory for British colonial interests. In Europe this was known as the Seven Years' War, and as the French and Indian War in the Americas.

   France was also involved in wars in Europe, where national expansion was a goal, mainly east to the Rhine, which the French saw as a natural border. Along these lines, France added Alsace in 1648, after the Thirty Years' War, and fought four more wars between 1667 and 1713 to add additional territory. One of these wars was the War of the Spanish

Succession, in which France tried to extend its influence over Spain. The Treaty of Utrecht prevented this in 1713. Britain was one of the nations involved in the war, but more to block the growth of French power than to achieve any territorial goals of its own.

Russia was involved in none of these conflicts in the late 1600s and early 1700s, concentrating instead on expansion attempts in the west and south to secure ports to end its status as a "landlocked" nation. In 1700 Peter the Great launched a 21-year war with Sweden, which ended with Russia gaining land along the Baltic Sea (where St. Petersburg was built as a port and capital of Russia). Later in the 1700s, one of Peter's successors, Catherine the Great, finally seized the north shore of the Black Sea from the Turks. As Russia expanded into Europe in the mid-1700s, it became involved in Europe's territorial conflicts, taking part in the War of the Austrian Succession in the 1740s and in the Seven Years' War in the 1750s and 1760s, but it gained no territory from these ventures. However, Russia took part in the partitions of Poland with Austria and Prussia in the 1770s and 1790s, and in this way gained additional territory in eastern Europe.

Chapter 22 (Modern Chapter 13)

TEST FORM A

Matching

1. g
2. a
3. h
4. c
5. d
6. b
7. f
8. e
9. j
10. k

Understanding Ideas

1. b
2. a
3. c
4. a
5. c
6. d
7. b
8. d
9. b
10. a

True/False

1. F
2. T
3. T
4. F
5. T

Practicing Skills

1. coal and metal
2. There are many canals and rivers, which made it possible to bring raw materials to factories and finished goods to markets.

Composing an Essay

1. Both capitalism and socialism are economic systems. In capitalism, the means of production are privately owned and are operated for the benefit of the owners. In socialism, the means of production are owned by the state and are operated for the benefit of all.
2. The middle class grew because industrialization required well-educated people to run the corporations and to serve as bankers, lawyers, doctors, and professors. As their numbers and their importance in industry increased, members of the middle class gained political as well as social power.

TEST FORM B

Short Answer

1. Britain had a large supply of such natural resources as coal and iron ore and rich sources of capital, including money, machinery, and equipment. The many rivers and harbors encouraged trade, and there was a large supply of labor as a result of population growth and migration to cities.
2. As a result of industrialization, women no longer worked on family farms, but instead took jobs in factories or as domestic workers. Better educational opportunities developed, leading to more independence for women.
3. As a result of industrialization, products no longer were made by skilled workers. Instead, work was broken down into easily learned steps, and machines helped workers produce more in a shorter time.

4. pressure from reformers, passage of reform laws, strikes, and collective bargaining by unions
5. The utopian socialists believed that people could live peacefully together in small cooperative settlements and work for the common good. Marx and Engels believed that utopian socialism was not practical and that inequality always caused a struggle between those who owned property and those who did not. They believed that the entire capitalist system needed to be destroyed.

Primary Source

1. about 16 hours
2. Children received only one meal a day and had a limited amount of time to eat it; they did not receive any other work breaks; and they were sometimes whipped.

Composing an Essay

1. Before the Industrial Revolution, Britain was an agricultural society in which people worked their own land to grow food for their families, and they grazed their sheep and cattle on common lands. After enclosure fenced in the common lands, large landholders added to their holdings, and small farmers either became tenant farmers or moved to the cities. Improvements in agriculture made it possible for large farmers to grow more crops on the same amount of land. Mechanization had a similar effect on manufacturing industries, making it possible for fewer people to produce more than did the skilled craftspeople of earlier times. Work was broken down into simple, easily learned steps, and workers could earn only as much as factory owners were willing to pay. They had to follow many rules and often worked in poor conditions. Businesses grew in size, and corporations became a common organizational type.
2. Industrialists and economists saw industrialization as bringing more benefits, while workers, reformers, and socialists focused more on the problems caused by industrialization. Industrialists felt that government should not try to regulate business, but should instead leave decisions about hiring, wages, tariffs, and trade to business owners. Economists supported this position based on the laws of supply and demand and competition. Workers, on the other hand, contended with low wages, lack of job security, and poor working and living conditions. Reformers argued that laws were needed to protect workers, while some socialists proposed setting up small cooperative settlements and others the destruction of the capitalist system underlying industrialization.

Chapter 23 (Modern Chapter 14)

TEST FORM A

Fill in the Blank

1. pasteurization
2. Sigmund Freud
3. Thomas Edison
4. romanticism
5. emigration
6. antisepsis
7. Walter Camp
8. Paul Cézanne
9. Alexander Graham Bell
10. Herbert Spencer

Understanding Ideas

1. c
2. d
3. d
4. a
5. b
6. a
7. a
8. b
9. c
10. c

True/False

1. F
2. T
3. F
4. F
5. T

Practicing Skills

1. by about 2 times
2. No, their populations did not grow as quickly.

Composing an Essay

1. The early sociologists were interested in adapting the theories of the biological sciences to the new field, which they say is operating by laws similar to the laws of nature. Herbert Spencer applied the theory of natural selection to human societies, contending that society had evolved through selection from lower to higher forms, and that the fittest societies survived while those that were less fit perished. This theory was known as social Darwinism.
2. The 1800s saw the growth of free public education in many countries. Laws were passed that required education for all children up to a certain age. Kindergartens and state universities became part of school systems. Science and other new subjects were offered, as were vocational and technical training. Girls received elementary education, and some secondary education was available. Colleges for women began to appear.

TEST FORM B

Short Answer

1. The development of electrical power inspired the inventions of the telephone and wireless communication.
2. Vaccines, new medicines, better sanitation, safer surgical techniques, and antisepsis allowed people to stay healthier and live longer.
3. Sociology is the social science that studies human relationships. The French philosopher Auguste Comte, who was one of the founders, stated that society operated according to laws and that sociologists should use the scientific method to study society. Later, sociologists adapted the theory of evolution to sociology.
4. The population of cities increased drastically. The cities were unhealthy and smelled of smoke, garbage, and sewage. Later in the century, various technological advances such as public sewers and paved streets made the cities more livable. Police departments were set up to protect city dwellers. Suburbs also developed and grew, populated mostly by more affluent people who could afford to travel to work.
5. Both realism and naturalism focus on the lives of ordinary people and deal with social and economic themes. Naturalism, however, focuses only on the ugly and unpleasant aspects of everyday life, while realism presents both good and bad.

Primary Sources

1. Wordsworth wrote about the lives of ordinary country people because he believed that their emotions are simpler and country life places less restraint on their expression.
2. application of imagination to real life and of an unusual aspect to the everyday feelings and emotions

Composing an Essay

1. Answers will vary. Some students may feel that science and technology have improved people's lives, while others may feel that something valuable was lost as a result of industrialization. Students should discuss the uses of electricity to produce power, allowing homes and streets to be lighted at night; rapid communication via telephone and the wireless; better and faster transportation; and medical advances that improve health and longevity. They should also discuss the retreat from reality of romanticism and the focus on the evils of industrialization and urban life by the realists and the naturalists.
2. Public education provided the numerous managers, professionals, engineers, scientists, and other skilled workers to run factories and businesses and to continue advancing science and technology. Without free education, only people with money would have been able to send their children to school, which would have limited the numbers of such workers and slowed technological and scientific advances. The social sciences began to explore similarities in human societies and defined culture as a set of beliefs we all share.

Chapter 24 (Modern Chapter 15)

TEST FORM A

Matching

1. g
2. c
3. j
4. b
5. a
6. l
7. e
8. h
9. d
10. k

Understanding Ideas

1. d
2. b
3. c
4. d
5. a
6. c
7. a
8. c
9. d
10. b

True/False

1. T
2. F
3. F
4. T
5. F

Practicing Skills

1. Gran Columbia, Paraguay, United Provinces of La Plata, Chile, Haiti
2. United Provinces of Central America, Peru, Empire of Brazil, Bolivia, Uruguay, Mexico

Composing an Essay

1. The factors include competition between the industrial Northeast, the agricultural South, and the frontier West. The issue of slavery divided people in these regions the most. The harvesting of cotton and tobacco in the South was believed to depend on slave labor. The issue of whether slavery should be allowed in new territories ultimately led more people to favor prohibiting it entirely. After Abraham Lincoln was elected president on an antislavery platform, southern states seceded from the Union, causing the war to break out.
2. American Indians were slave farm workers, miners, and servants on the haciendas, where they were often overworked and mistreated. They were highly susceptible to European diseases, and large numbers died. To meet their needs for labor, the Spanish and Portuguese imported slaves from Africa.

TEST FORM B

Short Answer

1. Great Britain granted Canada self-government and unified the separate colonies into one state, which they had not done for the American colonies.
2. After the revolution of 1830, Louis Philippe was chosen as king of France. His policies kept prices high, which benefited the wealthy but harmed workers. Workers were not allowed to organize into labor unions. Monarchists opposed the king because he was not a direct descendant of Charles X; Bonapartists wanted a revival of the empire of Napoléon; and republicans favored reforms, granting of political rights, and establishment of a republic. There were food shortages and unemployment. When Louis Philippe restricted freedom of speech, rioting broke out.
3. After Germany occupied Paris in the Franco-Prussian War, Germany demanded territory and money from France. Although most French people wanted peace, the republicans of Paris were angry when the treaty was accepted. As a result, socialists and radical republicans set up the Commune, which was a council to govern the city of Paris.
4. Charles III instituted policies that benefited Spain rather than the colonies. He limited colonial industries that competed with those in Spain and collected high taxes from the colonies to support his wars. The colonists resented these policies and called for independence.
5. Some of the large states split into smaller countries. Conflicts between upper-class creoles and liberal mestizos made orderly rule difficult, and rebellions and dictatorships resulted.

Primary Sources

1. The declaration states that men have not allowed women to vote, participate in making laws, own property, work at jobs that pay well and receive respect, or obtain higher education.
2. The delegates followed the format of the Declaration of Independence because it is the basis of American rights and freedoms.

Composing an Essay

1. The chapter title reflects the fact that all the countries covered were experiencing various inequalities and other social problems, and all took actions to try to solve these problems and extend more rights and freedoms to citizens. The Industrial Revolution led to new inequalities in Great Britain, and there were many restrictions on who could vote and hold political office. Great Britain was also denying political freedom to its colonies. In the United States, slavery was a major issue, and after a war was fought that resulted in freeing the slaves, voting rights for women became important. After the defeat of Napoléon, France moved back and forth between various types of government, and the revolutions resulted in slow progress toward voting and economic reform. The nations of Latin America gained political freedom from Spain and Portugal, and ultimately began moving toward economic growth.
2. Great Britain refused home rule to Ireland and followed economic policies that harmed Irish farmers. Later, some land reforms were put into effect. On the other hand, when Canadians protested colonial policies, Great Britain did give Canada self-government. British settlers mistreated the original inhabitants of Australia and New Zealand, which also became self-governing colonies. Spain treated the original inhabitants of its Latin American colonies very harshly as well, and also instituted economic policies that were harmful to the colonies. Unlike the case of the British colonies, however, the Spanish colonies were forced to rebel in order to obtain political freedom.

Chapter 25 (Modern Chapter 16)

TEST FORM A

Fill in the Blank

1. Zollverein
2. Russification
3. Balkan League
4. Young Italy movement
5. Alexander II
6. Schleswig
7. Giuseppe Garibaldi
8. William II
9. Francis Joseph I
10. Kulturkampf

Understanding Ideas

1. d
2. a
3. b
4. c
5. c
6. c
7. d
8. a
9. b
10. b

True/False

1. F
2. F
3. T
4. T
5. T

Practicing Skills

1. Hungary and Transylvania by Austria in 1699
2. Greece in 1829

Composing an Essay

1. Bismarck adopted the policies of some of his opponents so as to cut into their support, as when he granted reforms proposed by the socialists. He ignored rules that got in his way, such as when he collected money for a military buildup without the approval of parliament. He was quick to go to war and even manufactured evidence so as to have France declare war on Prussia in 1870. When the emperor opposed him, he threatened to resign, forcing the emperor to give in to him. However, this didn't work in 1890, and he was forced to go ahead with his threat.
2. Attempts to liberalize the Russian government failed because the czars feared that liberal ideas would lead to revolution. Alexander II did attempt several liberal reforms, but when radical groups engaged

in violent protest, he became more conservative. When he was assassinated by radicals, his successors overturned his reforms.

TEST FORM B

Short Answer

1. Students should discuss two of the following: Giuseppe Mazzini organized the Young Italy movement, was a Carbonari, and spread ideas of the risorgimento. Camillo Benso di Cavour was chief minister of Sardinia who made reforms within the kingdom, increased its political influence, won Lombardy from the Austrians, and annexed most of the Papal States. Giuseppe Garibaldi recruited a large army and captured Sicily and Naples.
2. The German states had to abolish tariffs and adopt uniform systems of weights, measures, and currency. They also had to join together politically and accept a single overall ruler, constitution, and national capital.
3. Political parties formed by dissatisfied groups gained more power and made policy demands that conflicted with Bismarck's policies. He feared that Catholics were disloyal and tried to control the clergy and schools, which created more opposition. Social reformers and socialists pressed for reform. When William II became emperor, he felt that Bismarck had too much power, and began to rein him in.
4. Russia's national and ethnic groups were the Belorussians, Ukrainians, Great Russians, Jews, Poles, Finns, and the conquered peoples of Central Asia and Caucasia. The "Russification" program of Czar Nicholas I forced the non-Russian people of the empire to use the Russian language, accept the Orthodox religion, and adopt Russian customs. Jews were killed or forced to flee from pogroms (riots) sponsored or allowed by the government.
5. The Dual Monarchy was formed in 1867 after Prussia defeated Austria and in response to Hungarian demands for independence. It was headed by Francis Joseph I, Emperor of Austria and King of Hungary, and by ministries that controlled war, finance, and foreign affairs. Austria and Hungary had separate parliaments. The two countries provided markets for each other.

Primary Sources

1. to be strong enough to preserve their rights and independence from other European nations
2. He felt that a constitution would work better because it is more permanent and more binding than a confederation.

Composing an Essay

1. In Italy and Germany, nationalism served as the underlying reason for the movement to unify the separate states. In Italy, the nationalists were also reformers, and unification meant freeing those areas ruled by Austria as well as bringing in states that were trying to undo reform. Some nationalists in Germany also favored reform, but unification occurred under the conservative rule of Prussia, whose chancellor, Bismarck, instituted reforms only when forced to. Nationalism in Austria-Hungary and the Ottoman Empire, by contrast, involved attempts by conquered peoples who wanted to form their own nations and rule themselves. In Russia, nationalism meant the attempt by the czars to maintain power over numerous ethnic groups and to keep Western ideas and ways out of the country.
2. Overall, nationalism had a negative effect on the peace and security of the world. All the countries engaged in wars in order to unify (Italy and Germany) or to maintain their empires (Austria, Russia, the Ottoman Empire). They competed with one another to build colonial empires (Italy, Germany, Russia) and they joined with one another in alliances to gain or defend territory. Conquered peoples wanted their freedom. Political tensions were especially high in the Balkans.

Chapter 26 (Modern Chapter 17)

TEST FORM A

Matching

1. b
2. f
3. e
4. j
5. c
6. h
7. d
8. g

Understanding Ideas

1. c
2. b
3. d
4. a
5. b
6. d
7. c
8. b
9. a
10. c

True/False

1. T
2. T
3. F
4. F
5. T
6. T
7. T
8. F

Practicing Skills

1. 1898: United States and Russia; 1913: United States, Russia, and Argentina
2. British India

Composing an Essay

1. The industrialized nations needed raw materials to make products, and they needed new markets to sell the products they made. They wanted to control both the sources of raw materials and the markets so that other countries could not interfere. Also, increased population meant that there was not enough work for everyone, and imperialism meant jobs for some of them in the colonized countries.
2. In both, the United States asserted control over the nations of Latin America, in particular the right to intervene in the governments. The Platt Amendment was about Cuba only, and prohibited Cuba from transferring land to any country other than the United States. The Roosevelt Corollary, by contrast, indicated that the United States would prevent other nations from endangering the independence of any countries in the Western Hemisphere.

TEST FORM B

Short Answer

1. Christian missionaries tried to convert people to Christianity. They also helped build schools and hospitals, taught in the schools, and cared for the sick. They shared their knowledge of medicine, hygiene, and sanitation.
2. Because building the canal cost a great deal of money and the ruler of Egypt spent a great deal of money to maintain his lifestyle, the country was deeply in debt. Consequently, Egypt chose to sell its stock in the Suez Canal to the British, which gave them control.
3. Settlers from the Netherlands, known as the Boers, lived in South Africa along with the Zulu people and other native peoples. The British seized the Cape Colony from the Dutch. When the Zulu fought the Boers to take control of the areas north and east of the Cape Colony, the British joined the war and defeated the Zulus. Later, they fought and defeated the Boers to take over more territory.
4. The British controlled Burma and Singapore. Burma was on the border of India, which made it desirable to the British. Singapore guards the entrance to a vital trade route at the Strait of Malacca.
5. The United States wanted a canal across Panama so that they could move battleships from one coast to the other more quickly. When Columbia, who controlled Panama at the time, refused to let the United States lease the land, some business leaders in Panama led a revolt to break free of Columbia. The United States kept Columbia from ending the revolt, which was successful, and the new Panamanian government allowed the United States to build the canal.

Primary Sources

1. that the Europeans are not really in charge, but just think they are
2. that it takes away his freedom and reduces the meaning of his life to just trying not to be laughed at

Composing an Essay

1. Answers will vary. The argument that imperialism benefited only the European nations will focus on the material and strategic rewards it brought—raw materials, new markets, jobs for Europeans, coaling stations, and control of trade routes—and the perceived duty that they must spread Western ideas and knowledge around the world. The argument that the people in the colonized regions also benefited will focus on the education, medicine, industrialization, and new ideas the colonizers brought with them. Students should supply examples from Africa, Asia, and Latin America.
2. The original residents of dependent colonies were ruled by outsiders and did not have their own government (for example, India). People in settlement colonies would have also been faced with colonizers who lived among them and who took the best of what was available for themselves (one example is Australia). In protectorates, the original residents might have believed that they were ruled by the government that was in place before the protectorate was set up, but in fact their local ruler had no power, and Europeans controlled the areas (Egypt, for example). Most people of a country that was within the imperialist's sphere of influence would probably have no knowledge of the imperialist nation's interests and would be affected only in that other countries would not enter or intervene in their nation's affairs (most Latin American nations are examples).

Unit 6 (Modern Unit 4)

TEST FORM A

Understanding Ideas

1. c
2. a
3. c
4. b
5. d
6. b
7. d
8. a
9. b
10. a

Fill in the Blank

1. Simón Bolívar
2. autocrat
3. capitalism
4. socialism
5. Suez Canal
6. Monroe Doctrine
7. William I
8. assimilation
9. Charles Darwin
10. realism

True/False

1. T
2. F
3. T
4. F
5. F

Practicing Skills

1. Germany and Great Britain
2. France

Composing an Essay

1. By leading to imperialism, the Industrial Revolution caused many of the nations of Asia to become colonies of European countries. In the case of Japan, the Industrial Revolution spread and allowed the Japanese to modernize quickly and become imperialists themselves. Those nations that did not become colonies of Europeans, like Siam and Japan, were influenced by Western ideas.
2. Technological advances such as the wireless telegraph made faster communication between distant lands possible. The steam engine was used to power railroads and boats, which connected distant parts of the world. The introduction of steel for modern weapons made conquests easier as well.

TEST FORM B

Short Answer

1. The British treated the native peoples as inferior, and they sometimes used brutal violence against them. This was the case with the Aborigines of Australia. If the native people resisted, as did the Maori of New Zealand, the Ashanti of West Africa, and the Zulus in South Africa, the British waged war against them. In South Africa, the constitution they imposed made it impossible for nonwhites to vote. On the other hand, in India they kept public order; built roads, bridges, and railroads;

established factories, hospitals, and schools; and worked to improve farming methods. However, these improvements were made for the perceived benefit of British colonists, not the native peoples.

2. The reformers objected to the working conditions in mines and factories, especially for children. Proposals for reform included regulating work hours, setting wages, and improving housing and factory conditions. John Stuart Mill proposed equality for all men and women and guarantees of individual liberty.
3. Coaling stations were places where ships, which ran on coal, could refuel. They were at strategic locations related to shipping routes and the distance ships could travel on one load of coal. They were important to imperialists because the navies were used to protect both widely scattered colonies and merchant ships.
4. Italian nationalists in the 19th century wanted to free Italian states from Austria, protect or reinstate the reforms made during the Napoléonic era, set up republics, and unify the Italian states as one country under one ruler. Nationalists also worked toward establishing a constitutional monarchy.
5. The growth of cities increased the entertainment choices for people. Sporting events became more organized and gathered audiences. Cultural activities were made available to more people, and vaudeville and comedy emerged. Art collections were made available for viewing in museums. Playgrounds for children were built, and public parks also became available.

Primary Sources

1. The dual mandate is first to provide profits to industry and secondly to, according to Western opinion, raise the cultural attitudes of native peoples to more enlightened and sophisticated levels.
2. by building roads and railroads, reclaiming swamps and deserts, ending starvation and disease, and ending the slave trade, wars between tribes, and human sacrifice

Composing an Essay

1. Socialists considered imperialism unacceptable for a number of reasons. The means of production were in the hands of outsiders and the wealth generated was sent out of the country to the foreign owners. People were not equal—there were social classes based not only on wealth but also on nationality. All native people, no matter what their economic status, were oppressed and unequal. A Marxist would probably point out that society in the colonies had already divided into two classes: a small number of colonists and a mass of native people.
2. Germany's unification was based on the nationalist feelings of the German people. In preparing for unification, the German states first put laws and taxes into place that encouraged the growth and spread of industrialization, and the states unified economically before coming together politically. After unification, Germany became an industrial giant. Political unification involved wars to build the German empire. To provide raw materials and new markets for industrialization—and to relieve the pressures of rapid population growth—Germany claimed colonies in West Africa.

Chapter 27 (Modern Chapter 18)

TEST FORM A

Matching

1.	a	**6.**	l
2.	f	**7.**	k
3.	g	**8.**	e
4.	h	**9.**	d
5.	j	**10.**	b

Understanding Ideas

1.	d	**6.**	c
2.	b	**7.**	b
3.	c	**8.**	a
4.	b	**9.**	c
5.	a	**10.**	d

True/False

1. T
2. F
3. T
4. T
5. F

Practicing Skills

1. Russia
2. Finland, Estonia, Latvia, Lithuania

Composing an Essay

1. Russia was economically very weak and did not have adequate food and armaments. The entrance into the war by the Ottoman Empire meant that supplies could not get into Russia. The corrupt government could not deal with modern war, and Russian losses were large. By the spring, the Russian people no longer had faith in the government, and they held street demonstrations. When the Duma pressed for reforms, the czar dissolved it. The army sided with the demonstrators, and the Duma refused to disband. Finally, the czar abdicated, and a provisional government was set up. In 1917, the Bolsheviks, a radical socialist group, overthrew the provisional government and took control of Russia as the Communist Party.
2. The United States wanted a treaty that was fair to all sides and that would not cause future wars. Many of the other Allies wanted to ensure that Germany would never be powerful again. France wanted security against another attack by Germany and wanted land. Italy and Belgium also wanted land. Great Britain wanted Germany's colonies in Africa and the near destruction of the German navy. Japan wanted Germany's Pacific colonies.

TEST FORM B

Short Answer

1. Bismarck was afraid that France would try to get revenge for its defeat in the Franco-Prussian War and would also try to regain Alsace-Lorraine, so he tried to keep France isolated.
2. the sinking of the *Lusitania*, which carried some American passengers, in 1915; British propaganda about German atrocities; interception of a telegram from Germany offering to help Mexico regain the southwestern United States; the death of Americans in submarine warfare by German vessels; and the overthrow of the czarist government in Russia, which meant that all the Allies were moving toward democracy, which was not true of all the Central Powers
3. The Allies were angry about the treaty and tried to get Russia to resume fighting Germany. They also feared that Russia would try to export revolution to Allied countries, and they supported the anti-Bolshevik forces with money, arms, and troops.
4. no secret treaties; freedom of the seas; removal of economic barriers; reduction of national armaments; adjustment of colonial claims; and establishment of an association of nations
5. The Germans were upset by the treaty and pointed out that it did not follow Wilson's Fourteen Points. The Germans said that they were not solely responsible for starting the war, and they did not want to pay reparations. However, they had no choice but to sign the treaty.

Primary Sources

1. peasants, soldiers, sailors, workers, and the various ethnic groups within Russia
2. They believed that a union would make Russia strong enough to withstand the middle class, whom they characterized as being imperialist.

Composing an Essay

1. One cause of World War I was competition for colonies from which to get raw materials and to which to sell finished products. In the Balkans, Serbia was trying to get access to the Adriatic Sea, which would allow freer flow of products. After the war began, Russia's weak economic condition ultimately caused a revolution and the withdrawal of Russia from the war.

2. Some national groups benefited from the war, while others did not. As a defeated nation, Germany was subject to treaty provisions that drastically reduced its power. Poland became a separate nation. Italy and France obtained self-determination for their nationals in the areas they took over from Austria and Germany, but the Austrian and German nationals there lost self-determination. The same was true of the new nations that were formed, such as Czechoslovakia and Romania (with ethnic Hungarian and German populations, respectively). The massacre of Armenians by the Turks stopped for a short time, but then resumed. Palestine, Transjordan, Syria, and Iraq became separate nations, but were run as colonies—supposedly only until they were "ready" for self-determination. The people of the four new Baltic states gained freedom from Russia.

Chapter 28 (Modern Chapter 19)

TEST FORM A

Fill in the Blank

1. Great Depression
2. Maginot Line
3. Social Security Act
4. command economy
5. Igor Stravinsky
6. Black Shirts
7. Comintern
8. Third Reich

Understanding Ideas

1.	c	**6.**	b
2.	d	**7.**	a
3.	a	**8.**	b
4.	d	**9.**	a
5.	c	**10.**	c

True/False

1.	F	**5.**	T
2.	F	**6.**	F
3.	T	**7.**	T
4.	F	**8.**	T

Practicing Skills

1. international trade and economic nationalism
2. that it is endangered by economic nationalism

Composing an Essay

1. Economic nationalism led nations to try to protect their industries by reducing trade with other countries by establishing tariffs on imported goods. The tariffs caused the prices of the imported goods to rise, so sales went down. They thus had less money to use to buy goods from the nations with tariffs or to pay off their war debts.
2. Both fascism and communism, in practice, are totalitarian systems headed by dictators. They both try to control people by means of force and by not allowing dissent to be publicly expressed. Communism promises to achieve a classless society and to improve the lot of workers. Fascism, on the other hand, promises to preserve existing social classes and the private property of the middle and upper classes.

TEST FORM B

Short Answer

1. A pandemic is an epidemic that affects a large part of the population over a large area. The influenza pandemic of 1918–1919 spread extremely rapidly, and by the time it ended, more than 20 million people had died.
2. The Labour Party leader formed a coalition government with the Liberal Party. The government set a tight budget, protected industry from foreign competition, and helped the construction industry.
3. Investors on the New York Stock Exchange rushed to sell their shares on Black Tuesday, in fear that bad economic news would cause the stock prices to fall. The sell-off had exactly that effect. People then began withdrawing money from banks, many of which did not have adequate cash reserves, and the banks demanded that people pay their loans. Many businesses and people were bankrupt as a result.

4. Instability and cultural tensions reappeared in these nations, which also faced severe economic problems. The Austrian government began moving away from democracy. The democratic governments of Hungary, Poland, Bulgaria, Romania, and Yugoslavia gave way to monarchies or dictatorships.
5. Stalin responded to the assassination by purging party members whom he believed to be disloyal, setting up public trials, and subjecting them to brutality and intimidation. He then expanded the purge to the population as a whole.

Primary Sources

1. to make Germany powerful
2. by building an army in violation of the Treaty of Versailles and by destroying anyone who opposes Germany

Composing an Essay

1. In literature, Oswald Spengler wrote that European civilization was dying, while Hemingway, Fitzgerald, and others wrote about their own generation, which they saw as having lost its moral grounding during the war. Popular culture reflected the desire of people to work less and enjoy life more. Movies offered escape and entertainment, as did spectator sports. People purchased luxury items and other consumer goods. Their desire to live in the present was shown by the use of credit instead of paying with cash. Investors "played" the stock market, buying and selling shares, often borrowing money to do so, instead of saving or investing for the long term.
2. Italy's fascist government, Germany's Nazi government, and the Soviet Union's communist government were totalitarian societies led by dictators. All disbanded competing political parties, and only members of the party in power held government positions. Democratic liberties disappeared. All three used secret police to control their populations. Mussolini instituted corporatism, in which major economic activities were formed into organizations that managed wages, prices, and working conditions. Hitler planned to achieve "racial purity" through the elimination of all Jews and others he considered impure. The ideology of the Soviet Union, unlike that of Germany and Italy, promised a classless society and equal treatment of all people, though the government did not live up to this ideology. The government discouraged religious worship and seized religious property. Hitler and Stalin sent political opponents—or those who were perceived to be opponents—to concentration camps.

Chapter 29 (Modern Chapter 20)

TEST FORM A

Matching

1. h
2. f
3. l
4. d
5. i
6. c
7. j
8. g
9. a
10. b

Understanding Ideas

1. d
2. b
3. b
4. a
5. c
6. d
7. c
8. a
9. d
10. b

True/False

1. T
2. F
3. F
4. T
5. F

Practicing Skills

1. 30%
2. 35%

Composing an Essay

1. Africans who served as soldiers in World War I brought home ideas about freedom and nationalism, and they organized anti-colonial protest movements. Although colonial rulers agreed to some reforms, Africans increasingly insisted on independence.

2. Mao Zedong and his followers put their beliefs to work by instituting land and tax reform, and by listening to the peasants about their problems. Ultimately, the peasants began to trust the Communists and joined their cause. Some peasants were able to keep the Communists informed about the movement of Nationalist troops.

TEST FORM B

Short Answer

1. Passive resistance in India involved boycotts of British goods and refusal to pay taxes.
2. Kemal wrote a new constitution that separated the religion of Islam from the government, abolished the position of caliph, made civil and social reforms, abandoned the Islamic calendar, prohibited wearing traditional clothes, established secular schools, and instituted economic programs.
3. political unification and an end to foreign influence; democratic government with universal personal liberties and rights; and industrialization, more equal distribution of land, and other economic improvements
4. Workers organized labor unions and went on strike for higher wages and improved working conditions. Young Japanese questioned traditional values. Work roles shifted and women entered the labor market.
5. New professional, government service, and commerce jobs as well as new university programs created opportunities for middle-class people and gave them more access to power. Their political parties emerged in several countries.

Primary Sources

1. that Japan cannot compete with England because it lacks colonies to supply food and raw materials, and the possibility that China might develop its own industries and no longer need Japanese trade
2. by entering China under the guise of trade, taking over the country's resources, and then proceeding to conquer the rest of Asia and beyond

Composing an Essay

1. The British were torn about Indian self-rule, but allowed elections of representatives, though Britain could veto any laws that were proposed. The British controlled India's defense, revenue, and foreign policy. On the other hand, Britain granted complete self-government to Canada, Australia, and New Zealand and made them, as well as South Africa and other former colonies, equal partners in the British Commonwealth.
2. Nationalist movements build on the beliefs and experiences of the people within them—the culture of those people. Examples include the desire of peoples in the Middle East for national homelands where their ancestors once lived; the disagreements between Western-educated Indians who were satisfied with British rule and the nationalists who wanted independence; Gandhi's peaceful and spiritual approach to resistance; the decision by Kemal to change the culture of Turkey by changing people's education, alphabet, and clothing, among other things; the discomfort of Africans with living under colonization while being taught about freedom; and Japanese militarism.

Chapter 30 (Modern Chapter 21)

TEST FORM A

Matching

1. e
2. f
3. i
4. g
5. k
6. j
7. c
8. b
9. d
10. a

Understanding Ideas

1. b
2. d
3. a
4. b
5. c
6. d
7. c
8. a
9. d
10. a

True/False

1. F
2. T
3. F
4. F
5. T

Practicing Skills

1. Hitler is on the left; Stalin is on the right.
2. that they really hated each other, but could pretend to get along when they had a reason to

Composing an Essay

1. The Austrian chancellor had come to an agreement with Hitler to enter into a union with Germany, but he regretted doing so and proposed that Austrians be allowed to vote on whether to go ahead with the union. Hitler refused; the chancellor resigned; and the German army took over Austria without any opposition.
2. The United States passed the Neutrality Act in 1935, resisting any involvement of the country in future wars. However, the power of the isolationists declined as people began to fear that the Nazis would take over the world. The U.S. government gradually passed laws and took action to help Great Britain, culminating in the Lend-Lease Act in 1941, which allowed the president to supply war materials to Great Britain on credit. On December 7, 1941, the Japanese bombed Pearl Harbor, drawing the United States into the war.

TEST FORM B

Short Answer

1. The League of Nations played a very minor role, occasionally condemning aggression, but not taking any military action. This was the case when Japan invaded China, when Italy invaded Ethiopia, and when Germany marched into Austria and the Sudetenland.
2. The Soviet Union might have been an ally of Britain and the other Western nations aligned against Hitler. The pact gave Germany a military advantage by guaranteeing that it would not have to defend itself against the Soviet Union.
3. The Allies sent aid to Russia by opening a new route across Iran.
4. Japan attacked Pearl Harbor in order to destroy so much U.S. war material that the United States would be too badly damaged to fight the Japanese in the Pacific. At first, their plans worked, and they conquered almost the entire Pacific.
5. Mussolini resigned, and his successor dissolved the Fascist Party, began secret talks with the Allies, agreed to stop fighting the Allies, and declared war on Germany.

Primary Sources

1. that Britain might have to fight alone, that the fight would be long and difficult, and that the battle might reach their shores
2. He was telling the United States that Britain needed them to join the war effort.

Composing an Essay

1. The Spanish Civil War was in some ways a forerunner of World War II. In it, the Germans, Italians, and Soviet Union sent troops and war material, with the fascist nations opposing the communist nation. Germany and Italy saw the war as an opportunity to put a government friendly to them in power in Spain, which would physically isolate France, and also to threaten Great Britain.
2. Answers will vary. Some of the following should be included: strategy of total war on a much more massive scale than before; use of advanced technology and weapons, including bombing of civilians and the use of the atom bomb; blitzkrieg; violations of human rights; genocide as a major action of the war. World War II was the most destructive war in history, and by the end, people accepted the killing of civilians in war.

Unit 7 (Modern Unit 5)

TEST FORM A

Understanding Ideas

1. c
2. a
3. b
4. d
5. d
6. a
7. c
8. c
9. b
10. c

Fill in the Blank

1. Mohandas Gandhi
2. Woodrow Wilson
3. Franklin Roosevelt
4. Benito Mussolini
5. Mustafa Kemal
6. Vladimir Lenin
7. Hideki Tōjō
8. Francisco Franco
9. Chiang Kai-shek
10. Mao Zedong

True/False

1. T
2. T
3. F
4. T
5. F

Practicing Skills

1. Riga, Hamburg, Bremen, Leipzig, Berlin
2. Finland, Czechoslovakia, Hungary, Bulgaria, Latvia, Germany

Composing an Essay

1. European nationalism before World War I caused rivalries between nations that were seeking new colonies and control of trade. Also, European peoples living within the large empires of Austria-Hungary and the Ottomans were seeking independence. Their actions served as the spark that turned the tensions in Europe into war. Prior to World War II, German, Italian, and Japanese nationalism caused those countries to seek to add to their territories and to strike out against Great Britain and France, which they saw as standing in their way. Germans were also angry about the Treaty of Versailles, which they saw as an insult to their nation.
2. The Great Depression caused the prices that Latin America received for its exported agricultural goods and raw materials to fall. The Latin American nations had to cut back on imports, and some of them halted payment of foreign debts. Unemployment and worker unrest spread, leading to coups d'états, many by the military, which set up authoritarian governments. Dissent was suppressed, and labor unions were stripped of their power.

TEST FORM B

Short Answer

1. Hitler's party held more seats in the Reichstag than did the other parties, but not a majority. The president of the republic named Hitler chancellor. His private Nazi army then terrorized members of the Reichstag and claimed that the Communists were responsible. The Reichstag gave him emergency powers to deal with the Communists, and he used these powers to become dictator.
2. When the Communists came to power, they seized farmlands from landlords and divided them among the peasants. They then tried to persuade peasants to form collective farms. When the peasants resisted, the government forced them to merge into collectives, resulting in a decrease in agricultural production.
3. Great Britain controlled Transjordan, Palestine, and Iraq after the end of World War I. They kept complete control over Palestine, and maintained a strong military presence in the other two countries after recognizing their independence. In Palestine, they promised both Arabs and Jews independent homelands.
4. The Second Spanish Republic began instituting a number of changes that alarmed Spanish conservatives. The fascist party called Falange picked up their support and used terrorism to preserve the power of the army, landowners, and church. When a group of socialists and Communists won a major election, Falangist uprisings led to a civil war between the two groups.

5. Hitler intended to unite the European continent under a single political and economic system. He planned to take over land in Eastern Europe for Germans to colonize and to use Russia's food and raw materials for Germany. He also planned to destroy the entire Jewish population of Europe.

Primary Sources

1. stop fighting, support German rules, bear the cost of the occupation, and release all German prisoners
2. occupy part of France and exercise its power there

Composing an Essay

1. The Versailles Treaty humiliated Germany, stripped it of land in Europe and its colonies, and obligated it to pay reparations. It created much resentment among Germans, as well as economic problems. The worldwide depression intensified these economic problems, and German anger combined with nationalism to encourage the growth of groups that promised to restore Germany to glory. When one such group, the Nazi Party headed by Adolf Hitler, came to power in Germany, Germany began to nullify the Versailles Treaty by reneging on its reparations, building a new army, and ultimately taking over neighboring countries. When Great Britain and France finally stood up to Germany, World War II broke out.
2. The League of Nations lacked authority to carry out all its peacekeeping duties, and the absence of the United States as a member also undermined it. Although it did condemn Japan's annexation of Manchuria, with the result that Japan withdrew from the League, and it did impose sanctions on Italy after the invasion of Ethiopia, it did not follow through with military action. It also did not react to Germany's violations of the Treaty of Versailles, including the annexation of Austria.

Chapter 31 (Modern Chapter 22)

TEST FORM A

Matching

1. b
2. i
3. h
4. e
5. f
6. j
7. a
8. g

Understanding Ideas

1. b
2. c
3. a
4. c
5. d
6. b
7. d
8. c
9. a
10. b

True/False

1. F
2. T
3. T
4. F
5. T
6. F
7. F
8. T

Practicing Skills

1. Security Council
2. Economic and Social Council

Composing an Essay

1. The two main disagreements between the Western democracies and the Soviet Union were over the boundaries of postwar Germany and war reparations. The Soviet Union wanted to hold on to the territory in Poland and on the Baltic Sea that it had taken over during the Nazi-Soviet Pact, and suggested that Poland should receive part of East Prussia in repayment. The Western democracies allowed this. The Soviet Union also wanted $10 billion in war reparations from Germany. The Western leaders let the Soviet Union take industrial equipment instead.
2. Khrushchev loosened the government's grip on the economy, allowing local factory and farm managers to be more in control of meeting production quotas. As a result, the economy expanded, and the Soviet Union did become more industrialized. He freed political prisoners and ended some of the terrorism of the secret police. On the political front, he attempted

to improve relations with the West, but crises in the 1960s worsened relations even more, and Khrushchev was forced to resign.

TEST FORM B

Short Answer

1. The three leaders agreed to temporarily divide Germany and Austria into zones of military occupation. They also agreed that Poland and the other countries under Soviet rule in Eastern Europe would have free elections and democratic governments friendly to the Soviet Union. They also discussed the proposed charter for the United Nations.
2. The Soviet Union took the role of exporter of communism. Among the countries to which they brought communist governments were Poland, Czechoslovakia, Yugoslavia, East Germany, Bulgaria, and Albania.
3. The West German "miracle" was the rapid pace of reconstruction and industrial development after being defeated in war. Industry flourished because of technological innovation, quality, and good labor relations, and the currency became one of the most stable in the world.
4. By fighting a long and violent war for independence, Algeria split public opinion in France and brought down the Fourth Republic. The result was that Charles de Gaulle wrote a new constitution and become president of the Fifth Republic.
5. The two major issues were anticommunism and civil rights. Joseph McCarthy and others made wild accusations that government officials and others were disloyal. Anticommunist hysteria developed. The push for civil rights by minorities was helped to some extent by government policies, but was reasonably successful mostly because of its own leadership.

Primary Sources

1. Marshall describes the industries of Europe as being totally destroyed and/or subverted to war production.
2. Aid is the only way to restore the health of the economy so as to provide fertile ground for democracy.

Composing an Essay

1. On the whole, the Western European countries reconstructed their economic bases more quickly. West Germany was the fastest to return to a preeminent economic position. Denmark, Norway, and Sweden prospered and established extensive welfare states. Italy had extensive agricultural and industrial growth at first, but then declined. France had lost farmland as well as towns and cities, but its economy slowly improved with the help of its own leaders and the Marshall Plan. Britain lost its colonies and tried to improve the condition of its citizens by forming a welfare state. However, it had outdated equipment and lagged behind the other Western European countries. In the Soviet Union, on the other hand, the command economy created problems, and while industrialization did take place, it did not translate into a better life for the Soviet people. Collectivization of farming delayed economic recovery. The same was true in Eastern Europe, although the Poles did resist collectivization of farming.
2. The Soviet Union kept a firm grip on the communist nations of Eastern and Central Europe. They turned these nations into one-party states. They imposed collective farming, which delayed economic recovery. They repressed revolutions in most of the countries that tried to become more independent, such as Hungary and Czechoslovakia. By contrast, the United States stayed away from the internal affairs of its allies, providing aid through the Marshall Plan, but not intervening when political crises occurred. The different treatment of France and Yugoslavia provide a good example of the differences between the two nations. When Yugoslavia objected to Soviet domination, the country was expelled from the

Cominform. When France opposed U.S. and British interests, it remained a member of NATO.

Chapter 32 (Modern Chapter 23)

TEST FORM A

Fill in the Blank

1. Cultural Revolution
2. Gang of Four
3. nonalignment
4. mixed economy
5. SCAP
6. zaibatsu
7. domino theory
8. Geneva Accord
9. ASEAN
10. Khmer Rouge

Understanding Ideas

1. a
2. d
3. b
4. a
5. c
6. b
7. d
8. c
9. c
10. b

True/False

1. T
2. T
3. F
4. F
5. T

Practicing Skills

1. the Chinese protesters who want democracy
2. that it is not dead, even if the protester is

Composing an Essay

1. Deng Xiaoping was a moderate whose plan to reform the economy and improve agriculture, industry, science and technology, and national defense led China to move toward a market economy. That resulted in a more open society and more involvement with the West. This encouraged many Chinese people to push for democracy. In that vein, a demonstration in favor of ending government corruption, giving the people more say in government, and better conditions in the universities took place in Tiananmen Square. When students refused to leave, Chinese troops cleared the area, shooting and killing protesters.
2. According to the terms of the MacArthur Constitution, the Japanese were prohibited from building their military and the Japanese themselves wanted no return to a militaristic government. So even when the United States urged them to increase their armed forces so as to be able to defend themselves from a possible communist invasion, they refused, preferring to spend the money on industrialization and exports. After about 40 years, they did agree to provide the United States with assistance in case of a conflict near Japan—but not military forces.

TEST FORM B

Short Answer

1. Many Indians refused to back Great Britain in World War II because of its refusal to give them self-rule and because Britain did not consult them about India's role in the war. Because Britain needed to station troops in India to fight Japan, there was pressure to reach a settlement, and the British government proposed a plan involving independence following the war. Indian nationalists, including the Muslim League, rejected the plan and resisted Britain throughout the war.
2. The Red Guards were radical students who carried out Mao's Cultural Revolution by destroying art, books, and other artifacts of the "old ways," and beating, torturing, or killing people who did not completely follow Mao's teachings.
3. Japan's standard of living rose, as families could buy cars and modern appliances. Women won more legal, political, and social freedom, and more women joined the workforce. The family was no longer the center of Japanese life.
4. Both Laos and Cambodia unsuccessfully tried to remain neutral during the war. The United States bombed the part of the Ho Chi Minh Trail that went through Laos and Cambodia. In Laos, a communist government was ultimately set up and called on communist Vietnam for

help in controlling anticommunist forces. In Cambodia, the Khmer Rouge took over the government and engaged in genocide and other harsh measures against the Cambodian people.

5. The Four Tigers are South Korea, Taiwan, Singapore, and Hong Kong. The name refers to their very strong economies and major roles in world markets.

Primary Sources

1. conservative Islamic beliefs versus a more modern view of women

2. greater confidence of and a greater role for women, or political instability; the latter turned out to be the case, and there was another military takeover of the government

Composing an Essay

1. With the notable exception of Japan, most Asian governments were unable to sustain democratic governments and moved to authoritarianism, whether communist or noncommunist. There were three major reasons for this. (1) Most Asian countries have populations of different races, religions, and cultures, and the hatred between these groups periodically led to fighting. Governments had to rely on armies and police forces to maintain control, leading to a loss of civil rights. (2) Governments also worried about national security, which they saw as being threatened by reform. This was true of both communist and noncommunist governments. (3) All Asian countries desired rapid economic growth, and they thought that government control would promote faster growth.

2. Most students will say that it did not. Former British colonies (Burma, Pakistan, India), Dutch colonies (Indonesia), United States colonies (Philippines), and French colonies (Vietnam, Laos, and Cambodia) all experienced political instability and authoritarian governments. Other students may argue that all the French colonies became communist, which was not true of the others, and that India maintained an elected government.

Chapter 33 (Modern Chapter 24)

TEST FORM A

Matching

1. f
2. c
3. h
4. b
5. j
6. l
7. a
8. g
9. e
10. k

Understanding Ideas

1. c
2. b
3. c
4. a
5. d
6. b
7. c
8. d
9. a
10. b

True/False

1. F
2. F
3. T
4. F
5. T

Practicing Skills

1. grazing livestock

2. no, because they're included with desert and waste land

Composing an Essay

1. As a result of the Cold War, both the Western democracies and the Soviet Union tried to influence the African nations to favor their side. Some African states, like Guinea, were able to use this to their advantage: when de Gaulle withdrew French aid upon Guinea's declaring independence, Guinea turned to the Soviet Union, so frightening de Gaulle that he restored the aid. Others suffered as a result, as did Angola, for example, when the United States, Cuba, and the Soviet Union supported different sides in Angola's civil war. Even more confusing was the situation in Ethiopia and Somalia, both supported by the Soviet Union. When Somalia invaded Ethiopia, the Soviet Union sided with Ethiopia, and Cuba sent troops there.

2. Nasser, the Egyptian leader, tried to play the Western democracies against the

Soviet Union in order to get the most money possible for building the Aswan High Dam on the Nile. He delayed so long that the offer by Britain and the United States was withdrawn, which he saw as an insult. His reaction was to nationalize the Suez Canal and to refuse Israeli ships passage. Israel, Britain, and France tried to overthrow Nasser and take over the canal and succeeded in seizing the Mediterranean end, where they sank ships to block the canal. Egypt did the same on the other side. The United States, fearing that the Soviet Union would be drawn into the crisis, intervened, and the invasion ended. Britain and France withdrew, Egypt later blockaded the canal, and the United Nations sent a force to patrol the cease-fire line. The result was that Nasser became a hero to the Arab world.

TEST FORM B

Short Answer

1. He changed his mind because Guinea, the one colony that did choose independence, turned to the Soviet Union for help. This worried de Gaulle, so he reversed his position.
2. Ethnic conflicts caused civil wars in Nigeria, Burundi, and Rwanda, leading to massive death and destruction. So many refugees fled to Zaire from the civil war in Rwanda that the war engulfed that country as well.
3. Jordan benefited when it took over the part of the proposed Palestinian state that had not been taken by Israel.
4. Israel captured additional land and defeated all the invading Arab armies. As a result, many Palestinians no longer believed that the Arab governments could recapture Palestine, and they turned instead to their own guerrilla organization.
5. Saddam Hussein, the leader of Iraq, accused Kuwait of taking more than their share of oil from a jointly owned field and invaded that country, annexing it formally. There was fear that Iraq would invade Saudi Arabia next, and a coalition of nations sent troops to defend that country. When Iraq failed to withdraw its troops from Kuwait, the defensive troops went on the offensive in an attack against Iraq.

Primary Sources

1. as employers who exploit them and the police, soldiers, and security forces that mistreat them, as well as the fortunate beneficiaries of a democratic way of life
2. They are frustrated because they see democracy and its benefits daily, but they do not get to participate in it and are treated as a captive people.

Composing an Essay

1. Most students will say that it did make a difference. The French colonies were treated as being part of France, and although Algeria waged war to gain independence and France tried to resist giving independence to the others, France did finally grant them independence. Belgium and Portugal, on the other hand, strongly resisted independence for their colonies, and long, bloody wars were fought before their colonies were freed.
2. Some Arab alliances have been very short-lived. Egypt and Syria merged into the United Arab Republic in 1958, but by 1961 Syria had withdrawn from the alliance because of fear of domination by Egypt and because it disagreed with Egyptian policy on everything other than Israel. Others have waxed and waned depending on circumstances; in particular, various Arab nations have signed peace treaties with Israel, while others have remained adamant in their refusal to do so. OPEC, which includes all oil-producing nations, not only Arab nations, has been an alliance since 1960, although some members have disagreed with its policies at times.

Chapter 34 (Modern Chapter 25)

TEST FORM A

Fill in the Blank

1. NAFTA
2. Organization of American States (OAS)
3. Sandinistas
4. contras
5. PRI
6. Operation Bootstrap
7. desaparecidos
8. Shining Path
9. Contadora Principles
10. women, workers

Understanding Ideas

1. c
2. d
3. a
4. c
5. b
6. d
7. b
8. a
9. c
10. b

True/False

1. T
2. F
3. F
4. T
5. F

Practicing Skills

1. east central coast of South America
2. People in the United States receive more than 150 percent of required calories.

Composing an Essay

1. The lower and middle classes supported Castro because he promised to make changes that would improve their lives. These included educational and agricultural reforms, improved health care, restoration of civil liberties, and open elections. He also wanted to free Cuba of American influence, which was a popular cause with people in these classes.
2. Colombia's fortunes have fluctuated in this period. Immediately after World War II, the country experienced economic and political turmoil. When the two major parties agreed to share office, they ushered in a period of democracy and a stable economy. However, when Colombian drug producers and dealers began making money selling drugs in the United States and Europe, the civil fabric tore once again. Political terrorism by both communist and right-wing factions added to the problems.

TEST FORM B

Short Answer

1. The growth of cities has caused financial problems as governments have had to provide water, sewage, electricity, roads, and public transportation. There are severe shortages of both housing and jobs, and many poorer migrants live in shantytowns in which diseases spread.
2. The state of Mexico's economy has varied since World War II. The discovery of oil reserves in the 1970s significantly boosted the economy, but financial problems, a slump in the oil market, and a massive earthquake reversed that. Recovery appeared to begin in the late 1990s.
3. Arias proposed a peace plan for Central America. He called for an end to all fighting in the area, an end to foreign aid to rebels, and economic reforms.
4. Castro denied freedom of the press and executed some of his opponents. Land reform redistributed income and property, and the government took over U.S.-owned agricultural estates and businesses. He reformed education, boosting literacy, but he did not make other promised social reforms.
5. Argentina's military government invaded the Falkland Islands, which were owned by Great Britain. To Argentina's surprise, the British defended the islands and defeated the Argentinean government, which made way for free elections.

Primary Sources

1. because the Communists do not persecute the poor and do try to solve problems of poverty, hunger, illiteracy, and lack of housing
2. He is fighting for an end to right-wing authoritarian government and for government by the people.

Composing an Essay

1. To a very large extent, the United States has taken an anti-communist position in Latin America, intervening in the internal affairs of numerous countries to remove communists from power or preserve anti-communist governments. Students should mention events in some of the following countries in support of this: Nicaragua, El Salvador, Panama, Cuba, Dominican Republic, Haiti, Grenada, and Chile. The United States has been more successful than not in maintaining non-communist governments. The other roles of the United States have been as a colonizer in Puerto Rico and as a provider of aid to the government of Colombia fight the drug lords.
2. Economic reforms have included developing national industries, obtaining foreign loans, and hosting foreign corporations. For the most part, these reforms have had limited success, especially during economic downturns. The imposition of economic controls by the government has also been only partly successful, causing inflation in some instances. Another type of economic reform by Cuba is allowing a limited number of private investments and limited foreign investment. Most of Latin America continues to experience high unemployment, inflation and heavy debt.

Chapter 35 (Modern Chapter 26)

TEST FORM A

Matching

1. h
2. d
3. f
4. j
5. c
6. k
7. a
8. g
9. i
10. b

Understanding Ideas

1. c
2. a
3. b
4. b
5. d
6. c
7. d
8. b
9. a
10. a

True/False

1. F
2. F
3. T
4. F
5. T

Practicing Skills

1. 370,300; China and the United States
2. 478,300; Yugoslavia, Croatia, United States, Sweden, Netherlands, Denmark

Composing an Essay

1. For the most part, the United States and Canada have maintained very friendly relations. The border between the two countries is not defended, and extensive trade flows in both directions. There have been disputes about fishing rights, environmental concerns, and U.S. involvement in Canada's economy. NAFTA was a point of contention, but Canada did sign the agreement.
2. Boris Yeltsin was faced with moving the new Federation of Russia from communism to democracy. There was high inflation and unemployment, inadequate housing, and not enough food. The military was poorly paid and had poor living conditions, and organized crime flourished. Several separatist movements attempted to break away. Ongoing economic problems caused political turmoil, and nationalists and communists gained support.

TEST FORM B

Short Answer

1. The Vietnam War strained the U.S. economy. Many lives were lost, and the American people were divided over support for the war. Ultimately, the American people began to lose faith in their leaders.

2. The Maastricht Treaty set up the European Union. Trade barriers were eliminated among member nations, and the members agreed to cooperate in defense and foreign relations. They also accepted the idea of a common currency.
3. Thatcher took a conservative approach to economic matters and a firm approach to foreign relations. She eliminated some social programs and cut funding to others. She eased government controls on business and reduced the power of labor unions. Her foreign relations approach is illustrated by her use of force to defend the Falkland Islands.
4. Government control of the economy was eased, as were restrictions on dissent, so that people could speak openly. The size of the armed forces was reduced and the occupation of Afghanistan ended.
5. The Bush administration froze the assets of individuals, groups, and companies with suspected terrorist affiliations. Secretaty of State Colin Powell led the effort to build an international coalition against terrorism and to isolate the Taliban regime. The United States military began an offensive against the Taliban and al Qaeda network in Afghanistan.

Primary Sources

1. The West Germans were thrilled that their country was once again uniting and that people were free to move around the entire country. This meant, among other things, that families could be united.
2. The anxiety was caused by fear that even more refugees would pour into West Germany, which would be very expensive. They had made no plans to deal with the refugees.

Composing an Essay

1. There were nationalist separatist movements in Canada, Spain, and Great Britain. In Canada, French Canadians have used peaceful means to increase their political power, and barely lost a referendum to remove Quebec from Canada. In Spain, the Basques have used violent means to make their case for separation, as have both the Irish Republican Army and Protestant groups in North Ireland.
2. A number of national groups were able to form their own republics when the Soviet Union broke up, but there are ongoing struggles among some of them, such as Azerbaijan (Muslim) and Armenia (Christian). The Muslim Chechens declared independence, but Russia rejected their declaration and there has been violence since. Ethnic conflict has remained a problem in Eastern Europe, particularly in the former Yugoslavia, where Eastern Orthodox Serbia has tried to dominate the Roman Catholic Croats and Slovenians and the Muslims of Bosnia and Herzegovina as well as ethnic Albanians.

Chapter 36 (Modern Chapter 27)

TEST FORM A

Fill in the Blank

1. Jackson Pollock
2. George Balanchine
3. Federico Fellini
4. Maya Angelou
5. Bertolt Brecht
6. Yury Gagarin
7. Alpha
8. Rachel Carson
9. Alan Shepard
10. antibiotics

Understanding Ideas

1. c
2. d
3. b
4. c
5. a
6. d
7. a
8. b
9. c
10. b

True/False

1. F
2. T
3. T
4. F
5. F

Practicing Skills

1. Bangladesh; has the highest infant mortality rate and the shortest life expectancy
2. Japan; has the longest life expectancy and is tied with the United States for the lowest infant mortality rate

Composing an Essay

1. Experimentation has been a major part of modern culture. In painting and sculpture, artists like Jackson Pollock, Andy Warhol, and Louise Nevelson pushed the boundaries of style. Architects used new materials, technology, and styles. Serious music used new kinds of sound, and popular music took on new characteristics. Dramatists and novelists also broke new ground.
2. Many more nations moved toward democracy during the last years of the 20th century, including South Korea, Taiwan, the Philippines, South Africa, and many countries in Latin America. On the other hand, authoritarian rule seemed entrenched in China, Cuba, and a number of Muslim countries.

TEST FORM B

Short Answer

1. Serious drama, whether experimental or realistic, focused on social criticism, attacking modern society for its absurdity, class system, family problems, and racism, among other problems.
2. Authors criticized the racism, commercialism, materialism, and insensitivity of American life. Outside the United States, novels looked at the effects of colonialism and the difficulties of life under communism.
3. They have made possible many products that make life easier or more convenient, especially the computer, which has led to improvements in nearly all aspects of life.
4. The destruction of forests, wetlands, and other areas in order to accommodate population growth and industrialization has led to reduced biodiversity. The loss of plants and animals could damage both the environment and the people in it.
5. political, ethnic, racial, or religious intolerance and/or actions

Primary Sources

1. It saves the lives of children, keeps people from being malnourished, and improves the quality of life.
2. Technology has caused pollution, used up irreplaceable resources, and has the potential to harm the Earth even more.

Composing an Essay

1. Answers will vary. Some students may say that the changes are both good and bad. Examples of good changes are improvements in medicine and sanitation, faster travel, development of labor-saving devices, computers, and better communications. Examples of bad changes are pollution and other environmental damage, differences in the lives of the haves and have-nots, the use of technology to harm and terrorize people, and possible misuse of medical advances such as genetic research and cloning.
2. Students who feel that the future looks promising will probably focus on the increase in the number of countries with democratic governments, the opportunities provided by improved science and technology, and the growth and spread of cultural forms. Those who feel threatened by the future will likely look at possible misuses of science and technology, ethnic and religious conflict, the unequal distribution of resources, and poverty and terrorism around the world.

Unit 8 (Modern Unit 6)

TEST FORM A

Understanding Ideas

1. d
2. a
3. a
4. c
5. b
6. c
7. d
8. a
9. c
10. b

Matching

1. h
2. l
3. j
4. g
5. e
6. b
7. a
8. i
9. d
10. f

True/False

1. T
2. F
3. F
4. F
5. F

Practicing Skills

1. four
2. Estonia, Latvia, and Lithuania

Composing an Essay

1. The nations of Europe faced both economic and political problems. The economies of all the countries were in shambles, and farmlands as well as factories were damaged to a greater or lesser extent in most. Former colonies were fighting for independence. Germany was divided, and there was a threat of communist revolution, which occurred successfully across Eastern Europe and unsuccessfully in Greece. European governments rose and fell in conjunction with economic and colonial problems.
2. A major factor in the recovery of the Japanese economy was the occupation government of General MacArthur. Land reforms made it possible for small farmers to own their own land, and new farm machinery and improved seeds were made available. The huge industrial firms known as zaibatsu were broken up, making free trade possible. Also, the Japanese people's new focus on economic strength and apathy toward their military allowed them to direct all of their resources toward strengthening their economy and raising their standard of living.

TEST FORM B

Short Answer

1. They had command economies in which the government made all or most decisions. Industry was under government control and farms were collectivized.
2. The Communists wanted China to become a modern industrialized nation. They wanted to build up industry and give land to the peasants. Under government pressure, the peasants organized their land into collective farms, and the government also operated state farms.
3. Both Israel and the Palestinians believed that the British had promised them Palestine. The Arab nations wanted to destroy the state of Israel for this reason.
4. (Accept any of the following.) The New York Stock Exchange (NYSE) shut down for four days after the terrorist attacks. Once the market reopened, concerns about a potential war caused one of the worst weeks in the history of the NYSE. The airline industry was affected as well. Airlines were forced to shut down for several days and once they could fly again, they had to face tremendous cost increases in security. Thousands of workers in the airline industry lost their jobs, and tourism declined as people were reluctant to fly. Perhaps the most difficult economic impact was a low consumer confidence. Many Americans feared a recession.
5. Thatcher cut funding of social programs, converted many government-owned industries into private companies, eased other government controls on business, and reduced the power of labor unions.

Primary Sources

1. In the early 1990s, they saw capitalism as evil and violent because of the people who were associated with it, and they were afraid of it.
2. By 1996, they saw capitalism as something that could get them the goods they wanted, and they were eager to become part of it.

Composing an Essay

1. Answers will vary. Most students will say that the lives of most of the world's people have improved. They should cite conditions in 1945 among the nations that were involved in World War II (economic and political problems) and their colonies (independence movements, violence, difficulties of forming new governments). They should compare this to the decline of communism and the increase in the number of democracies in the world; industrialization and improved standards of living, especially among people in the West; independence of former colonies; and improvements in medicine, technology, and the like. Those who disagree may point to the large and increasing gaps between the haves and have-nots within and among nations, economic instability, the continued prevalence of dictatorships, and violence and wars. It is possible that some will also discuss spiritual values.
2. Establishing new governments proved very difficult and was complicated by communist revolutions in some nations (the Philippines, Vietnam, Laos, Cambodia, Cuba, Nicaragua, El Salvador, Grenada, Argentina, Peru). Dictatorships were common (Pakistan, Burma, Indonesia, Zaire, Ghana, Syria, Algeria, Panama, Haiti). Former colonies had raw materials, but no industry to speak of, and some, like Burma, experienced serious economic problems as a result. The same was true of those that had only one crop or mineral resource (Ghana, Zambia, Sudan, Zaire, Nigeria, Venezuela, Mexico, Colombia) when prices on that good dropped. Population growth and movement of people to cities compounded the problems. Colonial nations did not always prepare their colonies for self-rule and peace (e.g., the Belgian Congo). Although Britain did divide India and Pakistan into two nations prior to independence, there was violence among Muslims, Hindus, and Sikhs. In fact, a number of former colonies have experienced and continue to experience violent ethnic conflicts (India, Pakistan, Malaysia, Nigeria, Rwanda, Burundi). Disease has been a serious problem in Africa. Successes include the political stability and economic power of Singapore, the end of apartheid in South Africa, democracy and industrialization in Israel, democracy in Mexico, economic progress in Brazil and Chile, as well as periods of democracy and economic progress in many other former colonies.

Epilogue

TEST FORM A

Matching

1. d
2. e
3. i
4. a
5. g
6. c
7. f
8. h
9. l
10. b

Understanding Ideas

1. c
2. a
3. b
4. a
5. d
6. b
7. c
8. d
9. b
10. a

True/False

1. F
2. F
3. T
4. F
5. F

Practicing Skills

1. Allied Powers: United States, Japan, Great Britain, France, Belgium, Italy, Portugal, Serbia, Romania, Montenegro, Greece, Russia; Central Powers: Germany, Austria-Hungary, Bulgaria, Ottoman Empire
2. United States, British Empire, France, Italy, Germany, Austria-Hungary, Romania, Serbia, Ottoman Empire, Russia

Composing an Essay

1. All three wars involved groups in the society that disagreed with governments that were headed by monarchs. The British civil war pitted the Puritans against the monarchy after the king refused to put Parliament in charge of the army to put

down an Irish rebellion and arrested some of his opponents. It resulted in a new government led by Oliver Cromwell, the Puritan leader, and ultimately a restoration of the monarchy. In the United States, the group involved was the colonists, who were angry that Britain was taxing them without allowing them representation in Parliament. The result was the establishment of a new nation. In the case of France, the middle class and the poor wanted more voice in government. The king tried to escape and was beheaded. The French Revolution led to political turmoil, repression, the establishment of an empire by Napoléon Bonaparte, war, and ultimately restoration of a monarchy.

2. In the late 1800s, China was dominated by European interests and was headed by an emperor. In the early 1900s, the emperor was forced to abdicate, and a nationalist party made reforms. Since the lot of the peasants did not improve, the Chinese Communist party gathered strength and ultimately took over the government in the 1950s. Since then, the government has undergone periods of greater and lesser authoritarianism. The people of China have less freedom of speech than in the past, but there is also not as great an economic gap between the people at the top and the peasants.

TEST FORM B

Short Answer

1. In Europe, the result of nationalism was the unification of kingdoms in Italy and Germany into large, powerful nations. In Latin America, it led colonized people to fight for independence in Haiti, South America, and Mexico.
2. Imperialism was practiced by powerful nations whose nationalistic feelings led them to want the prestige and power of controlling colonies and who needed raw materials and new markets to maintain industrialization.
3. The Bush administration froze the assets of individuals, groups, and companies with suspected terrorist affiliations. Secretary of State Colin Powell led the effort to build an international coalition against terrorism and to isolate the Taliban regime. The United States military began an offensive against the Taliban and al Queda network in Afghanistan.
4. The Cold War was mostly caused by the Soviet takeover of the nations of Eastern Europe and its attempt to export revolution to other countries. The Western democracies opposed this and vied with the Soviet Union for allies.
5. A market economy involves competition among private businesses and individuals to determine what goods and services will be available. In a command economy, the government makes all economic decisions.

Primary Sources

1. No, it says only that the British government will "look with favor" on the idea and will try to facilitate its treatment, subject to other considerations.
2. Jews who were hoping for a homeland might have taken the letter as a promise of support, while Arabs who opposed such a homeland might have believed that it promised nothing other than to keep rights of the Jewish in mind.

Composing an Essay

1. Nationalism has caused kingdoms to unify into larger nations (Germany, Italy) and the peoples within larger nations to seek and obtain independence (groups within Austria-Hungary, for example). It triggered both world wars: World War I by setting off a series of alliances and World War II in that German nationalism was the basis of Hitler's anger and determination. Imperialism was also at fault in World War I in that it increased world tension and caused governments to form defensive alliances. Imperialism grew out of nationalism. Like nationalism, it has led to powerful nations taking over weaker peoples—colonizing them. And nationalist movements among the colonized people grew out of imperialism. Both nationalism and imperialism assume the superiority of some nations over others.

2. Answers may vary. Idealistic students may argue that the world has learned from the mistakes of the past and that the United Nations will hold the forces of nationalism and imperialism at bay. Other students will point out that nationalism was at the root of the breakup of the Soviet Union; that China's imperialism resulted in takeovers of Tibet and other nations, which have not broken away; that the nationalism of Middle Eastern nations is still leading to violent conflict; and that nations must still compete for resources.

Prologue

TEST FORM A

Matching

1. d	6. k
2. h	7. j
3. a	8. l
4. i	9. g
5. c	10. b

Understanding Ideas

1. b	6. b
2. c	7. d
3. d	8. a
4. c	9. c
5. a	10. a

True/False

1. F	4. F
2. T	5. T
3. T	

Practicing Skills

1. Africa
2. to Europeans, because East Asians and Europeans come from the same main "branch" of the "tree," while Southeast Asians developed along a different main "branch"

Composing an Essay

1. Both believed in the eternal nature of the soul and in people's continued rebirth, or reincarnation, and new lives during which they gain the knowledge and experience they need to reach a state of enlightenment, salvation, and peace. Both emphasized the importance of good actions and leading a moral life in making progress to reach this state. However, Buddhism did not accept the Hindu priests or gods.
2. At first struggles existed between landowners and soldiers and other nonaristocrats. Eventually, some leaders became tyrants, or people who rule unlawfully. As the tyrants' rule became harsh and unjust the people removed them from power. Eventually, in many city-states, some Greeks developed the idea that people should rule themselves. In Athens, tyrannical government was overthrown in 507 B.C. and a direct democracy was established. This is a government in which the all citizens play an equal role in decision-making.

TEST FORM B

Short Answer

1. As the number of people living in a place grew larger, society would become more complicated. Leaders would be needed, and it would be more important to have rules for living together. These things comprise government.
2. Early peoples who developed agriculture were drawn to river valleys because they needed a reliable source of water for their crops. Sumerian civilization developed in the Tigris-Euphrates Valley in Southwest Asia. Egyptian civilization developed along the Nile. In East Asia, Chinese civilization developed in the Huang Valley, and the Harappan civilization developed in the Indus Valley in South Asia.
3. The Greeks developed the idea that people should rule themselves. So in Athens, tyrannical government was overthrown and a direct democracy was established, a government in which all citizens play an equal role in decision-making. In Rome, the aristocracy set up a republic, a form of government in which the citizens elect their leaders.
4. The East African city-states were located on the coasts of the Red Sea and Indian Ocean. This location allowed them to develop trade with the Muslim merchants

of Arabia and Persia. The kingdoms of West Africa developed at the edge of the Sahara, along trade routes that crossed the desert. There they prospered from the exchange of gold mined in the south with salt that was mined in the desert.

5. The Inca maintained unity by building forts, covering their empire with paved roads, giving out food when crops failed, and minimizing cultural differences with conquered peoples through an educational system that taught them the Inca language, religion, and history.

Primary Sources

1. They coordinate cavalry and infantry well. Elite foot-soldiers are placed in front to lead the attack. The soldiers who fight together are related to one another as family or clan members.

2. Women encourage bravery by witnessing and honoring it. In addition, their fearful shrieks during battles motivate the soldiers to fight harder, as do the expectations—and even the demands—of women that their husbands and sons will be wounded in the fighting.

Composing an Essay

1. The Egyptians developed a calendar to keep track of the Nile's floods and used geometry to recalculate field boundaries after floods and to build their pyramids. They also developed the mummification process for preserving the dead. Early Indian physicians developed the technique of inoculation. Indian astronomers knew that the Earth rotated and mathematicians understood the concepts of abstract and negative numbers. Indian architects built domes. The early Chinese developed an extremely accurate calendar and built instruments to track the movements of the planets. They also developed standardized weights and measures and created a writing system. The Maya also built pyramids and developed a writing system, while the Aztec used mathematics and developed a calendar.

2. Early peoples were nomads who moved from place to place in search of food. As their technology improved, they became better at hunting and gathering food. This enabled some of them to settle in villages and start growing some of their food. Such people gave up their nomadic ways and domesticated animals as another food source. Over time, villages grew into large towns. As their farming methods improved, it took fewer farmers to feed larger populations. Over time, this led to a division of labor. Some people developed special skills such as making tools, engaging in trade, and creating calendars to help farmers and writing systems to help traders. These developments, along with the population growth that eventually turned their villages into towns and cities, advanced the cultures of such groups into civilizations.